Dawn of the
Bunny Suicides

VALEAS MUNDUM

Dawn of the Bunny Suicides

Andy Riley

ANDY RILEY IS THE AUTHOR/ARTIST OF:

THE BOOK OF BUNNY SUICIDES, RETURN OF THE BUNNY SUICIDES, GREAT LIES TO TELL SMALL KIDS, LOADS MORE LIES TO TELL SMALL KIDS, SELFISH PIGS, D.I.Y. DENTISTRY (AND OTHER ALARMING INVENTIONS), AND THE BUMPER BOOK OF BUNNY SUICIDES. ROASTED, HIS STRIP IN THE OBSERVER MAGAZINE, IS COLLECTED AS A HODDER & STOUGHTON HARDBACK.

HIS SCRIPTWRITING WORK INCLUDES BLACK BOOKS, THE GREAT OUTDOORS, HYPERDRIVE, LITTLE BRITAIN, THE ARMSTRONG & MILLER SHOW, THE ARMANDO IANNUCCI SHOWS, COME FLY WITH ME, THE 99p CHALLENGE, BIG TRAIN, THE FRIDAY NIGHT ARMISTICE, SPITTING IMAGE, SMACK THE PONY, GNOMEO AND JULIET, SO GRAHAM NORTON, HARRY AND PAUL, SLACKER CATS AND THE BAFTA-WINNING ANIMATION ROBBIE THE REINDEER.

LOOK OUT FOR NEW CARTOONS AT:
misterandyriley.com

ON TWITTER:
@andyrileyish

WITH THANKS TO:

POLLY FABER, GORDON WISE, CAMILLA HORNBY,
LISA HIGHTON & ALL AT HODDER AND
STOUGHTON, KEVIN CECIL,
ARTHUR MATHEWS AND ELLIOTT MILLER

FIRST PUBLISHED IN GREAT BRITAIN IN 2010 BY HODDER AND STOUGHTON
AN HACHETTE UK COMPANY

1

A CIP CATALOGUE RECORD FOR THIS TITLE IS AVAILABLE FROM THE BRITISH LIBRARY

HARDBACK ISBN 978 1444 71101 1 : TRADE PAPERBACK ISBN 978 1444 71102 8

PRINTED & BOUND IN ITALY BY L.E.G.O. SPA. HODDER & STOUGHTON POLICY
IS TO USE PAPERS THAT ARE NATURAL, RENEWABLE AND RECYCLABLE
PRODUCTS AND MADE FROM WOOD GROWN IN SUSTAINABLE FORESTS. THE
LOGGING AND MANUFACTURING PROCESSES ARE EXPECTED TO CONFORM
TO THE ENVIRONMENTAL REGULATIONS OF THE COUNTRY OF ORIGIN.

HODDER & STOUGHTON LTD.
338 EUSTON ROAD
LONDON NW1 3BH
WWW.HODDER.CO.UK

FOR

BILL & EDDIE

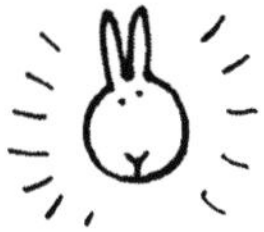

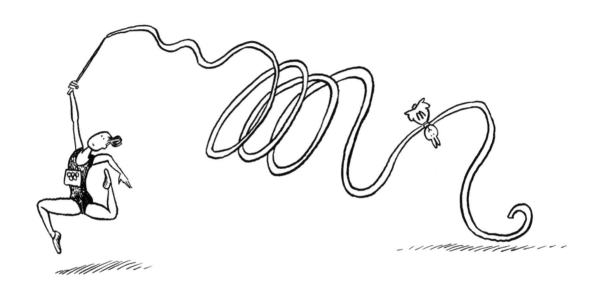

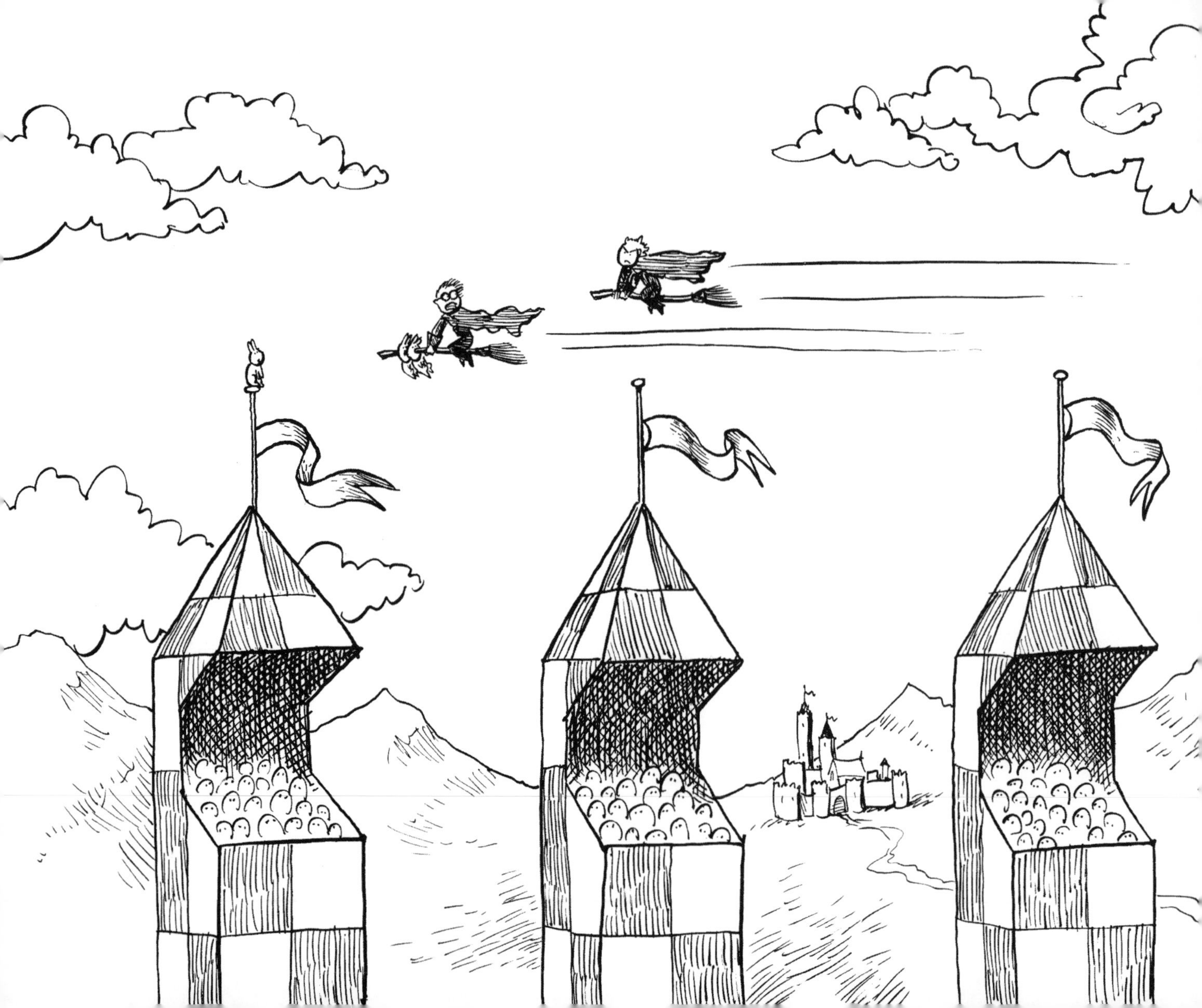

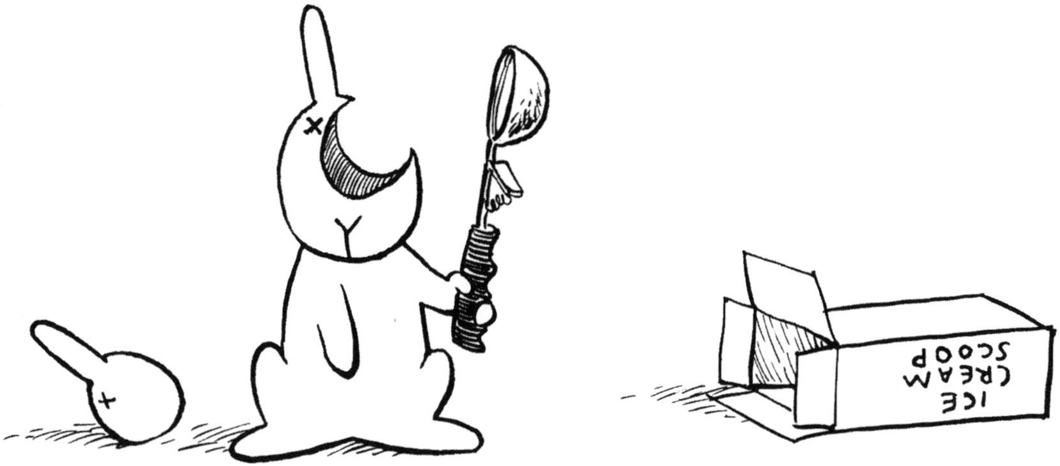
ICE CREAM SCOOP

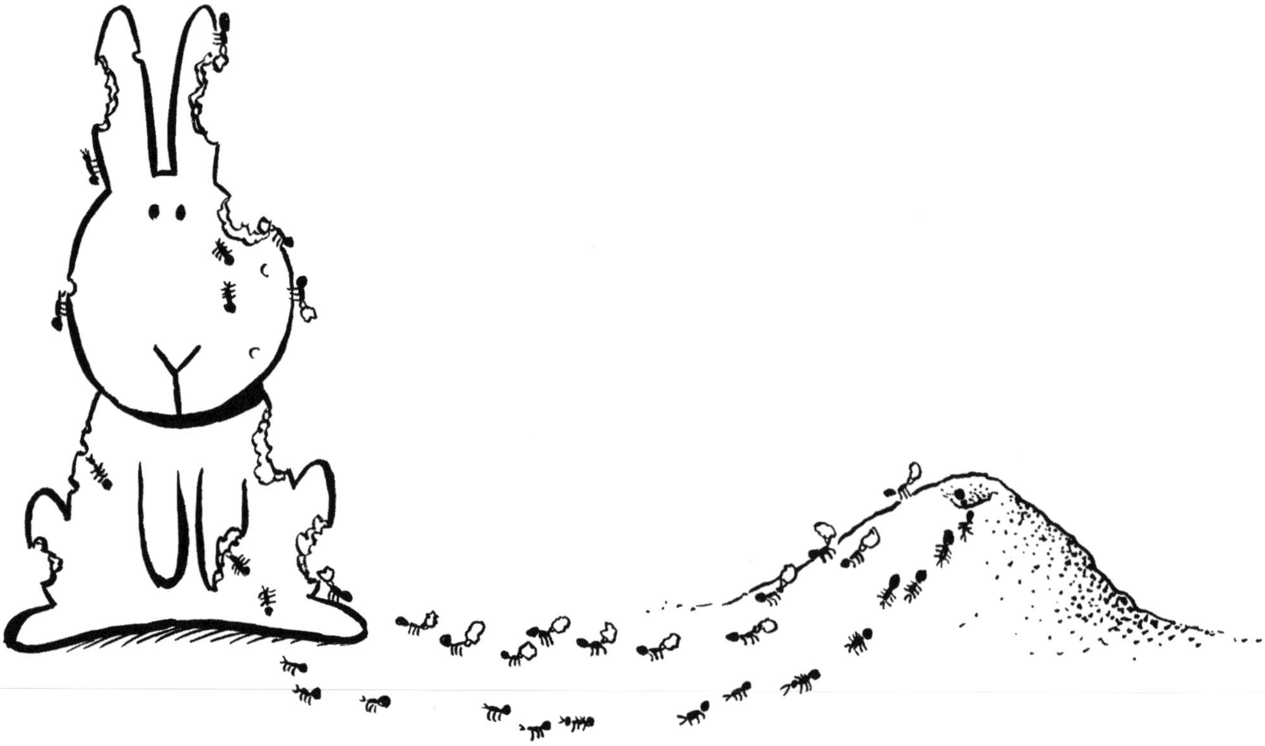

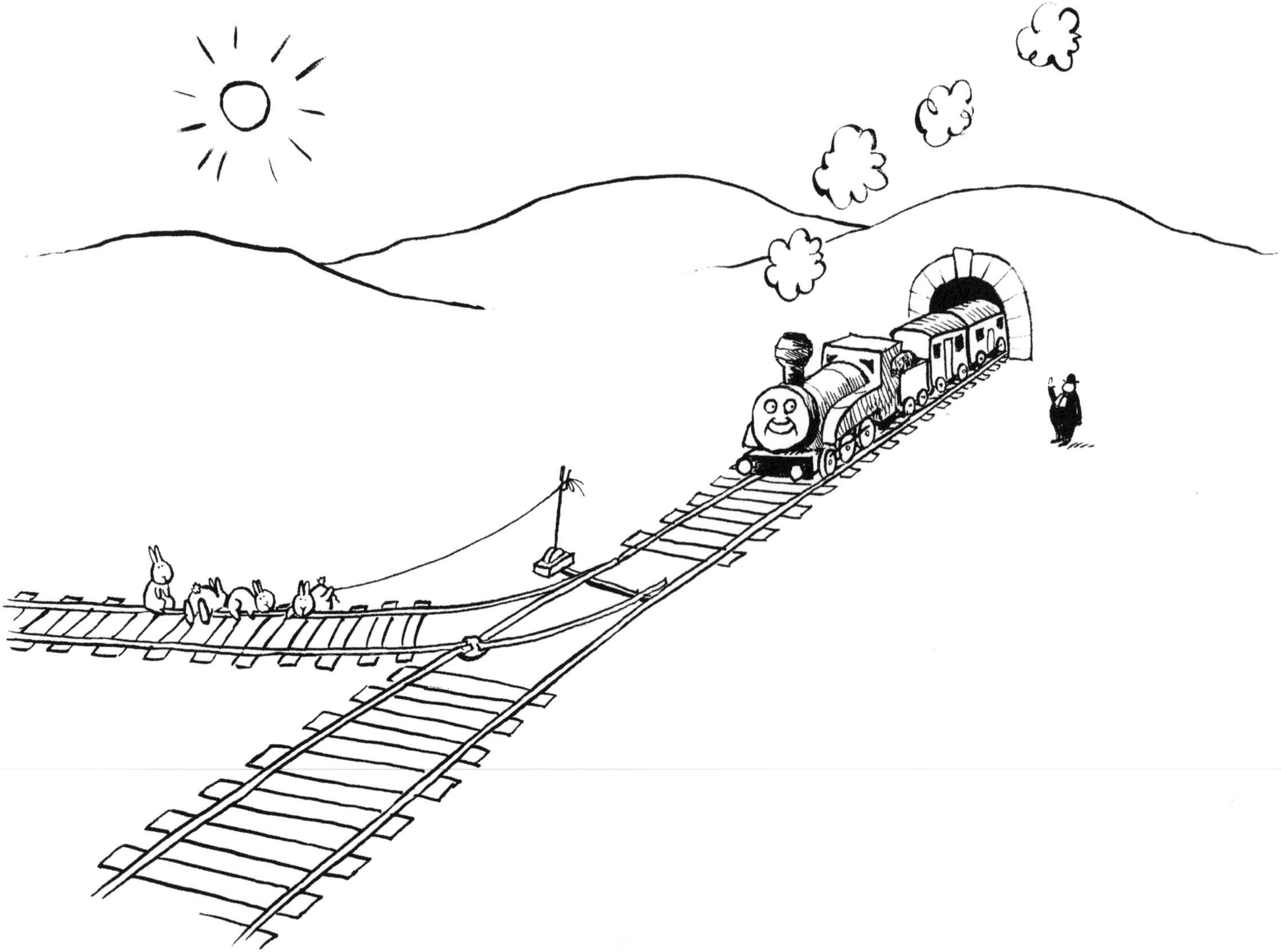

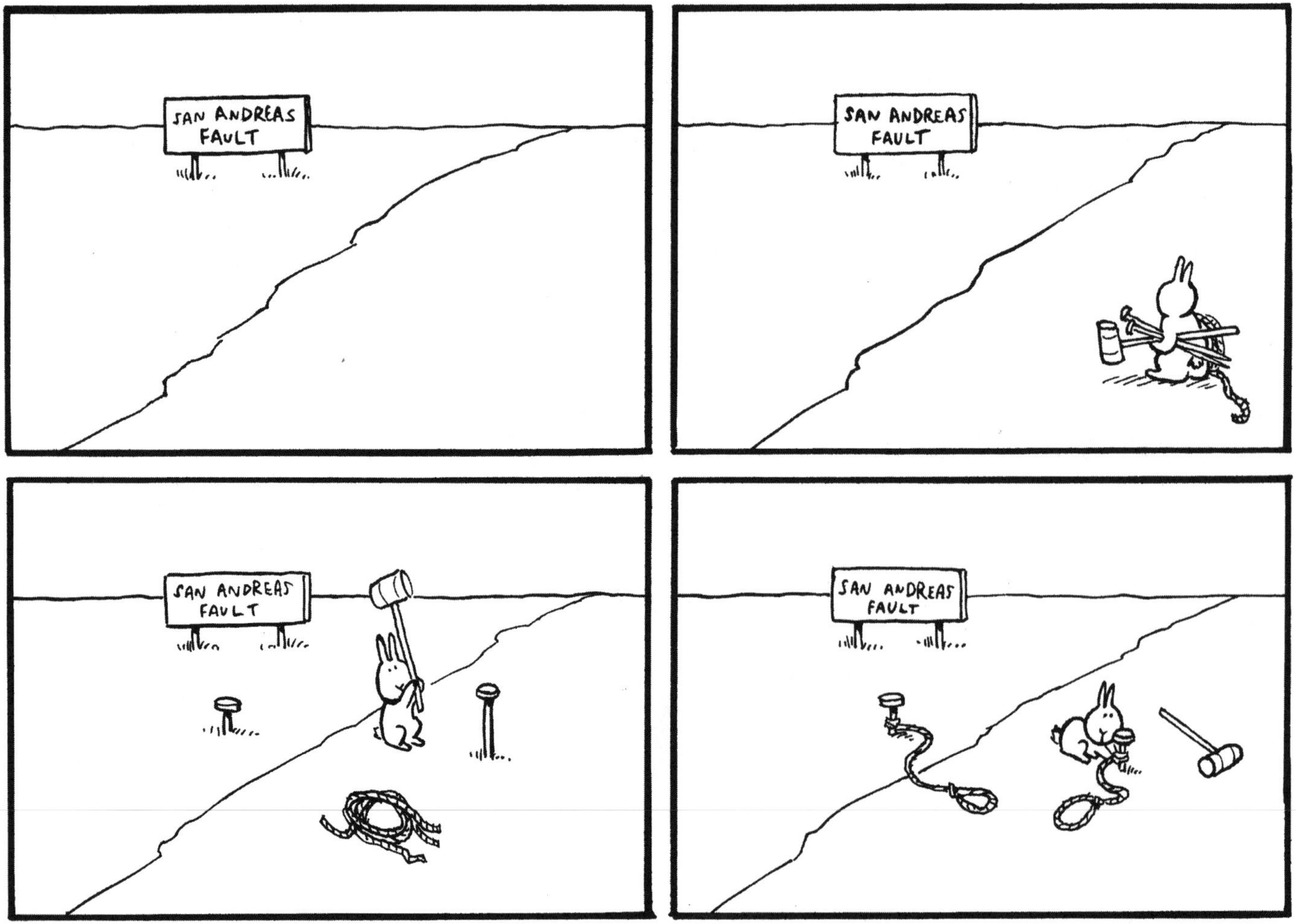
SAN ANDREAS FAULT
SAN ANDREAS FAULT
SAN ANDREAS FAULT
SAN ANDREAS FAULT

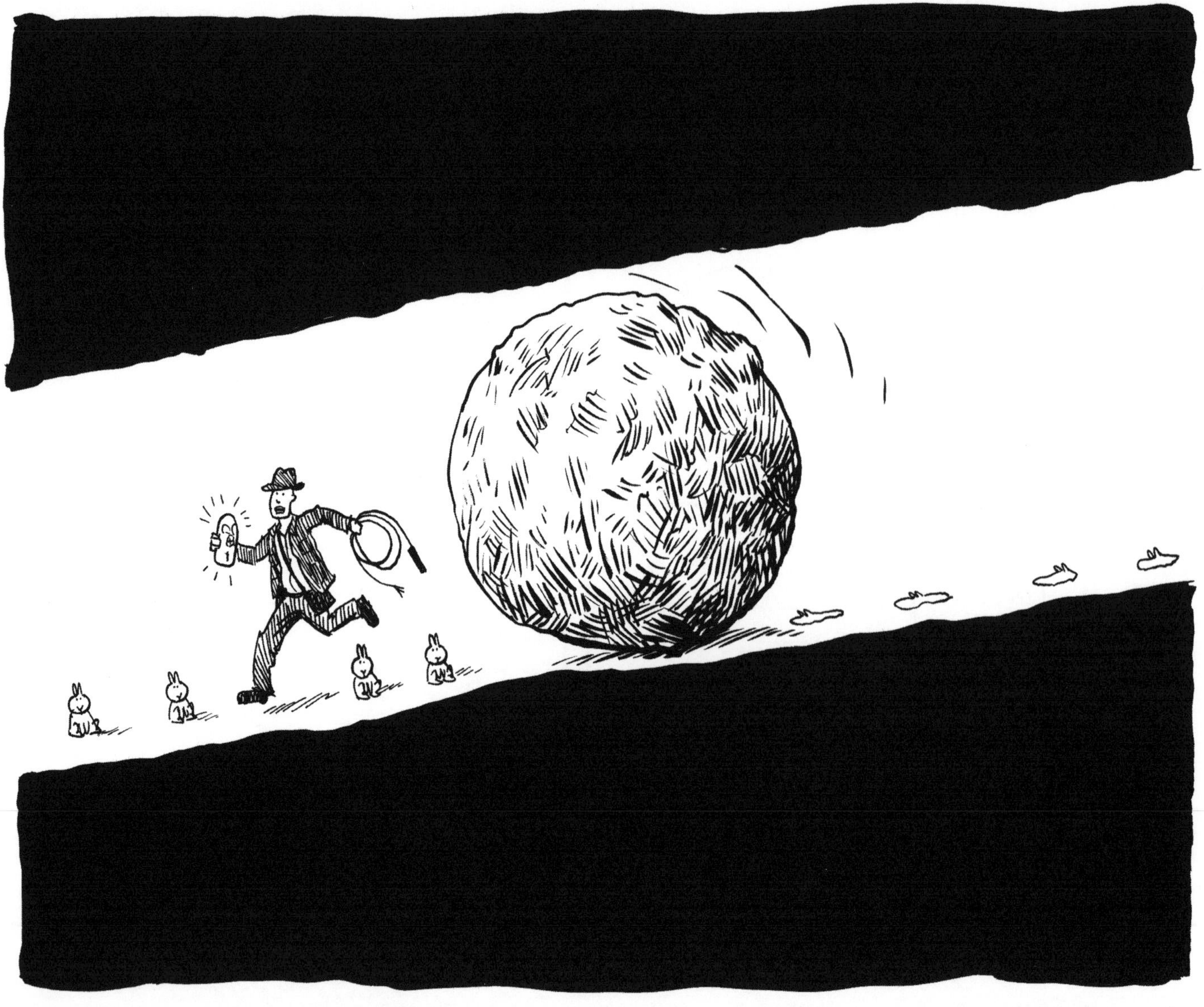

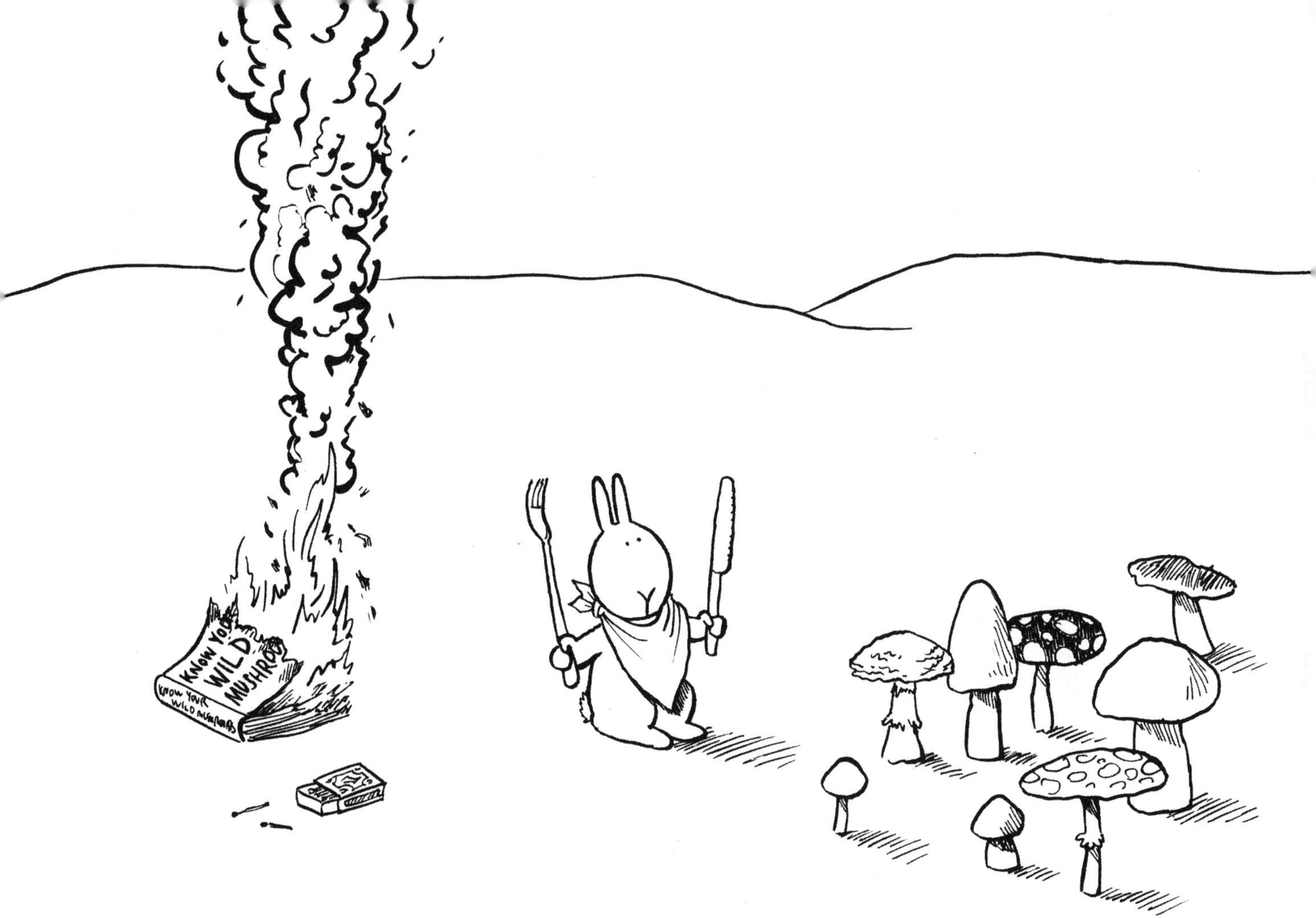
KNOW YO
WILD
MUSHROO
KNOW YOUR
WILD

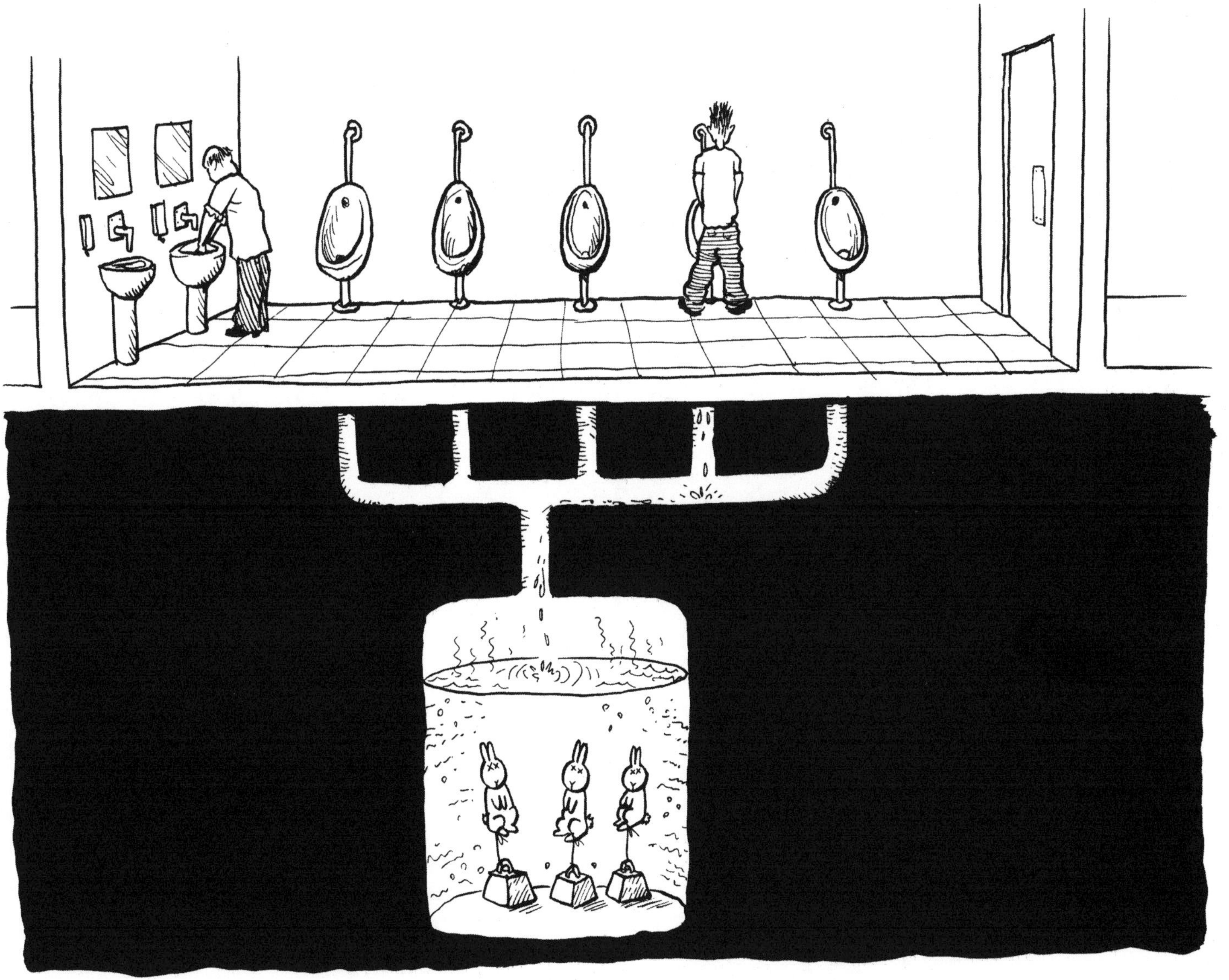

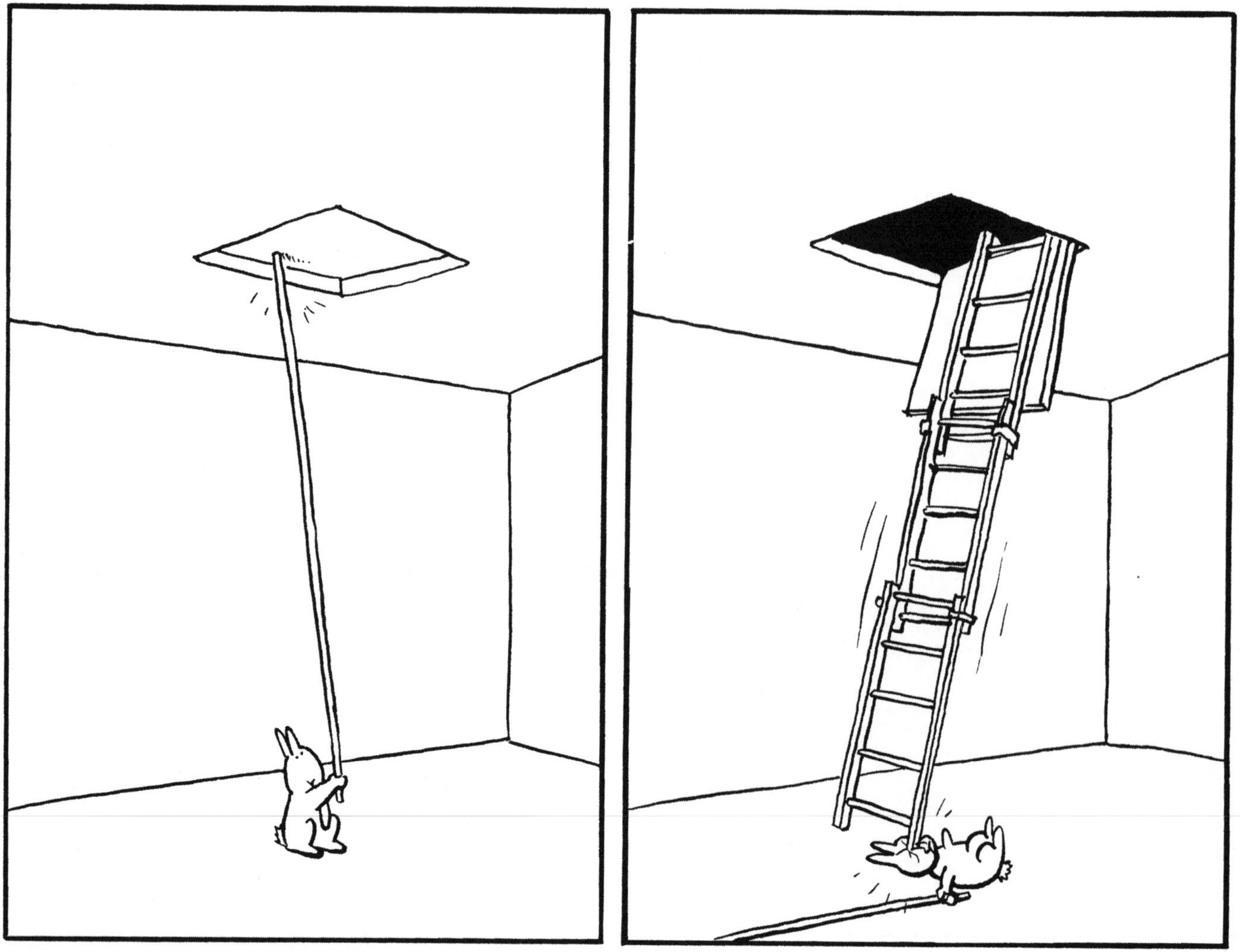

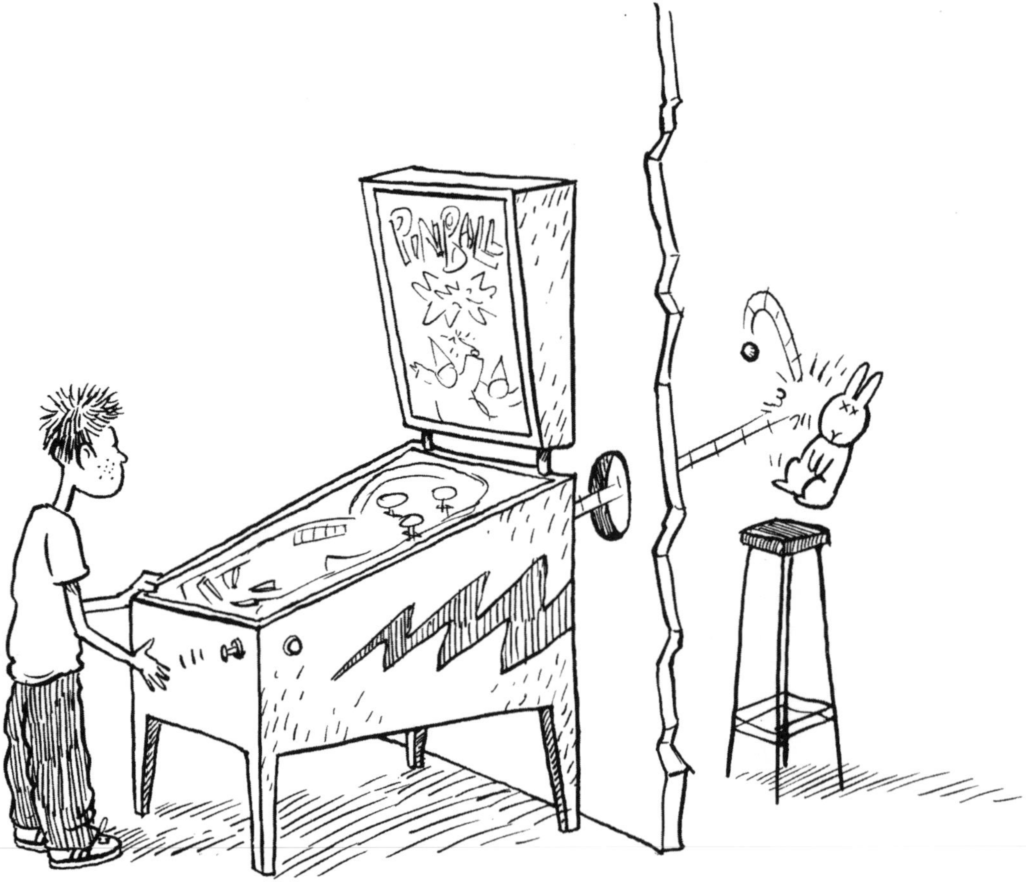
PINBALL

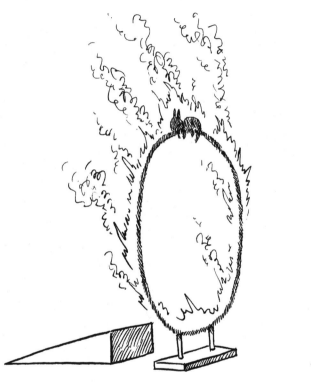

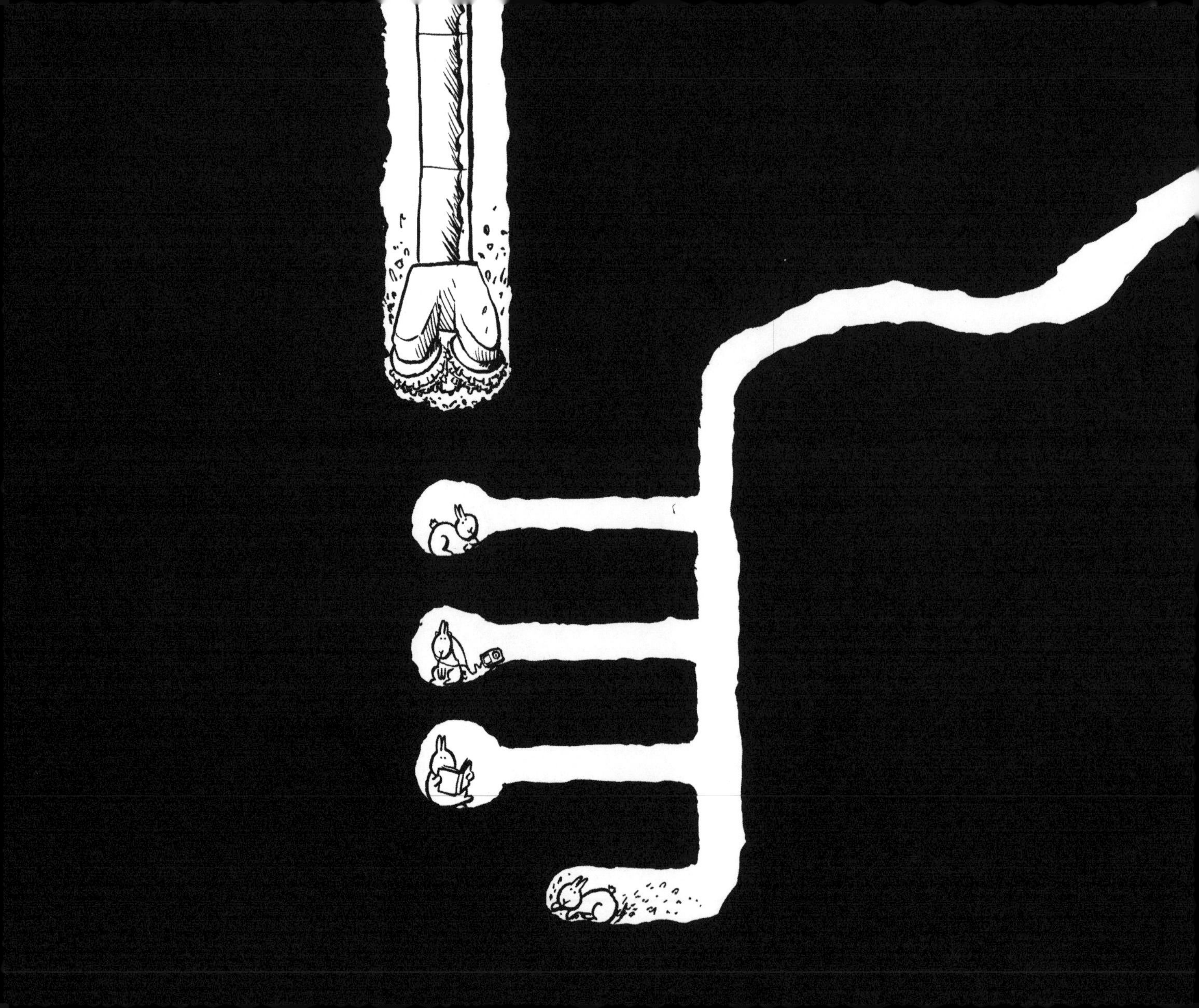

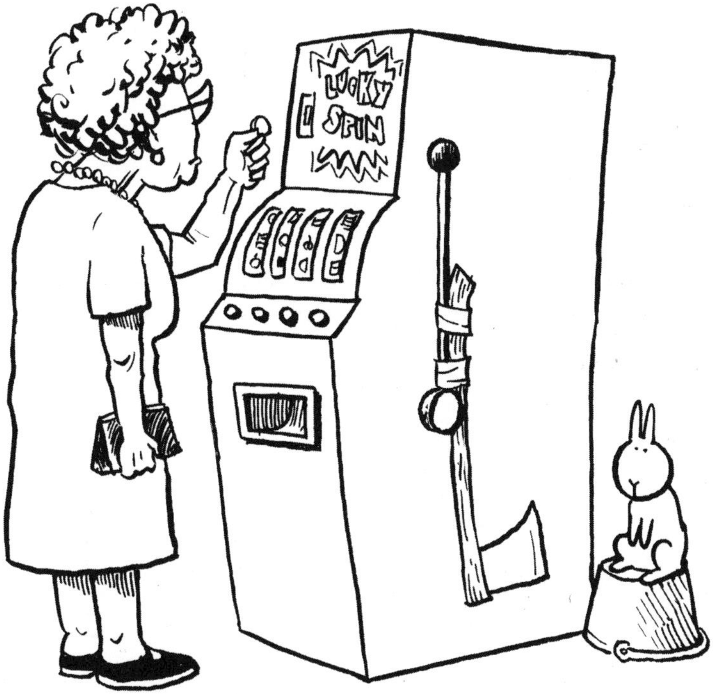
LUCKY
SPIN

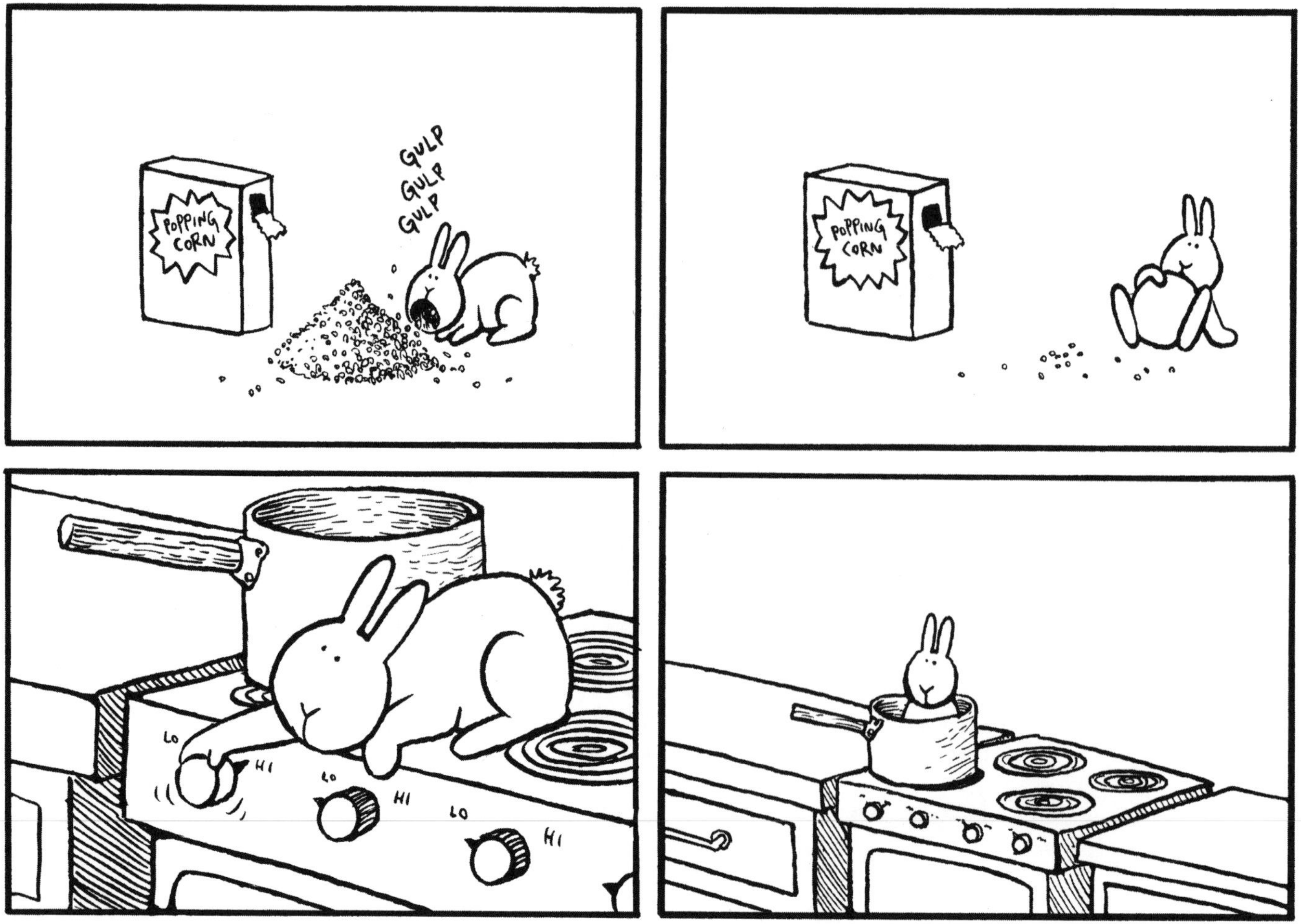
POPPING CORN
GULP
GULP
GULP
POPPING CORN
LO
HI
LO
HI
LO
HI

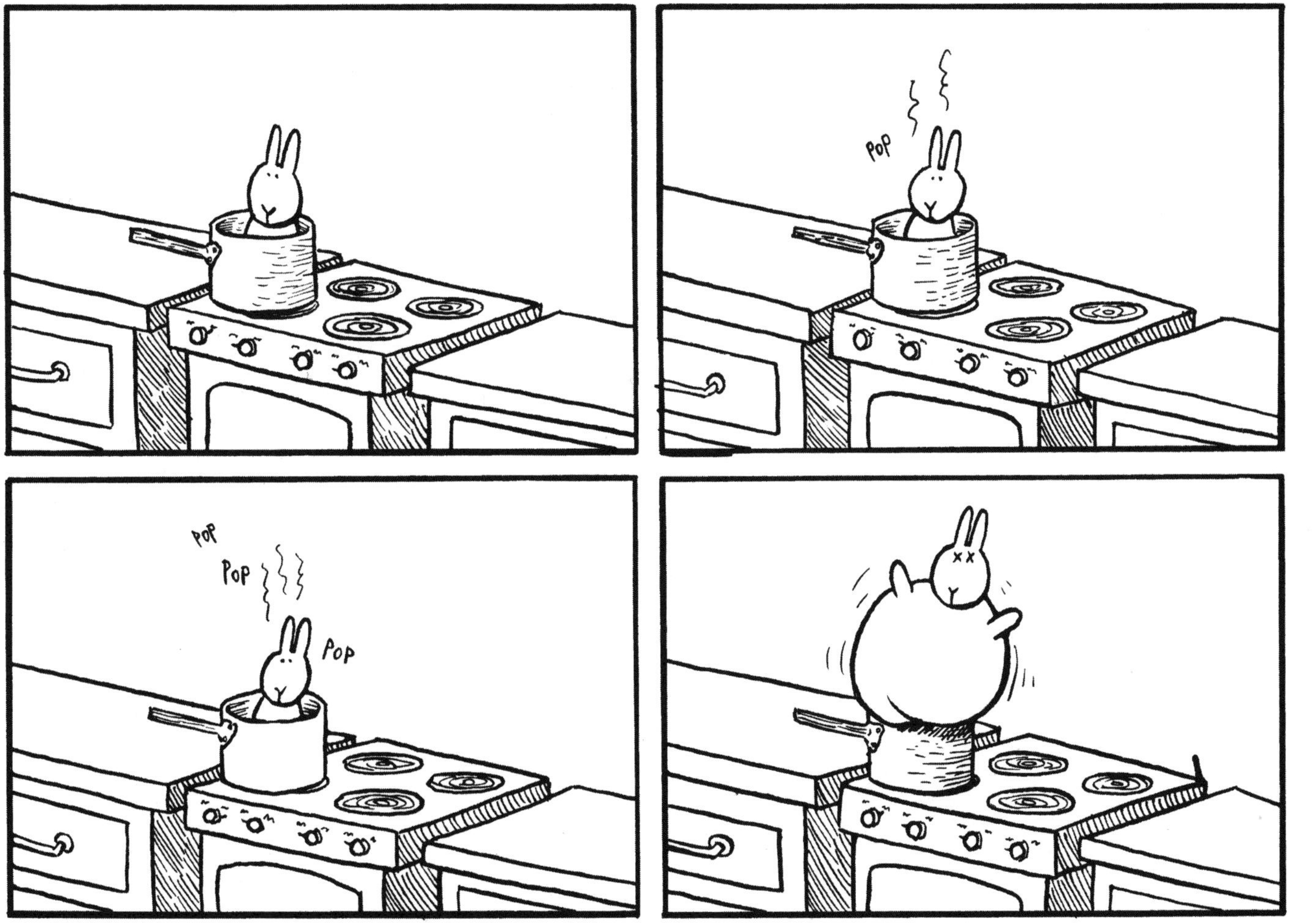
POP
POP
POP
POP

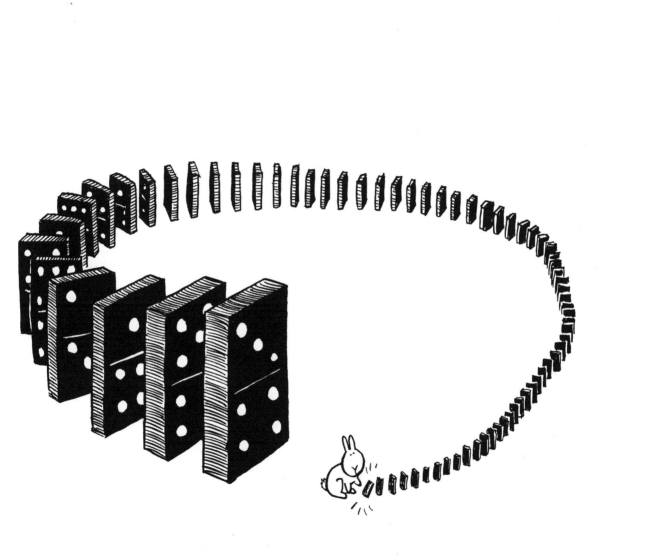

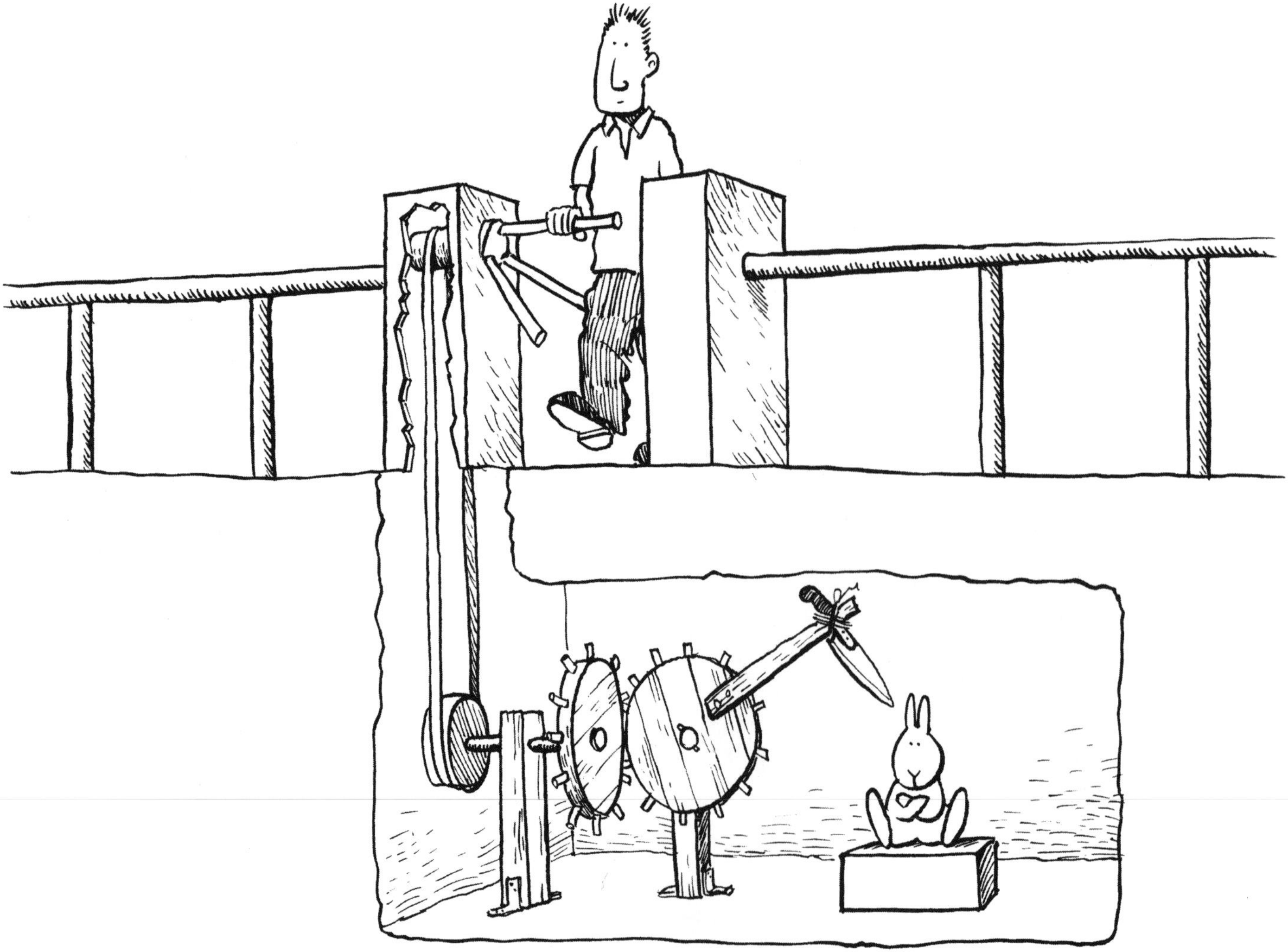

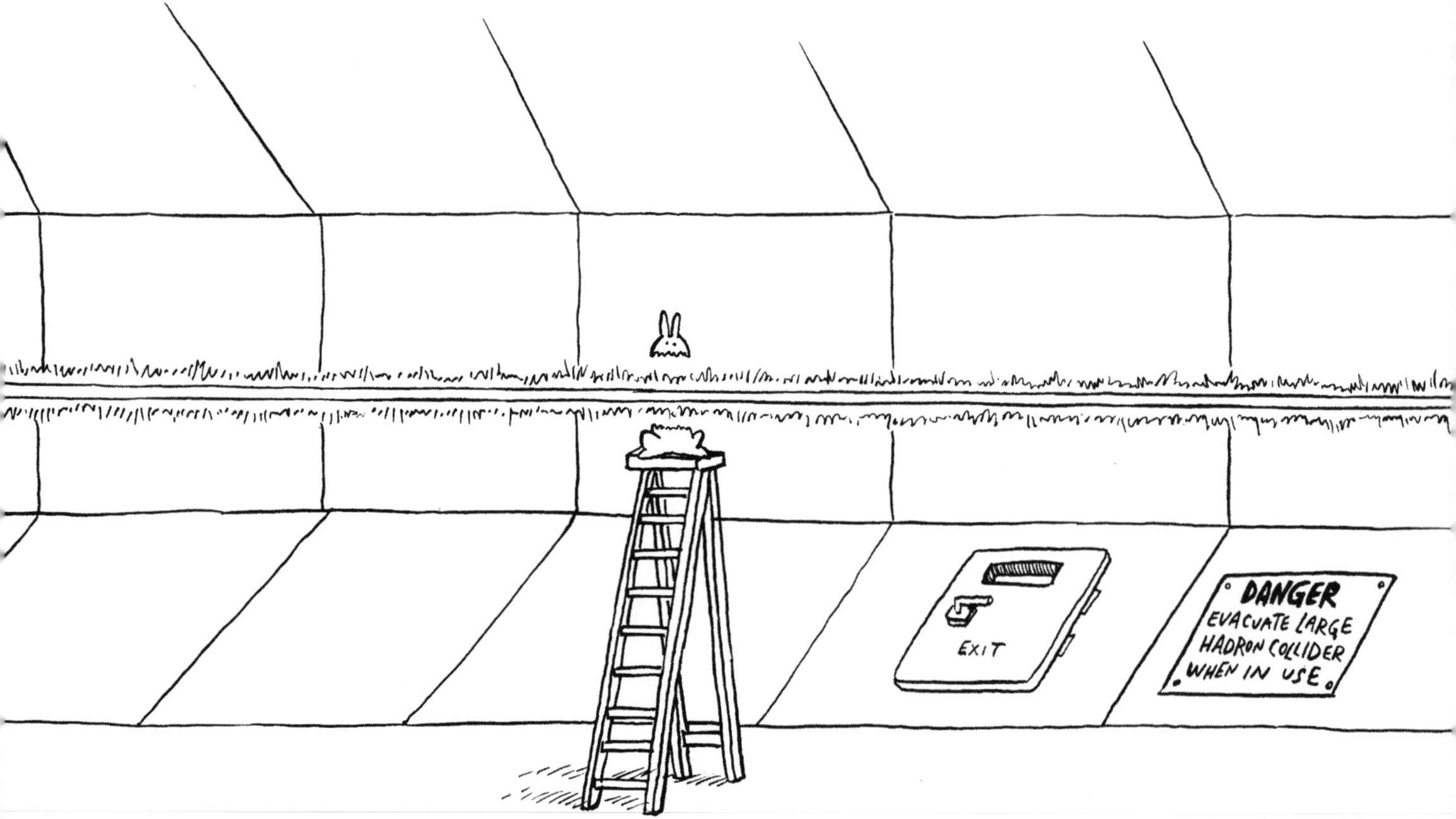
EXIT
DANGER
EVACUATE LARGE
HADRON COLLIDER
WHEN IN USE.

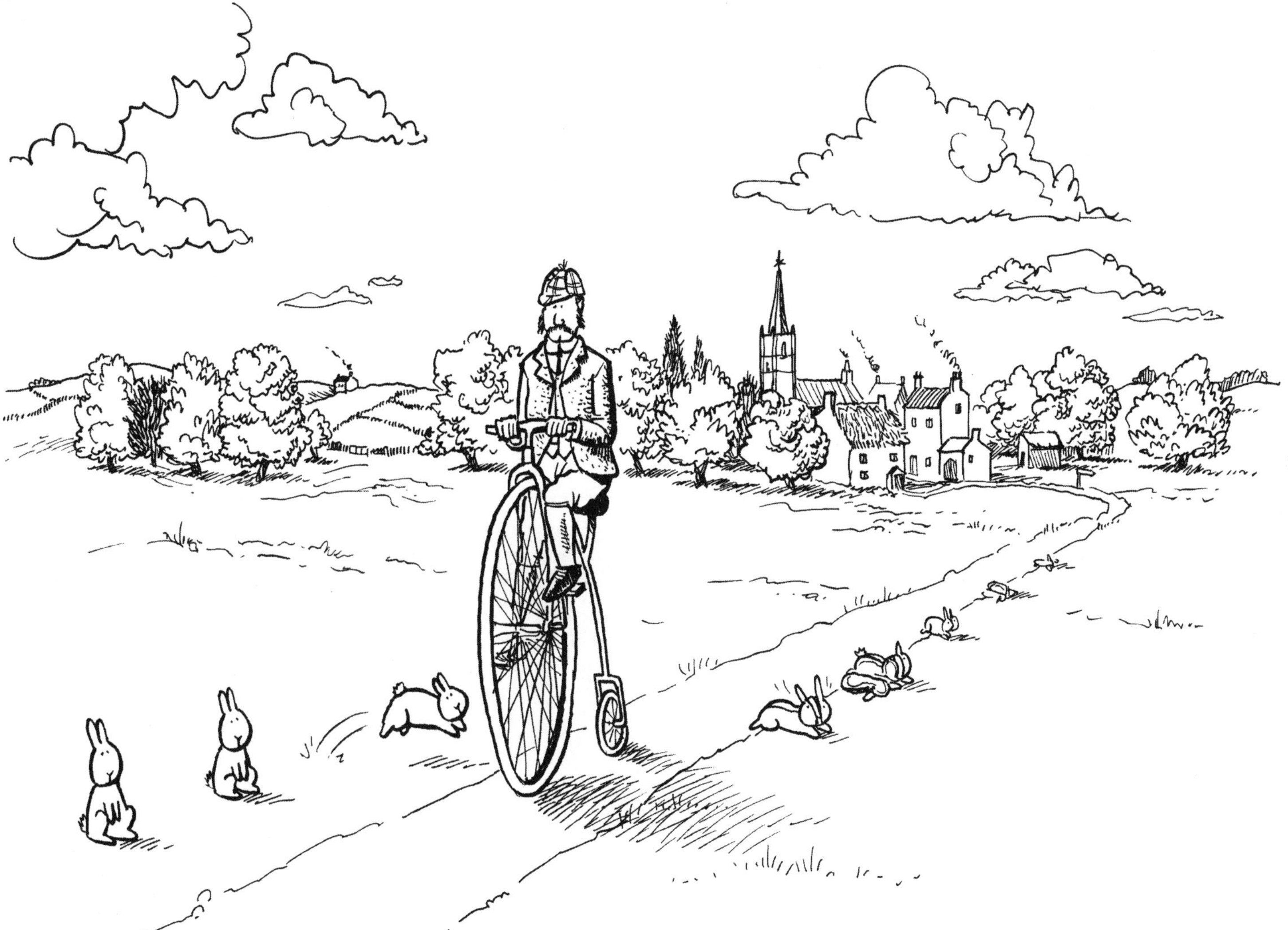

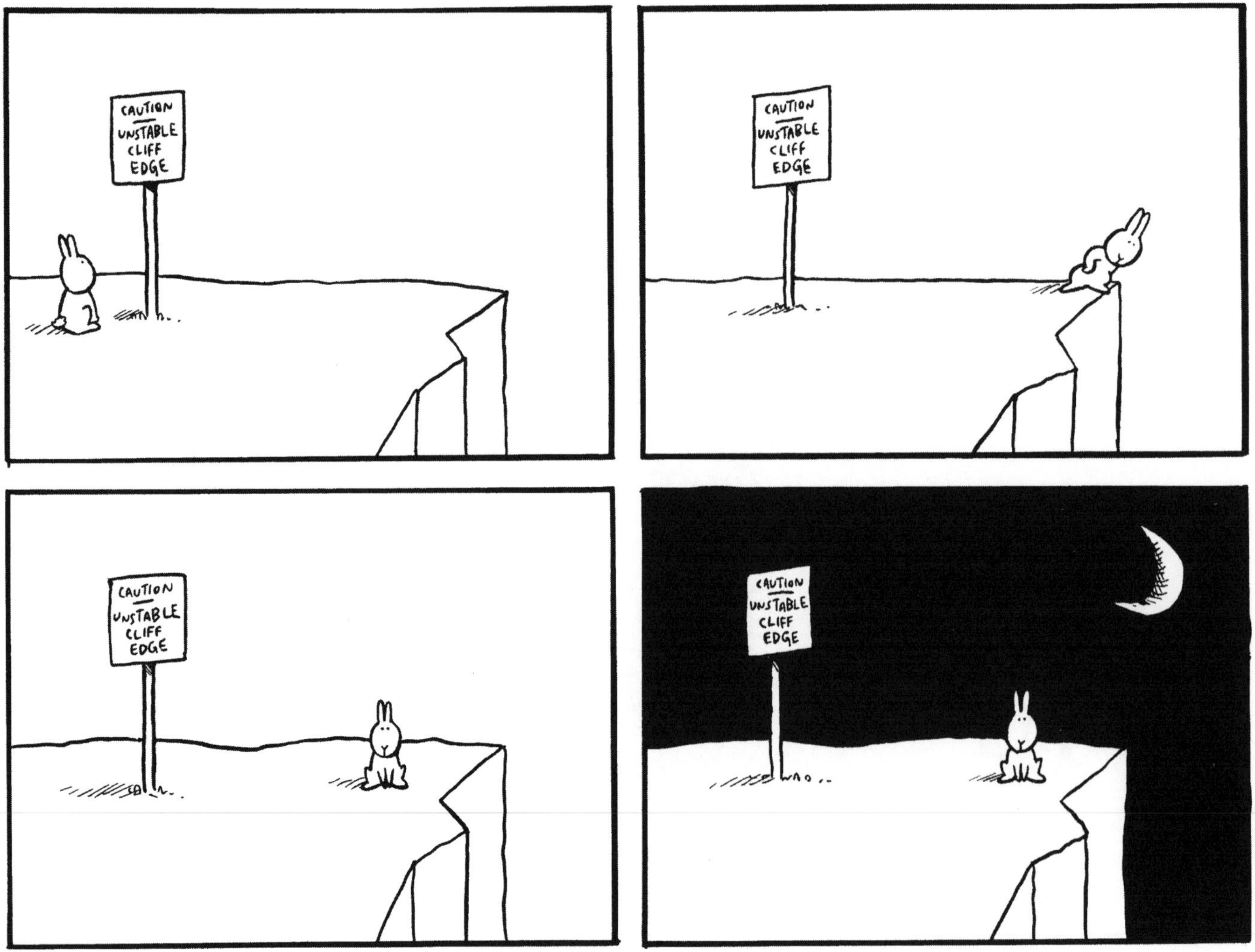
CAUTION
UNSTABLE
CLIFF
EDGE
CAUTION
UNSTABLE
CLIFF
EDGE
CAUTION
UNSTABLE
CLIFF
EDGE
CAUTION
UNSTABLE
CLIFF
EDGE

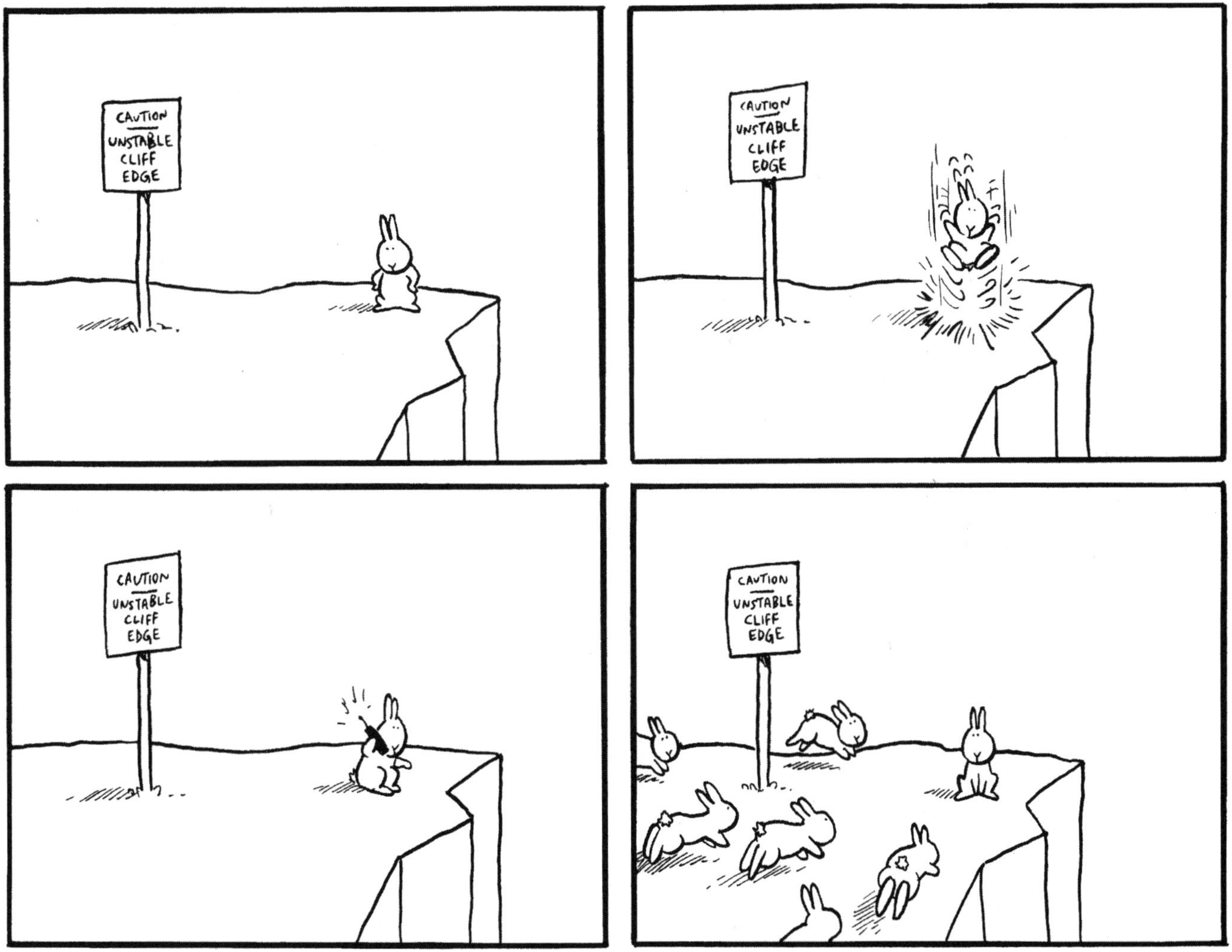
CAUTION
UNSTABLE CLIFF EDGE
CAUTION
UNSTABLE CLIFF EDGE
CAUTION
UNSTABLE CLIFF EDGE
CAUTION
UNSTABLE CLIFF EDGE

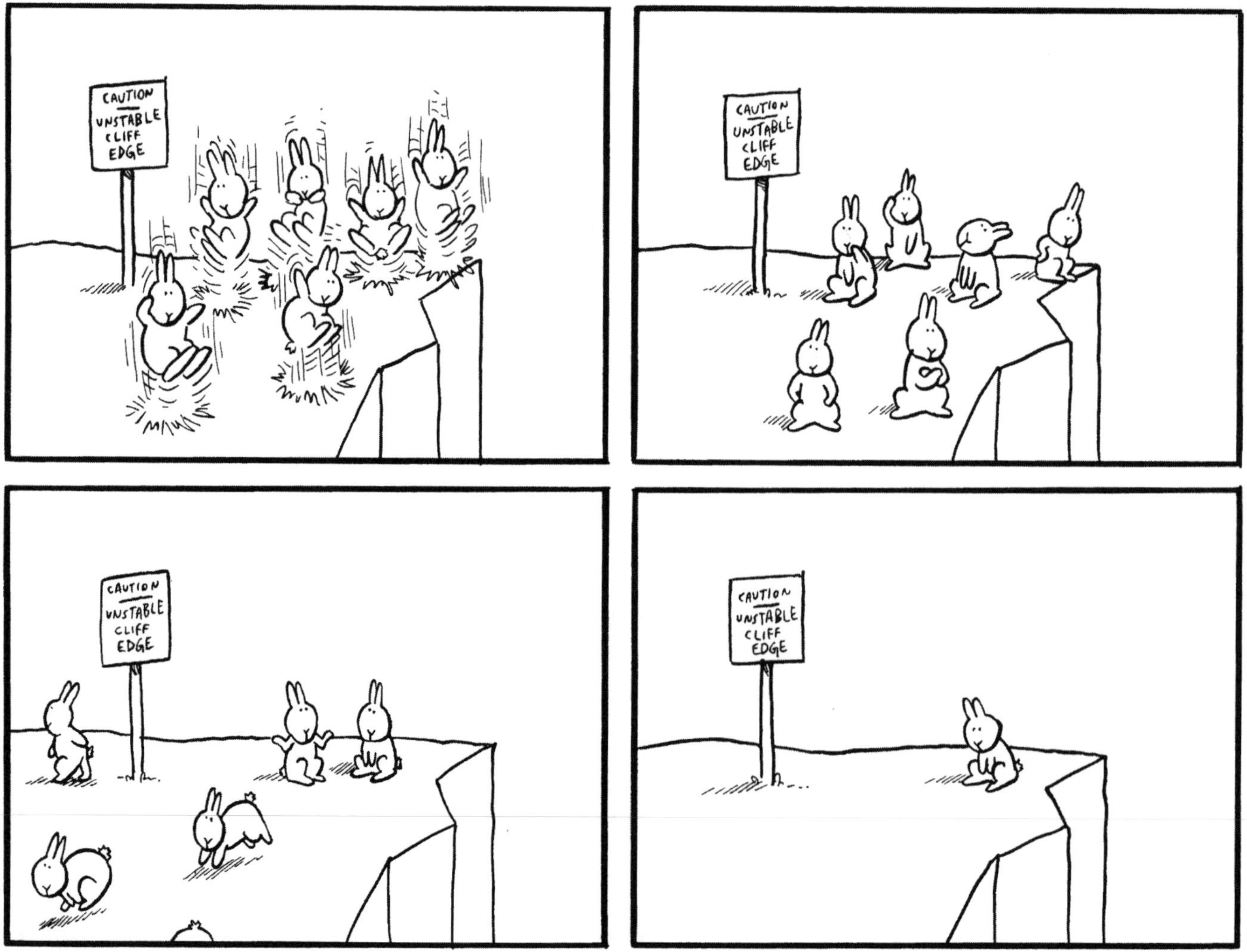
CAUTION UNSTABLE CLIFF EDGE
CAUTION UNSTABLE CLIFF EDGE
CAUTION UNSTABLE CLIFF EDGE
CAUTION UNSTABLE CLIFF EDGE

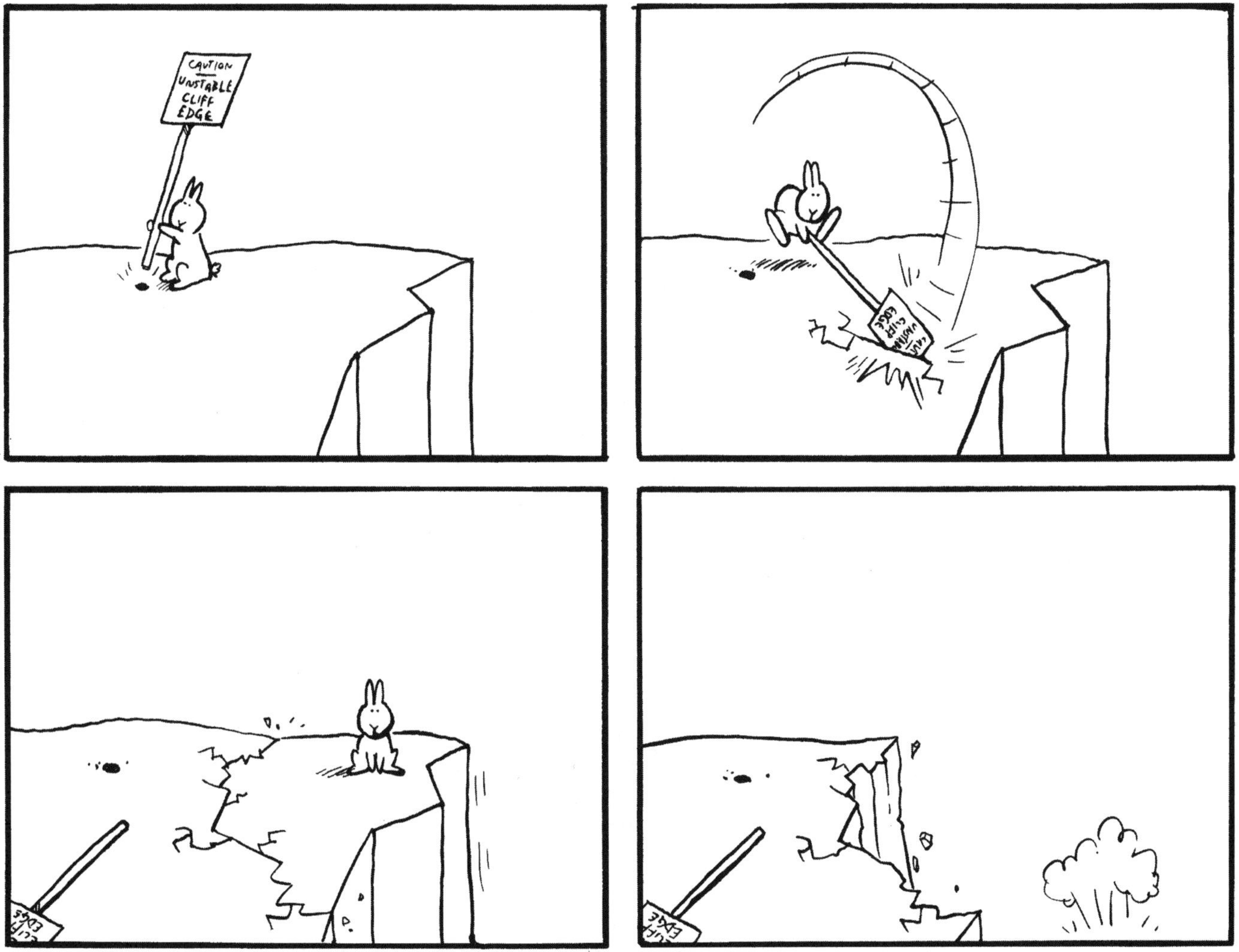
CAUTION
UNSTABLE
CLIFF
EDGE

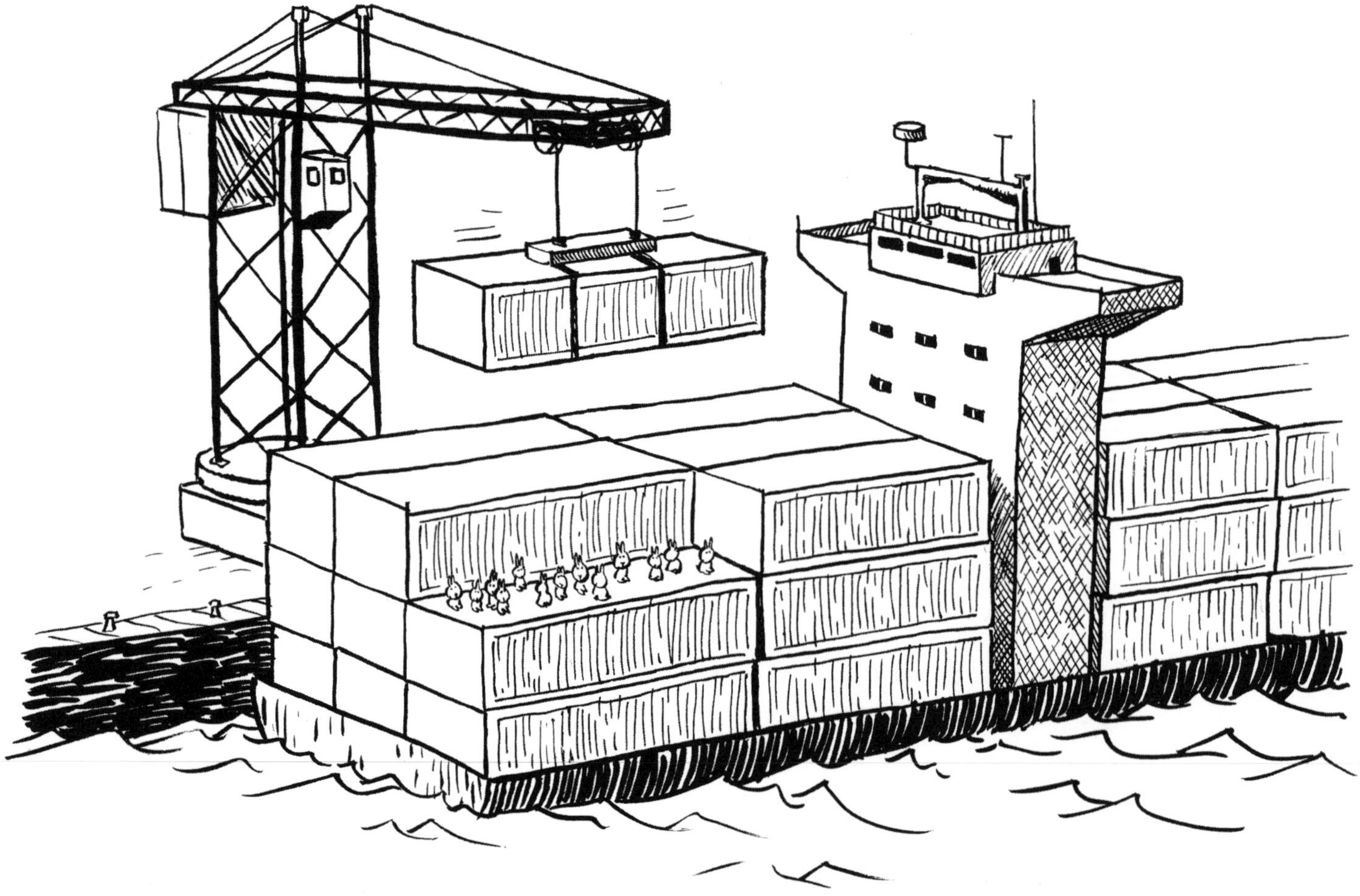

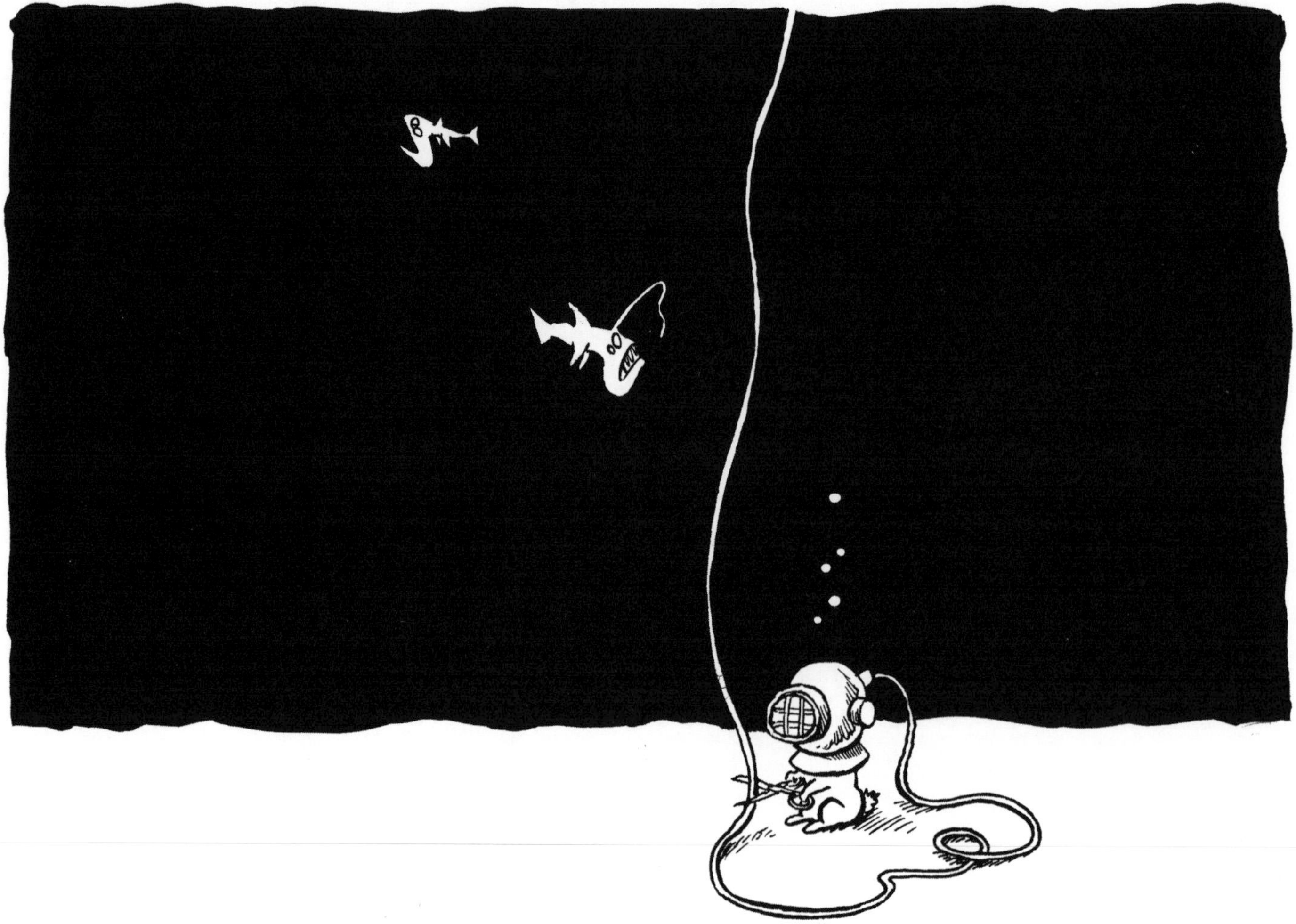

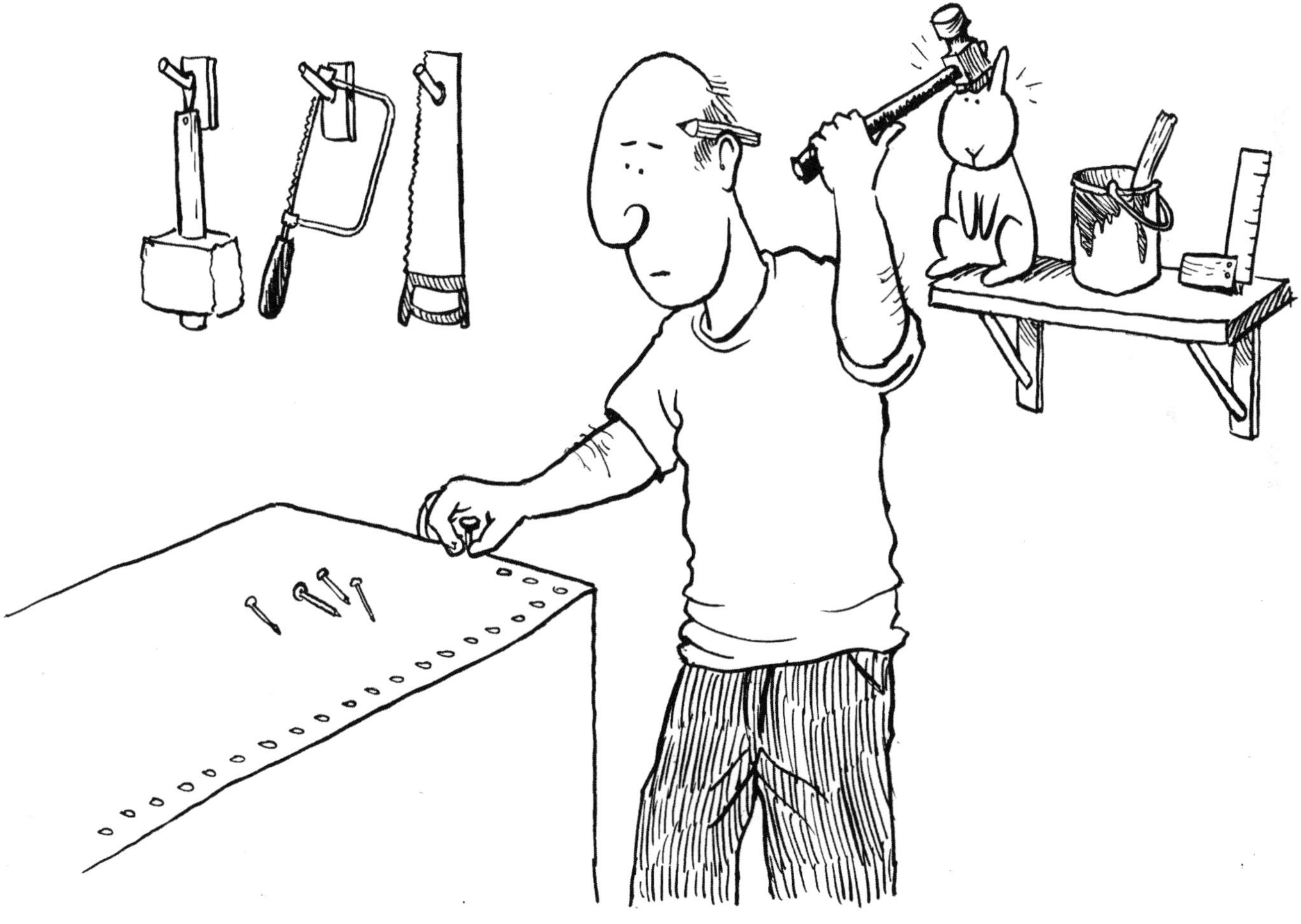

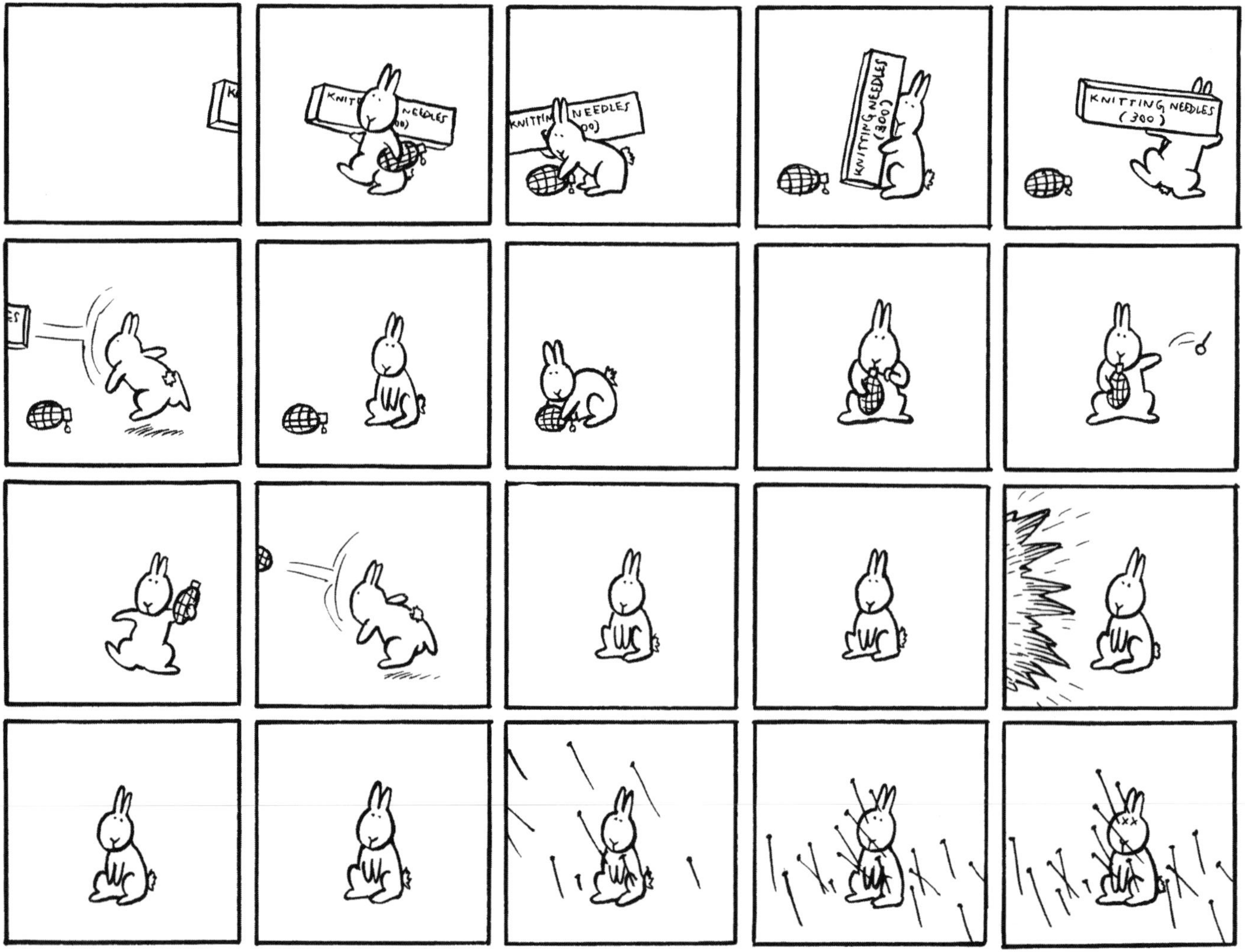
KNITTING NEEDLES
(300)
KNITTING NEEDLES
(300)

DRIVING
SCHOOL

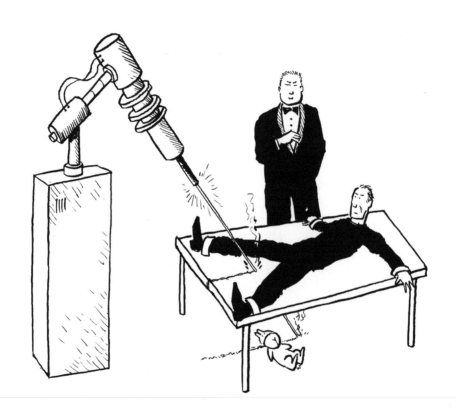

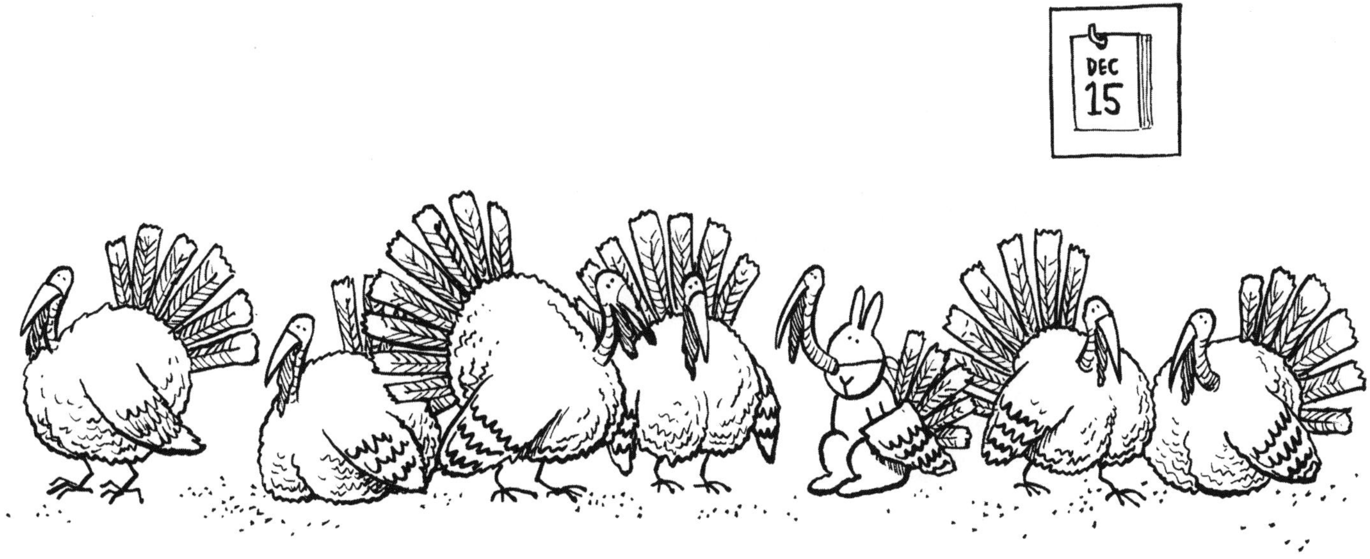
DEC
15

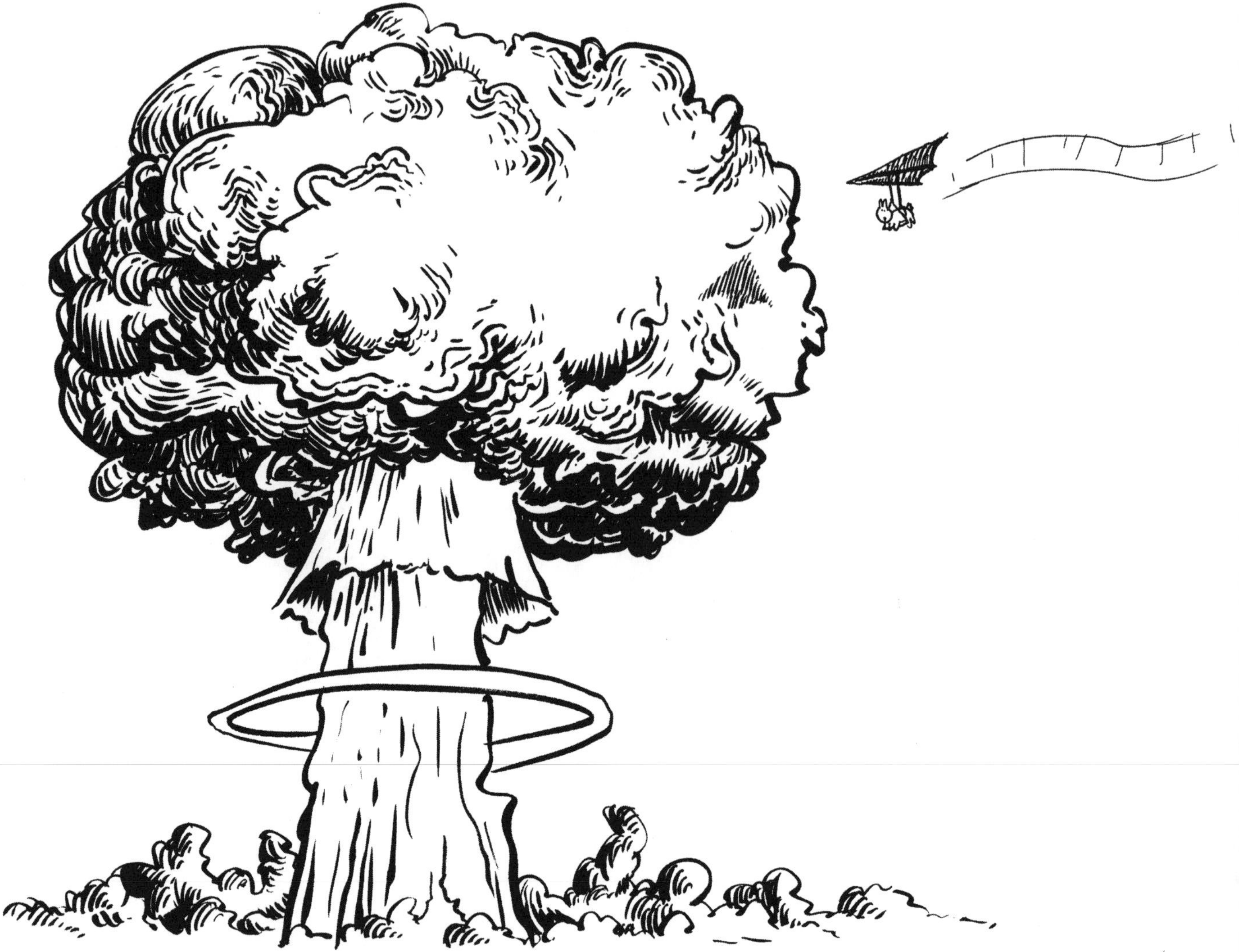

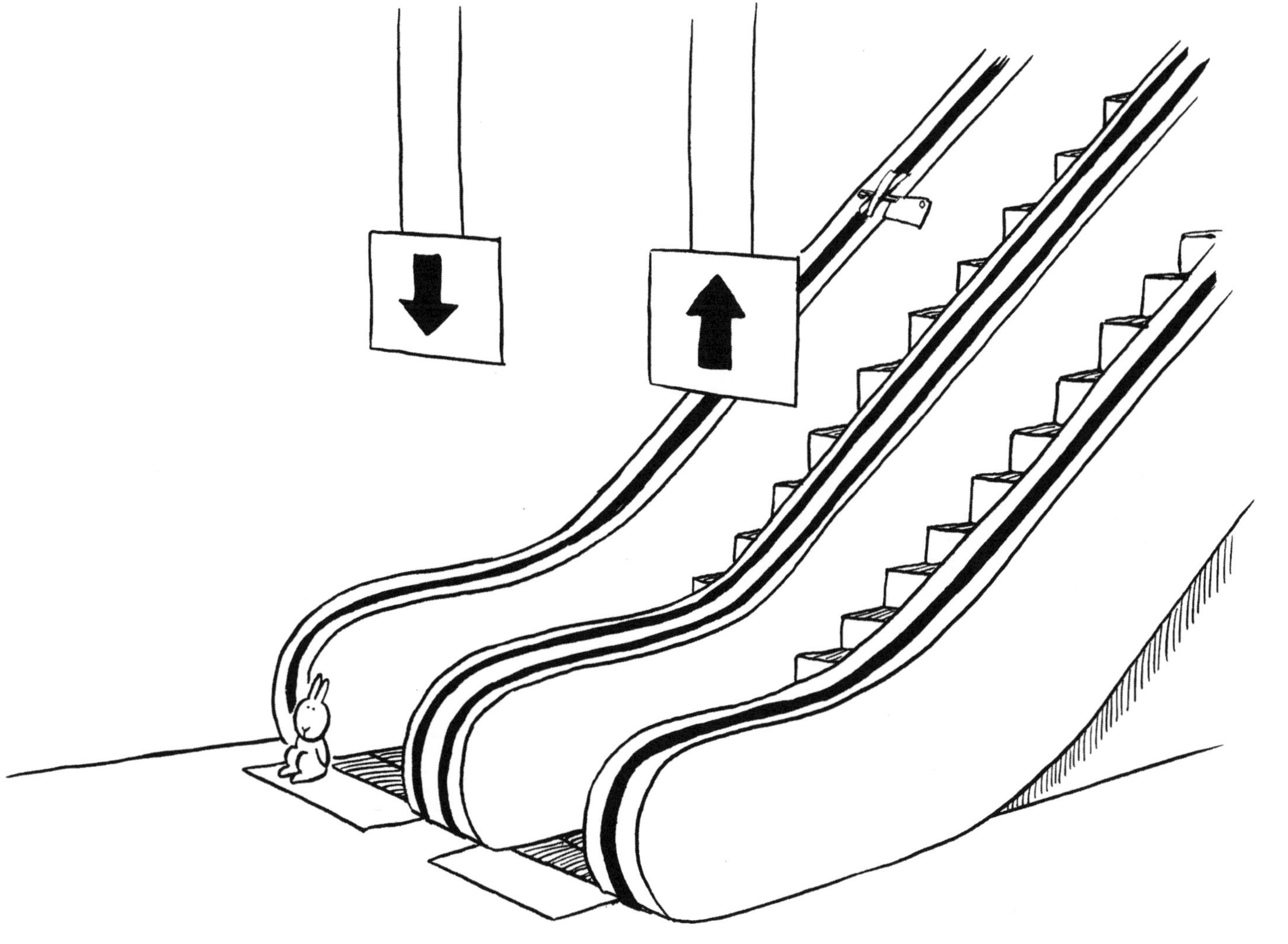

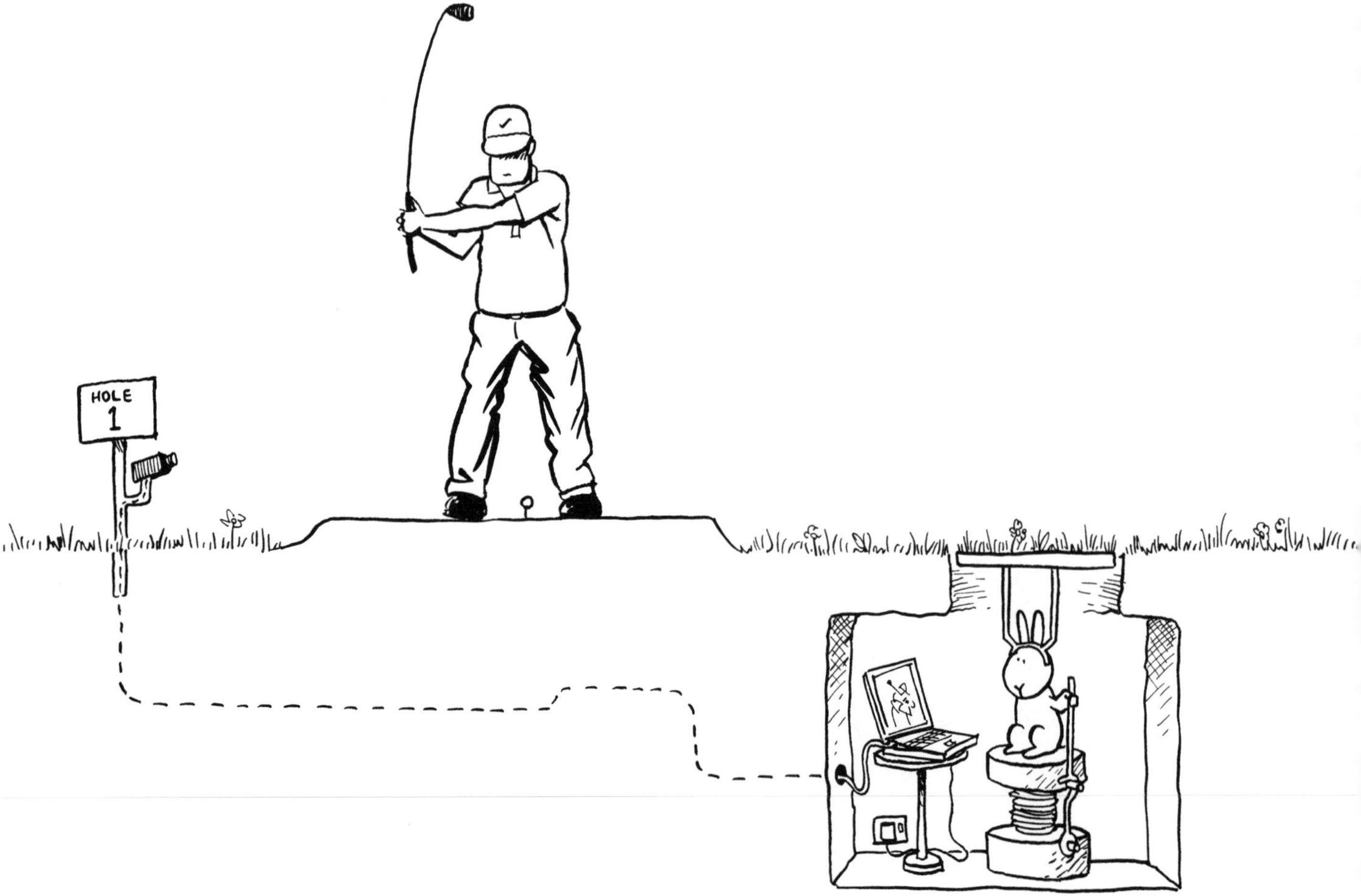
HOLE
1

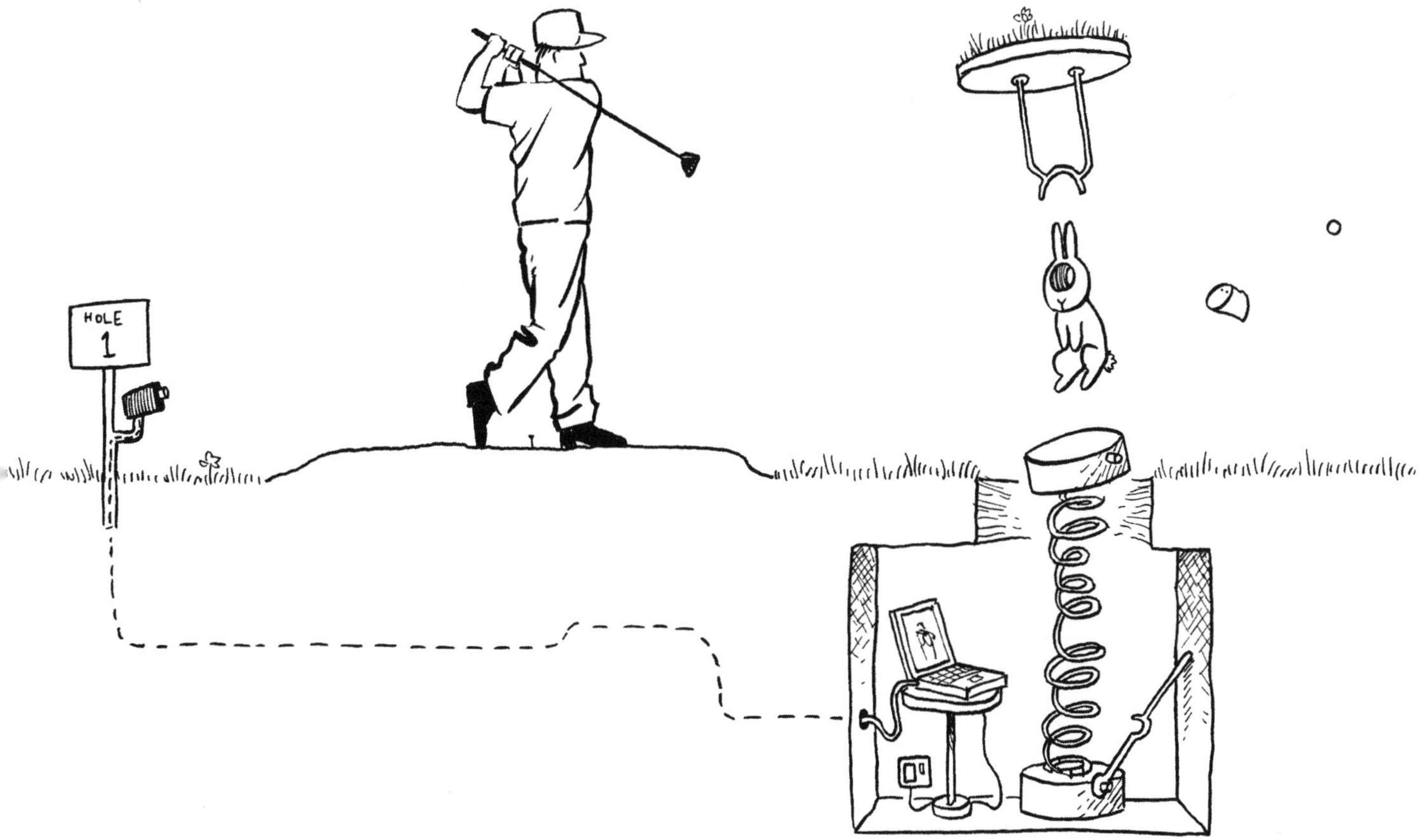
HOLE
1

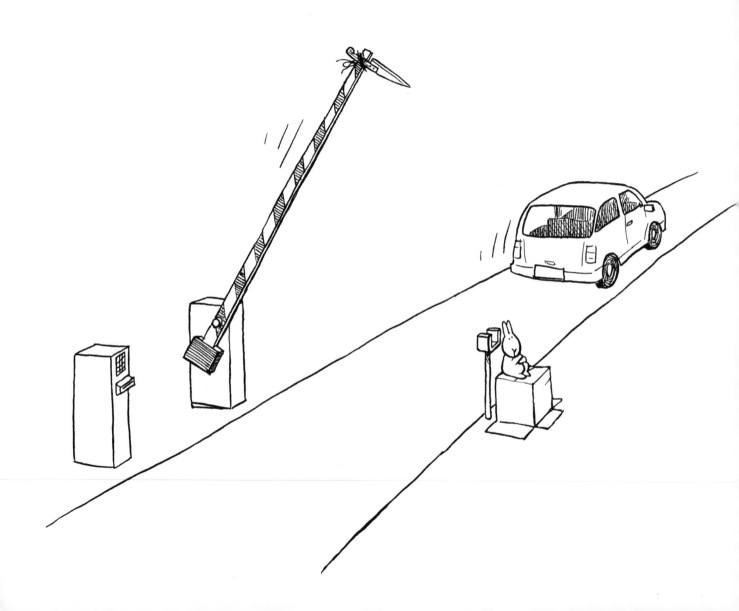

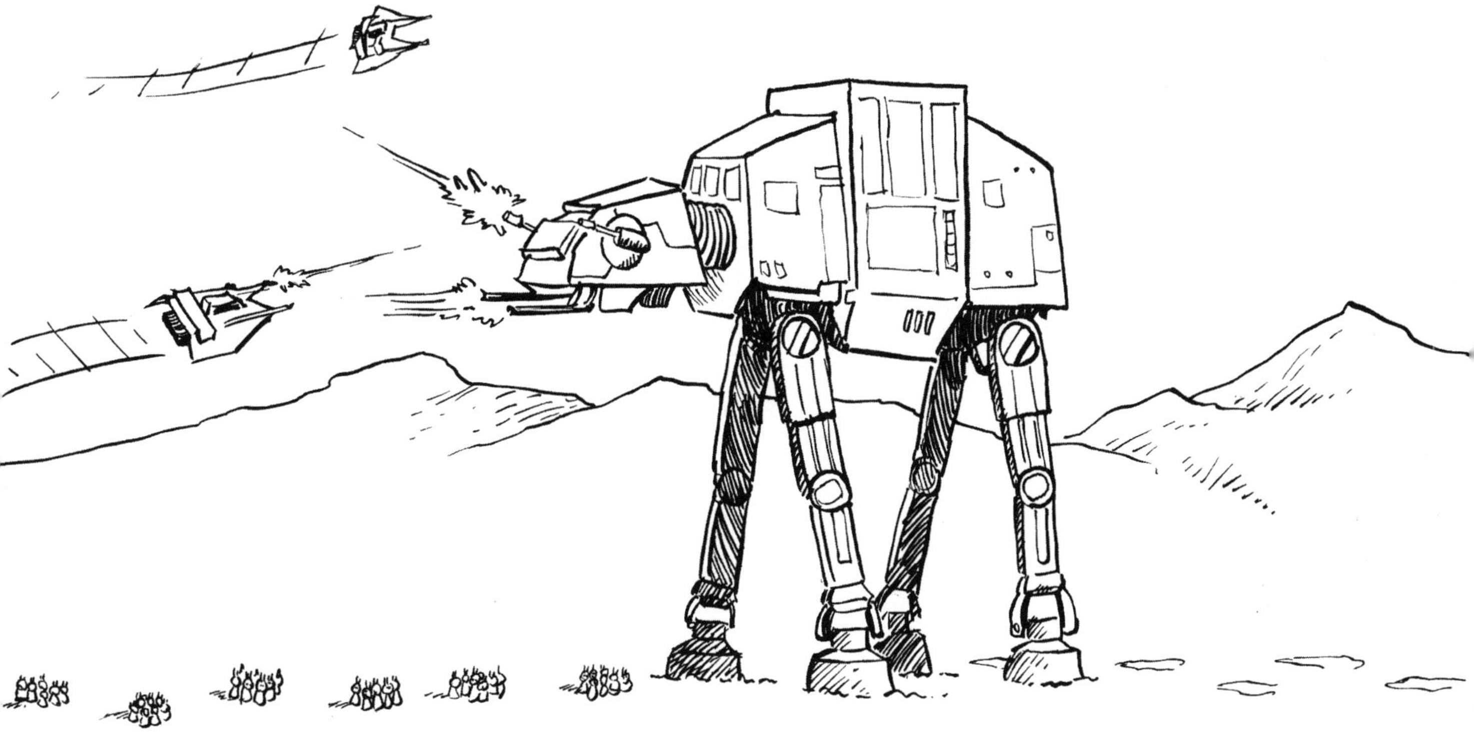

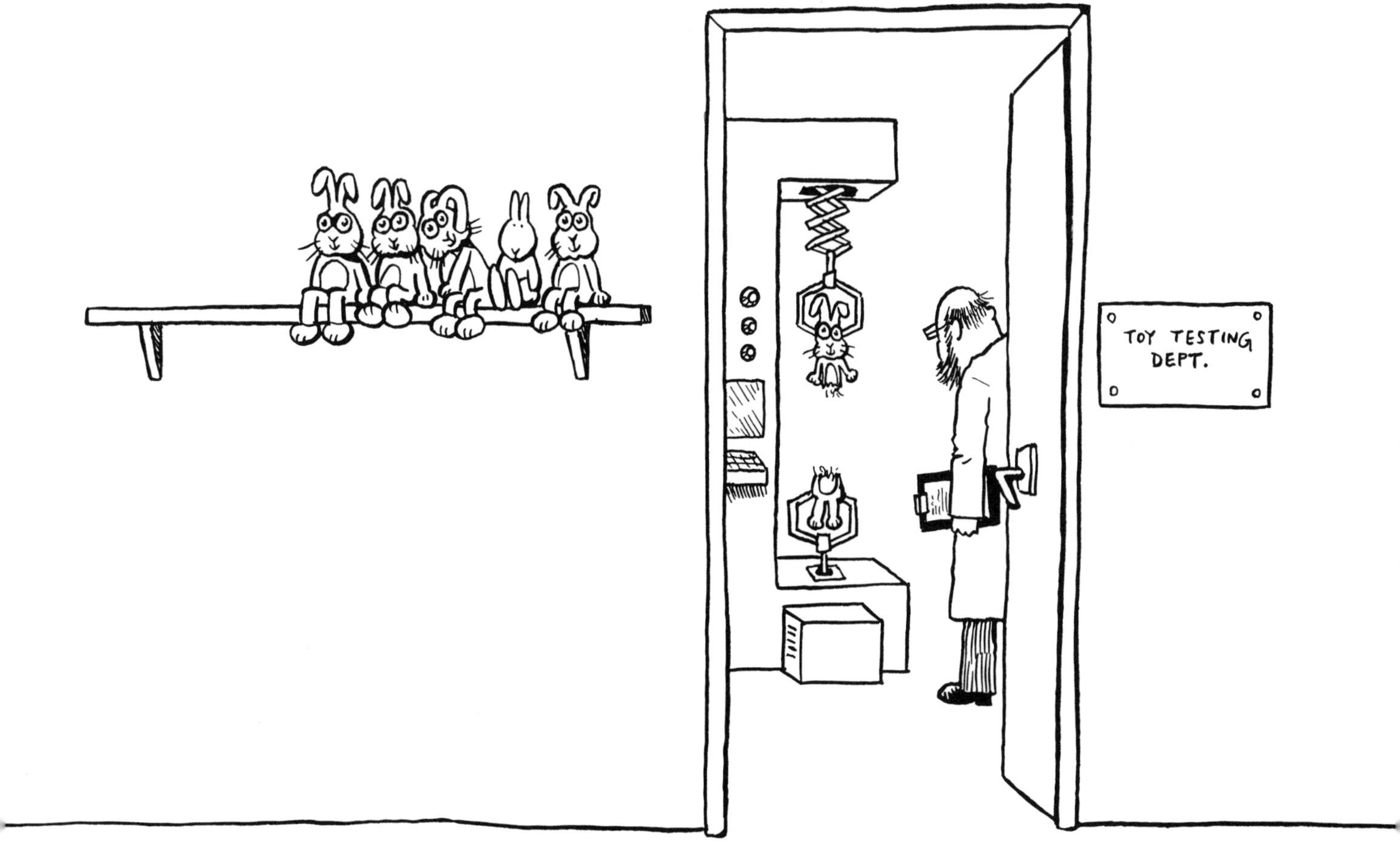
TOY TESTING
DEPT.

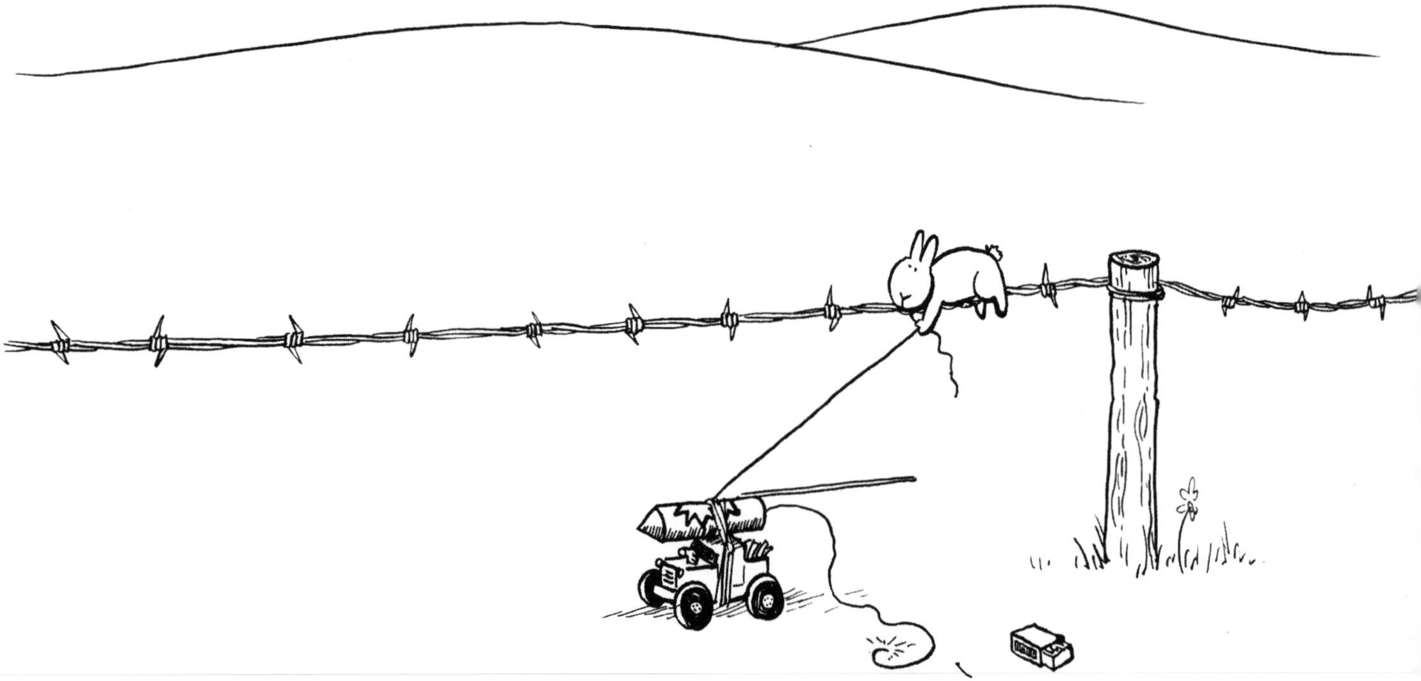

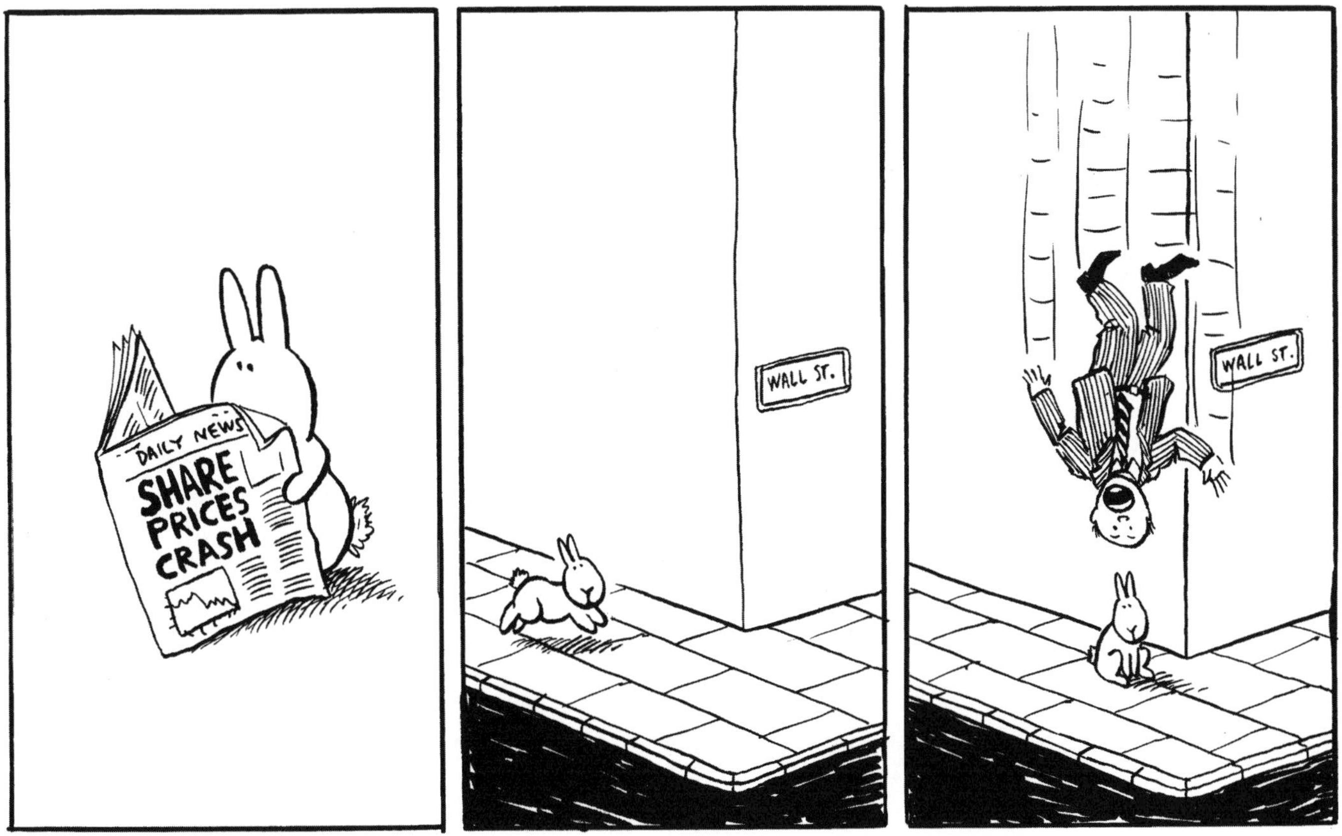

DAILY NEWS
SHARE PRICES CRASH
WALL ST.
WALL ST.

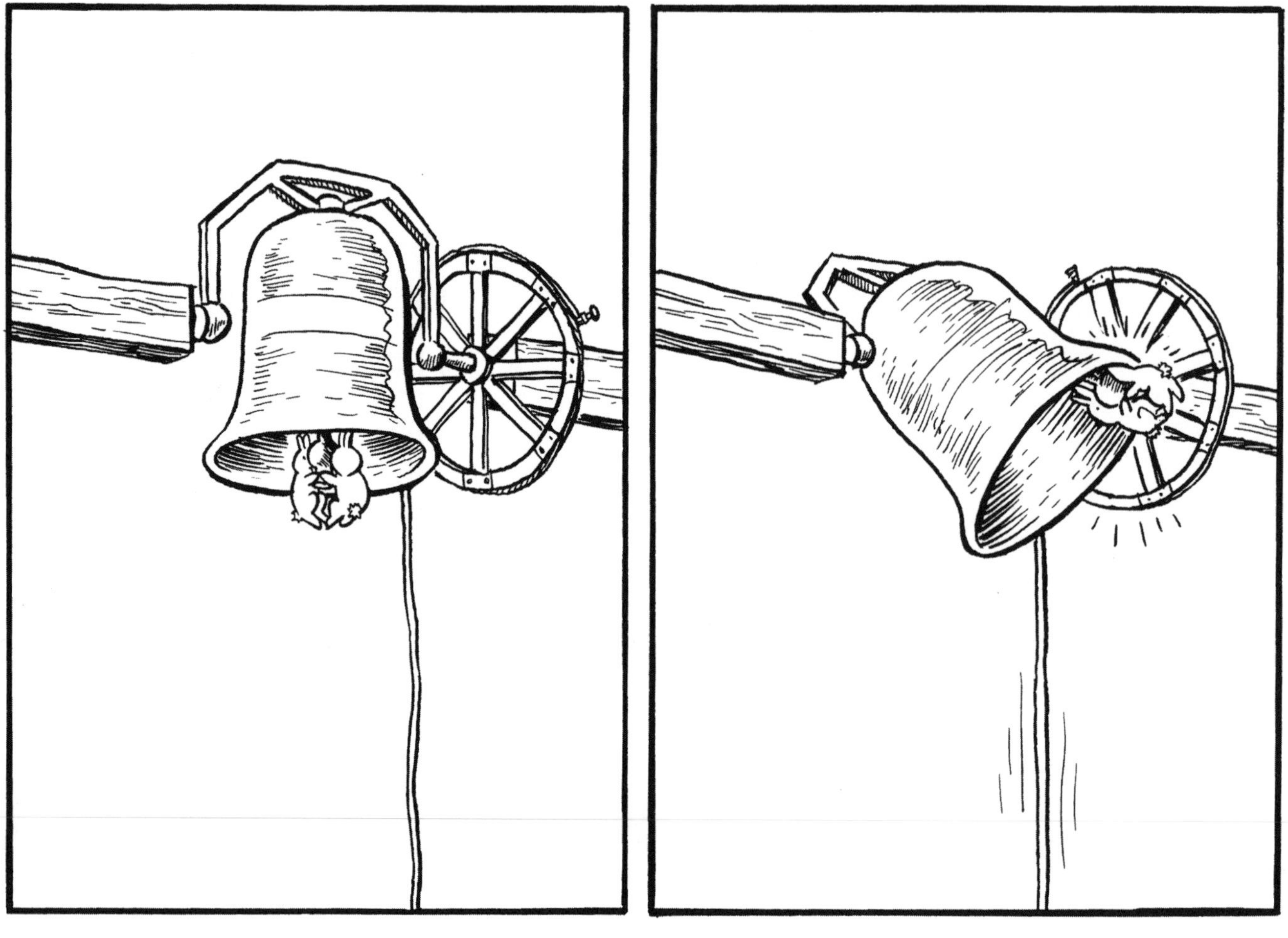

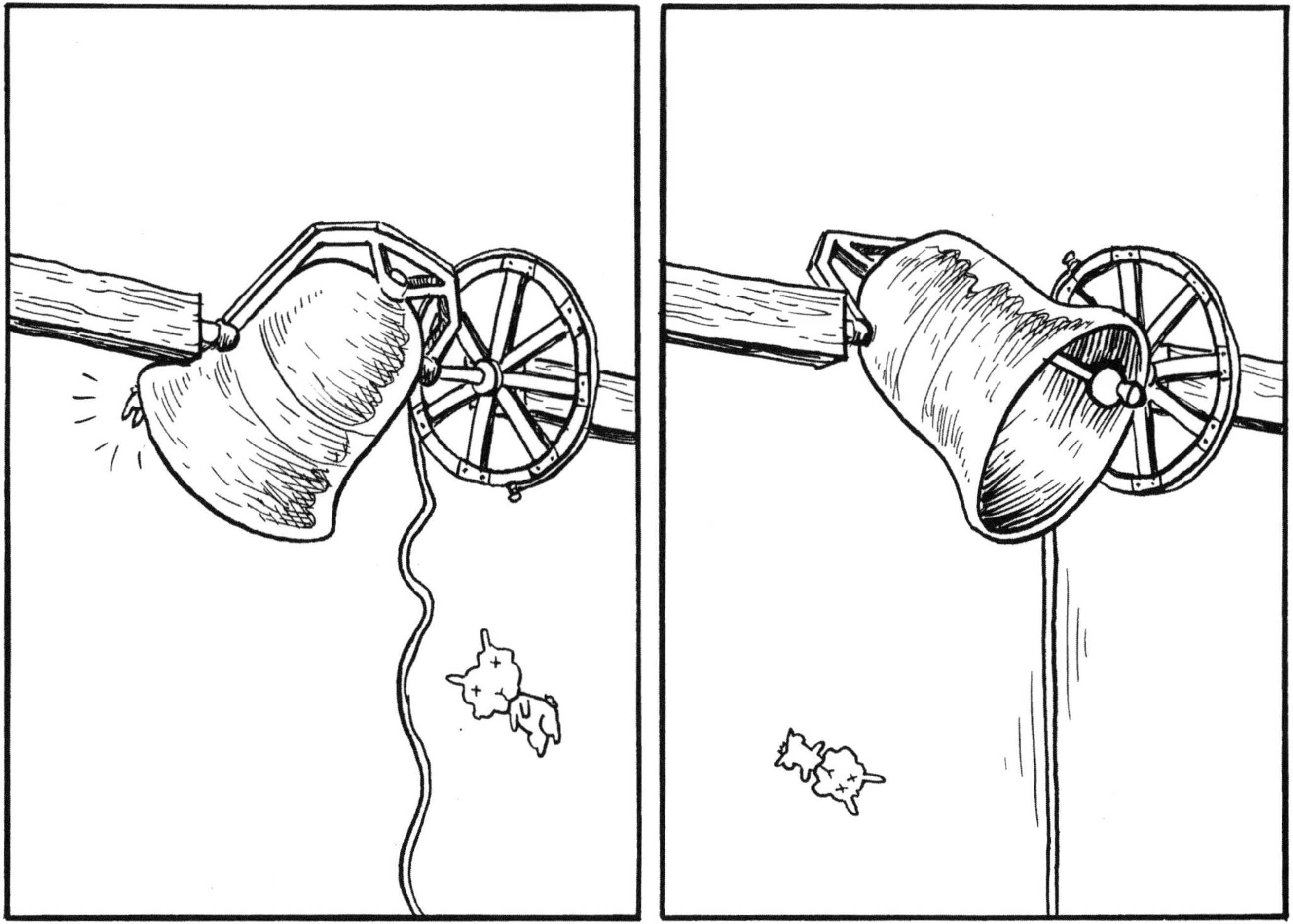

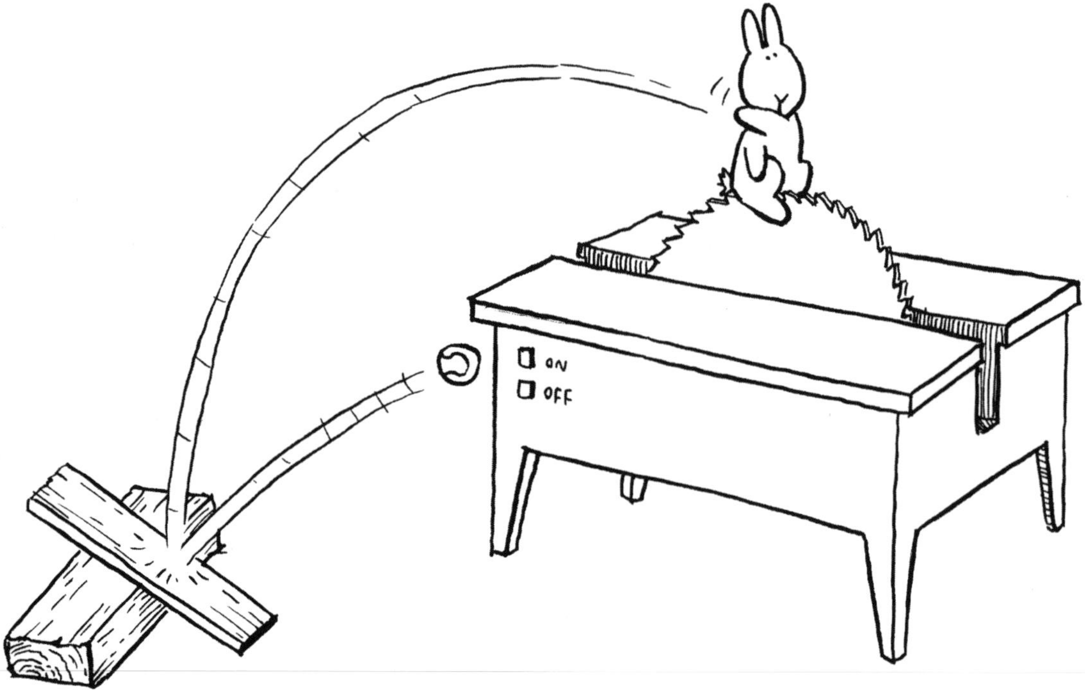
ON
OFF

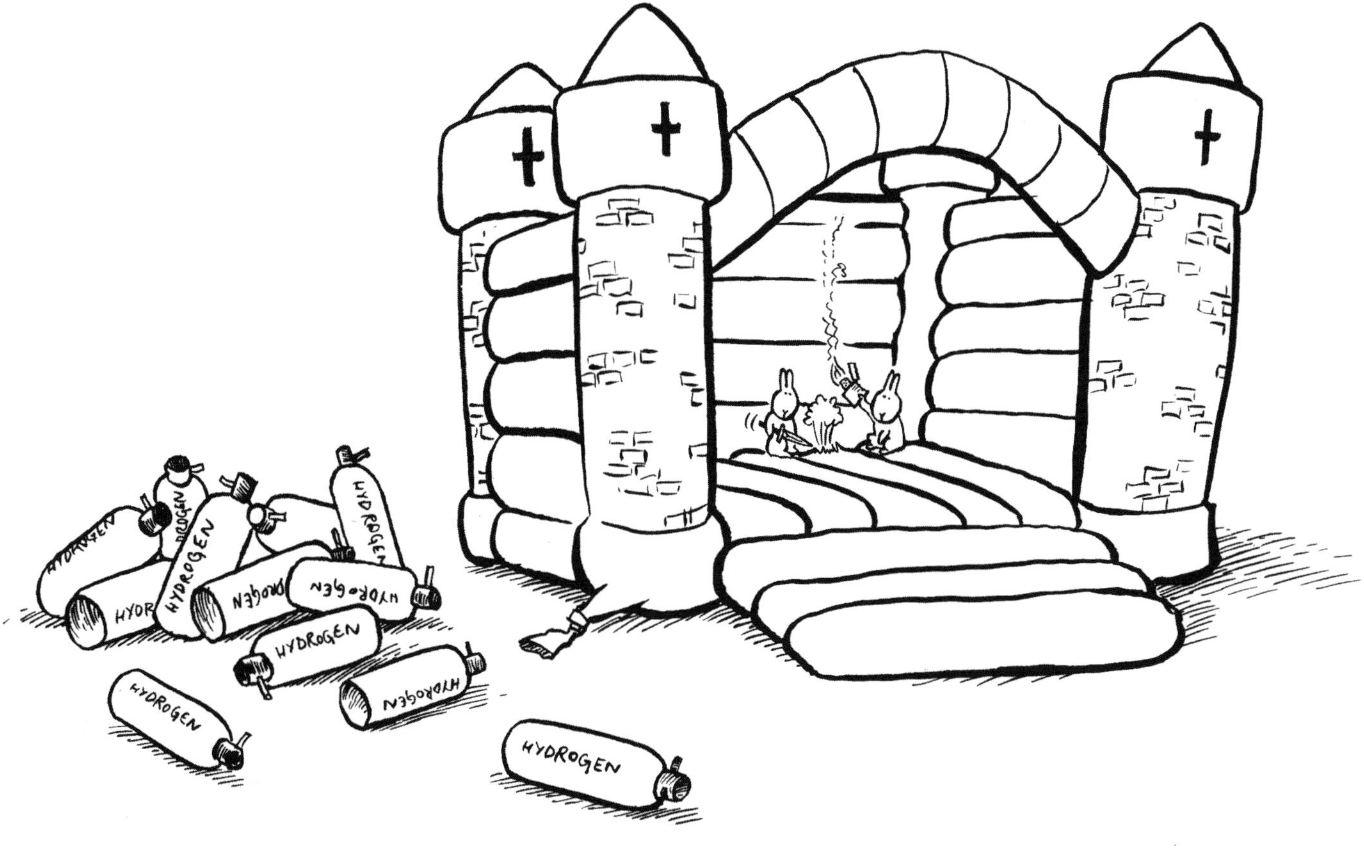
HYDROGEN
HYDROGEN
HYDROGEN
HYDROGEN
HYDROGEN
HYDROGEN
HYDROGEN
HYDROGEN

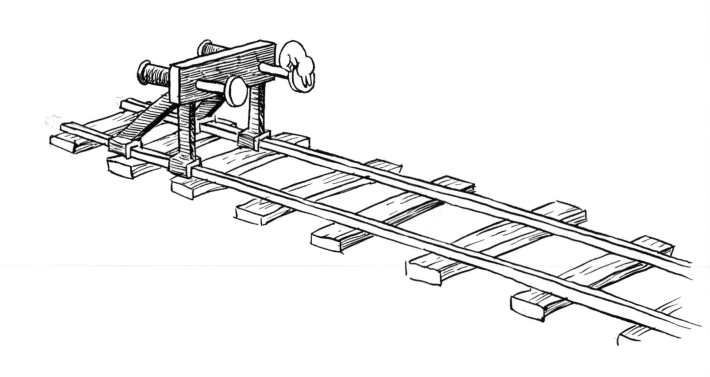

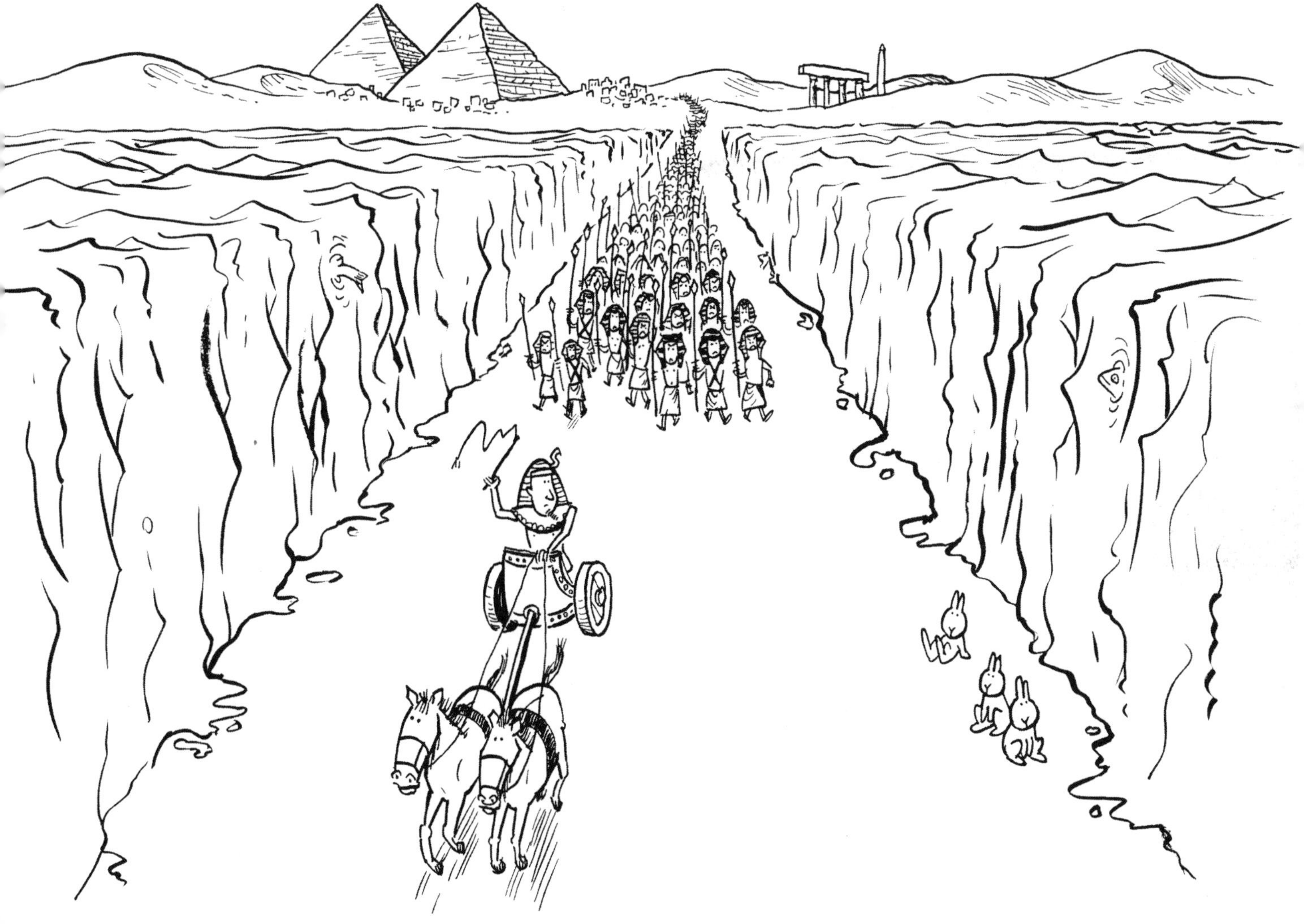

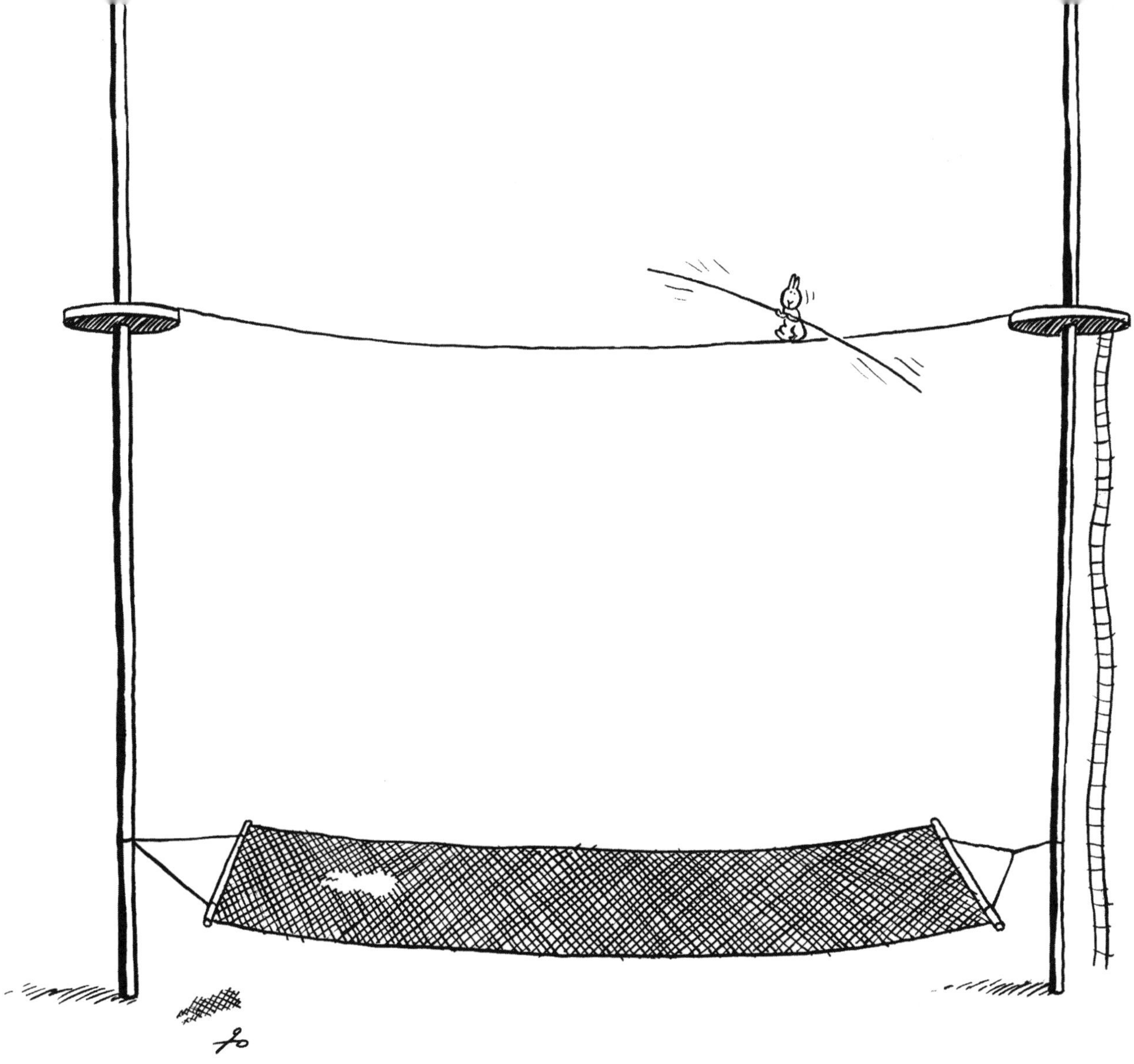

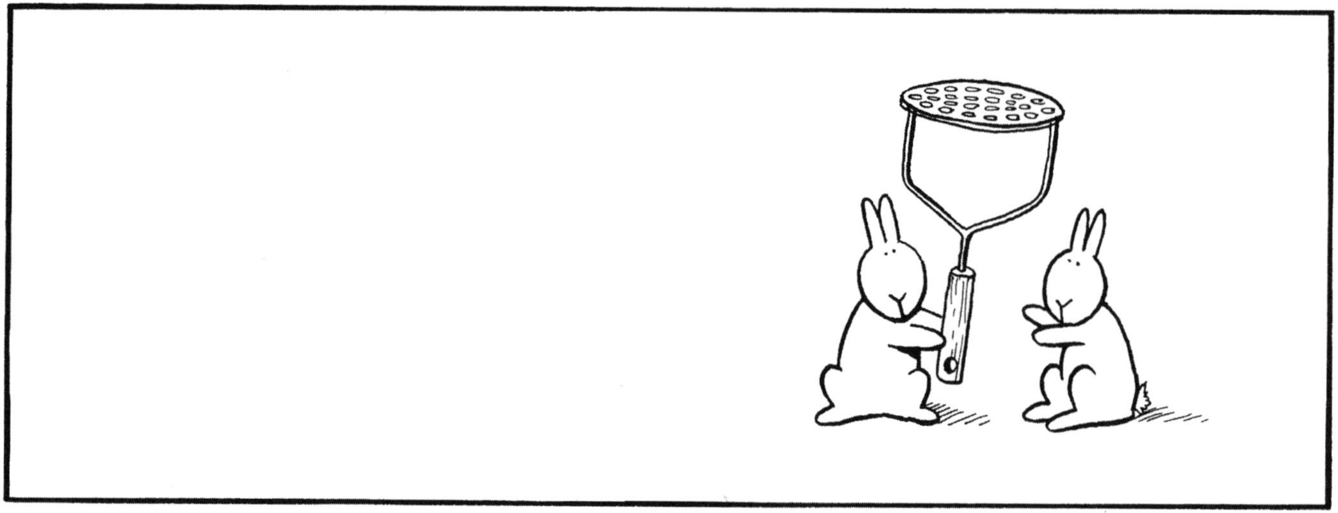
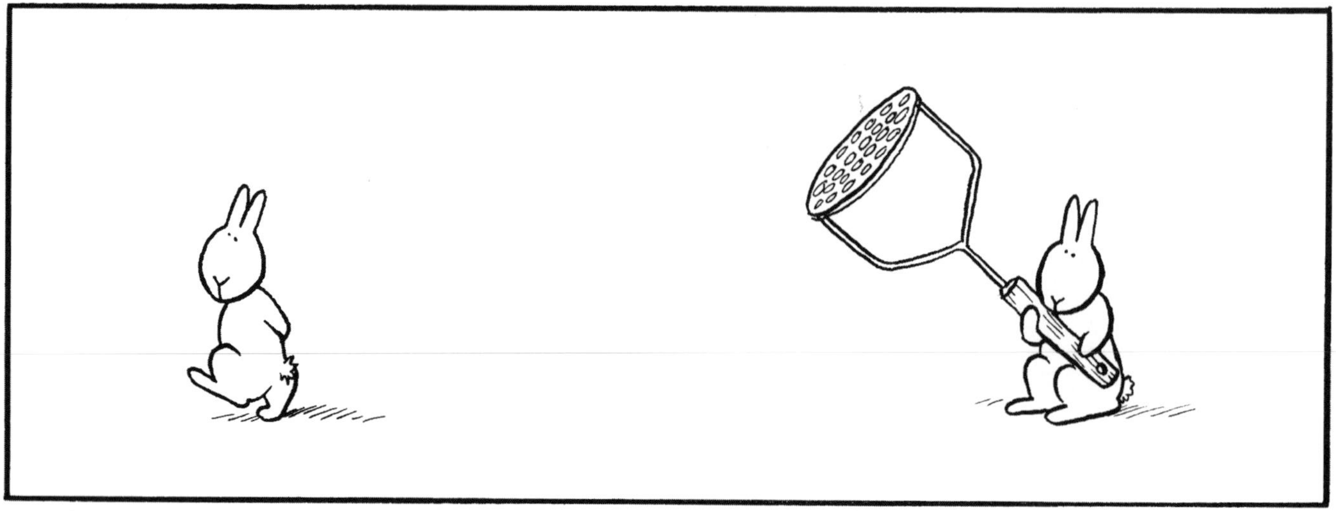

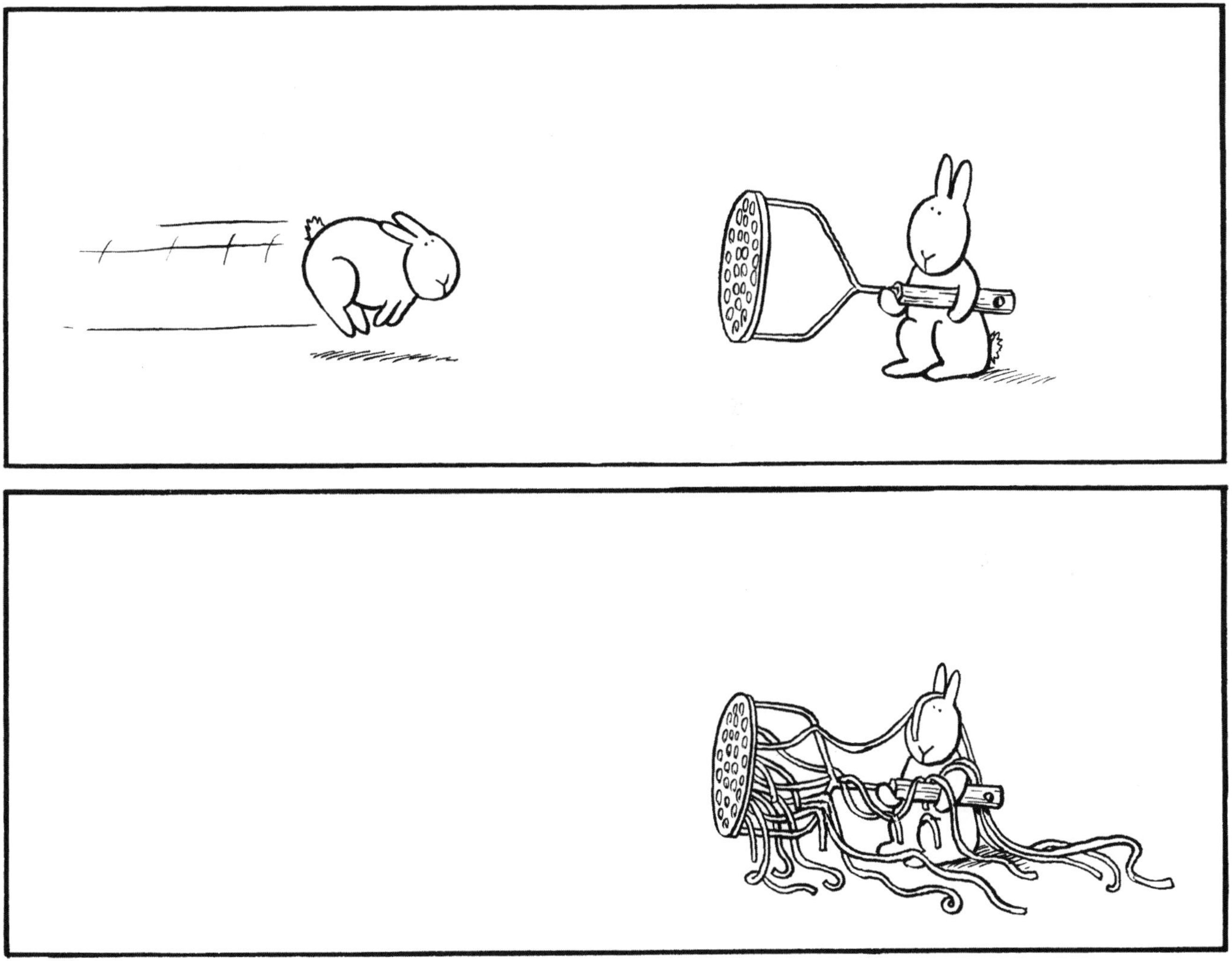

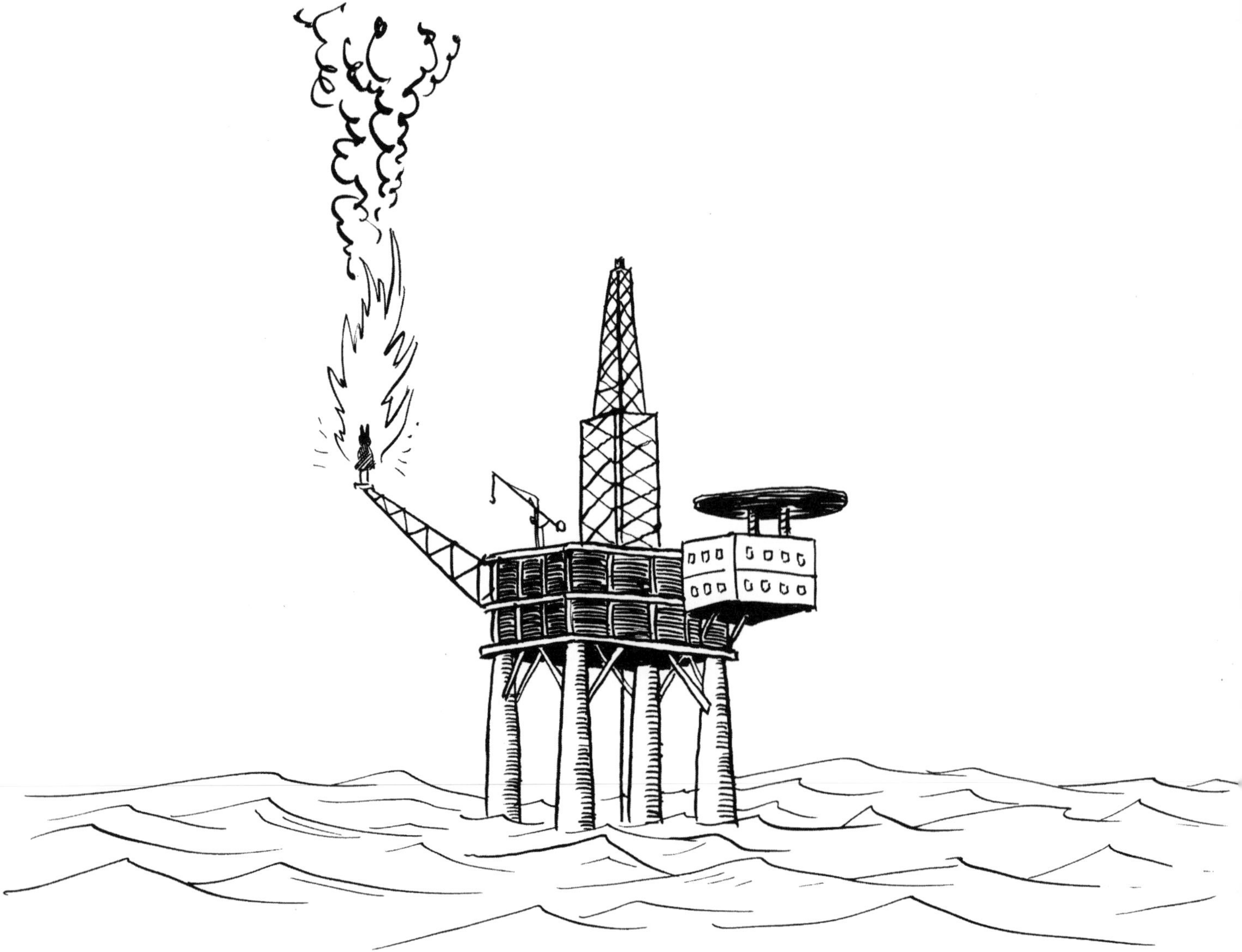

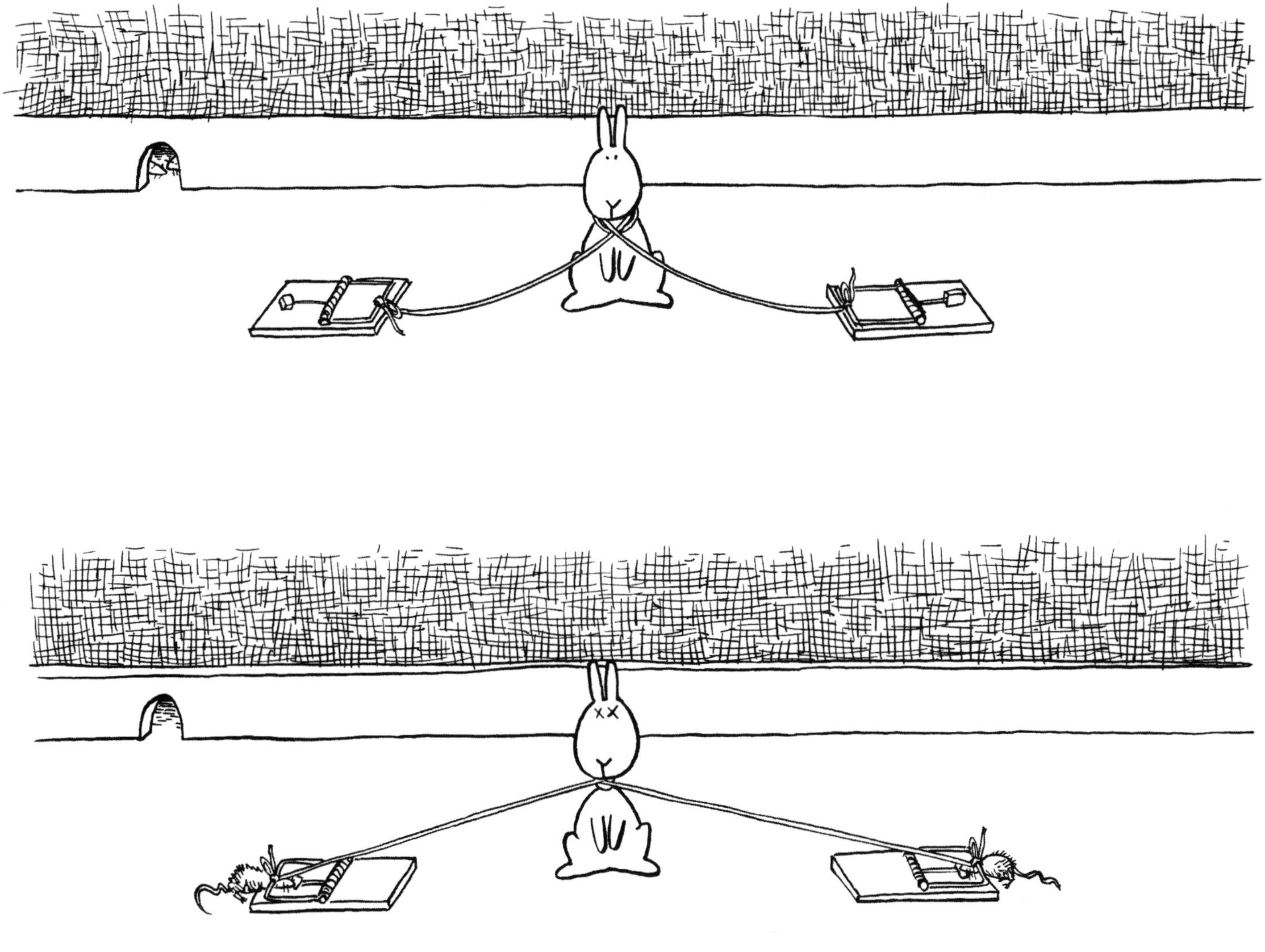

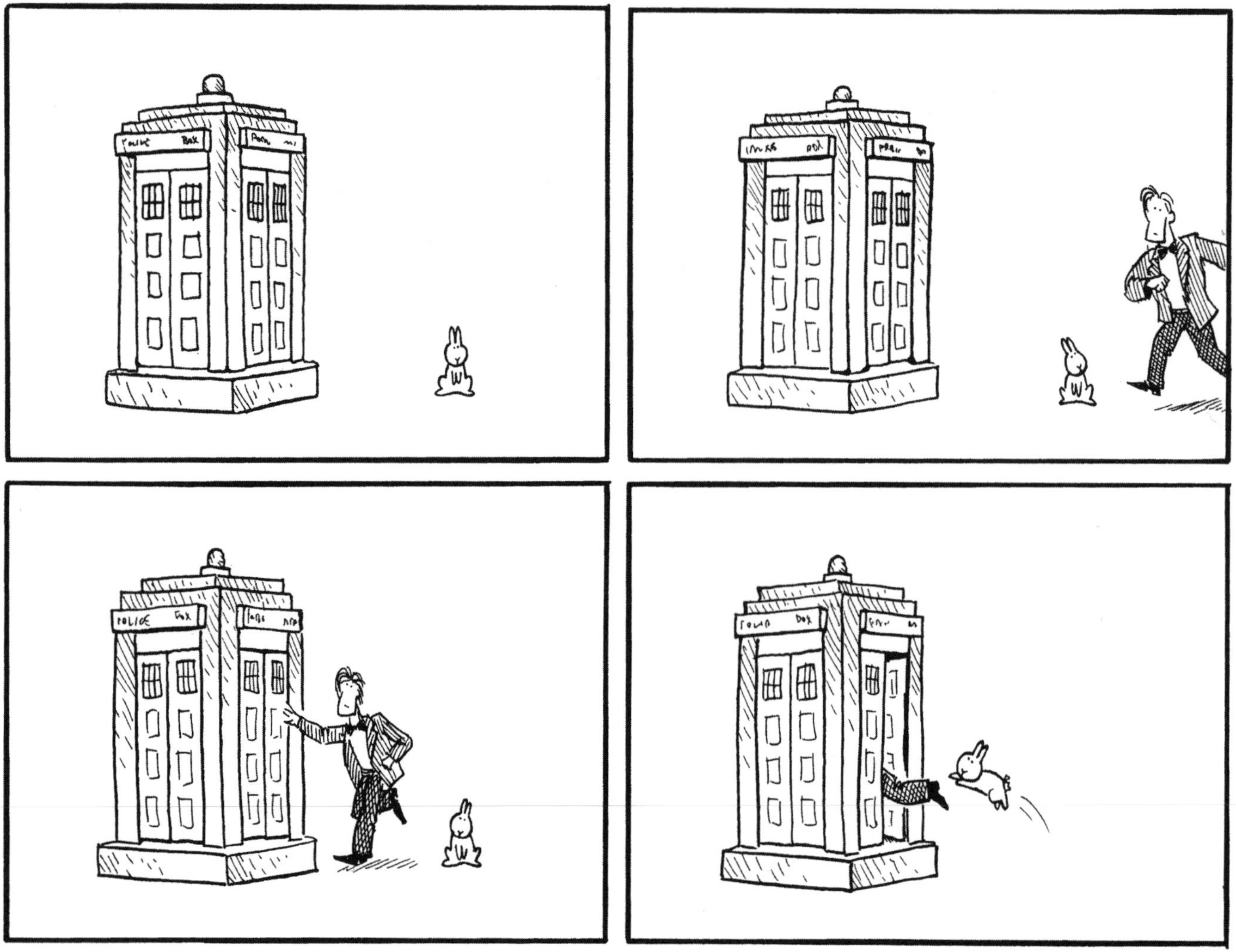

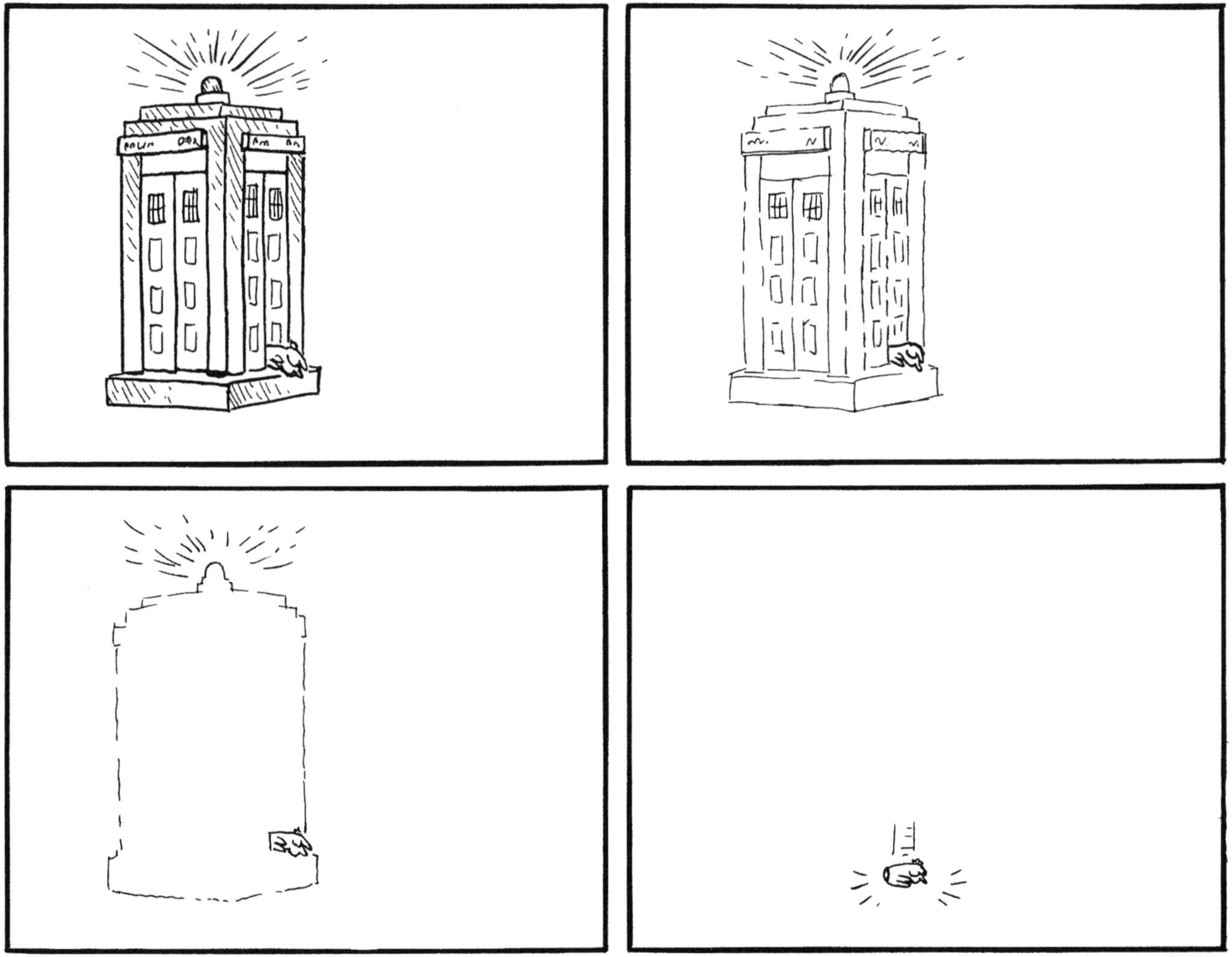

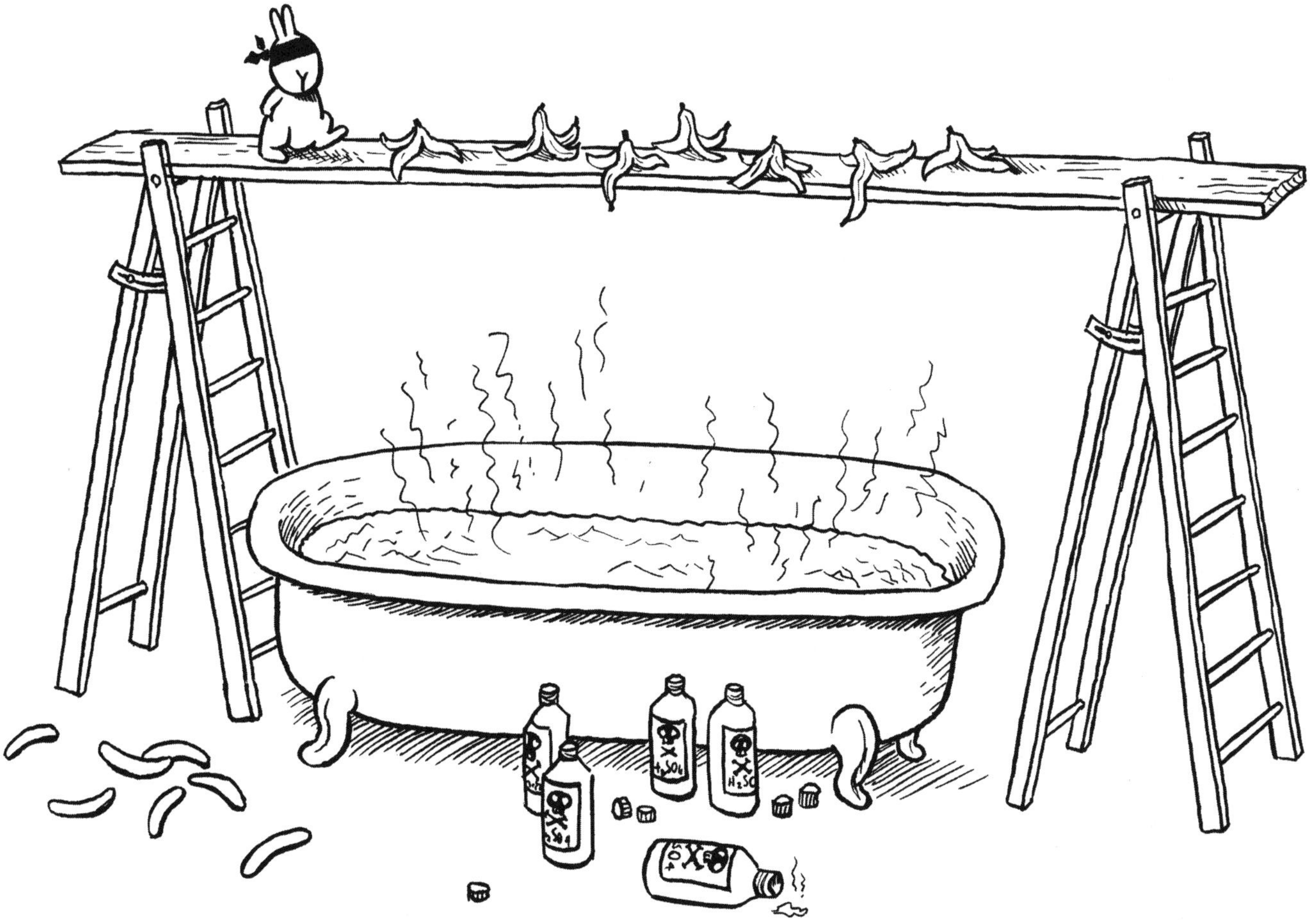
H_2SO_4

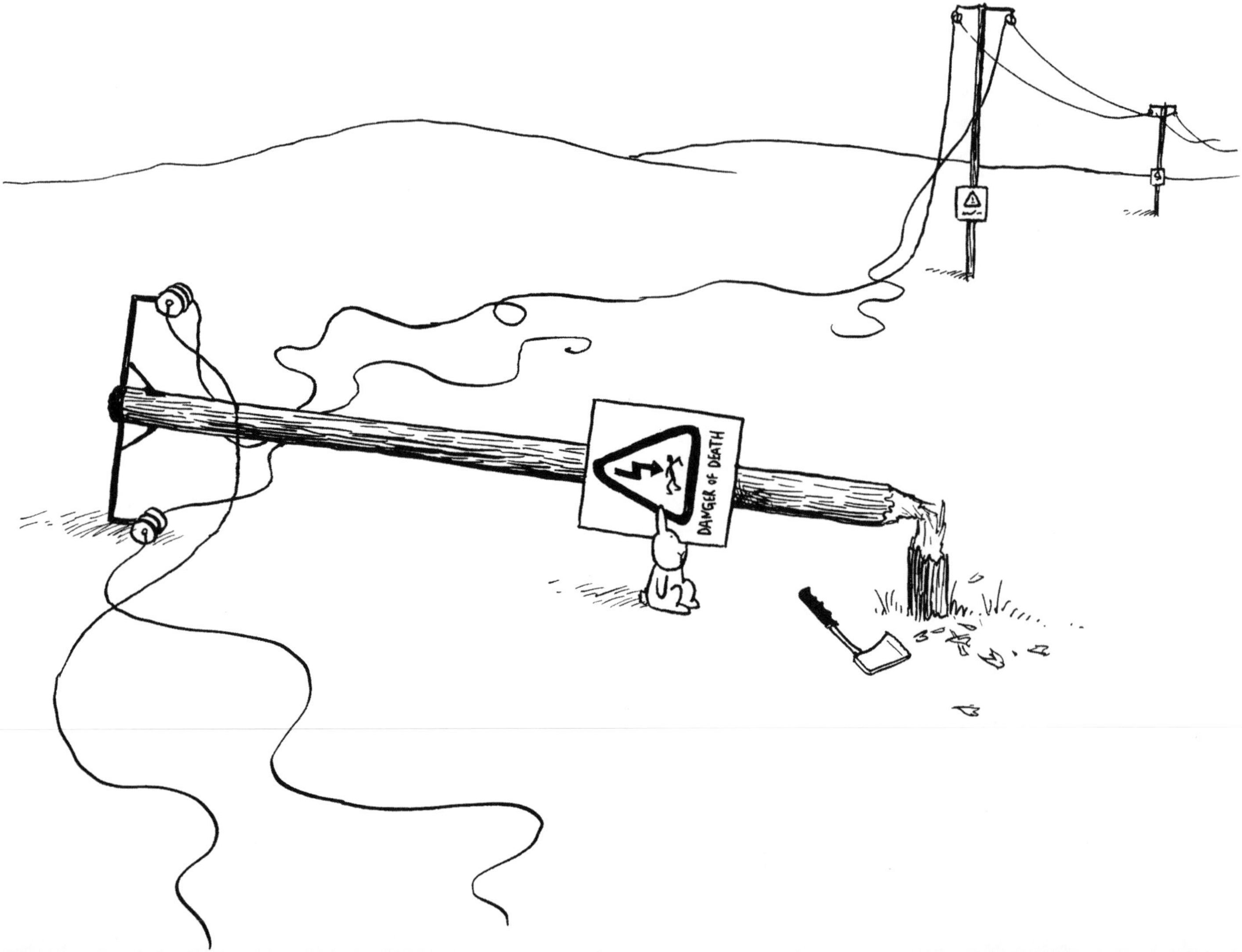
DANGER OF DEATH

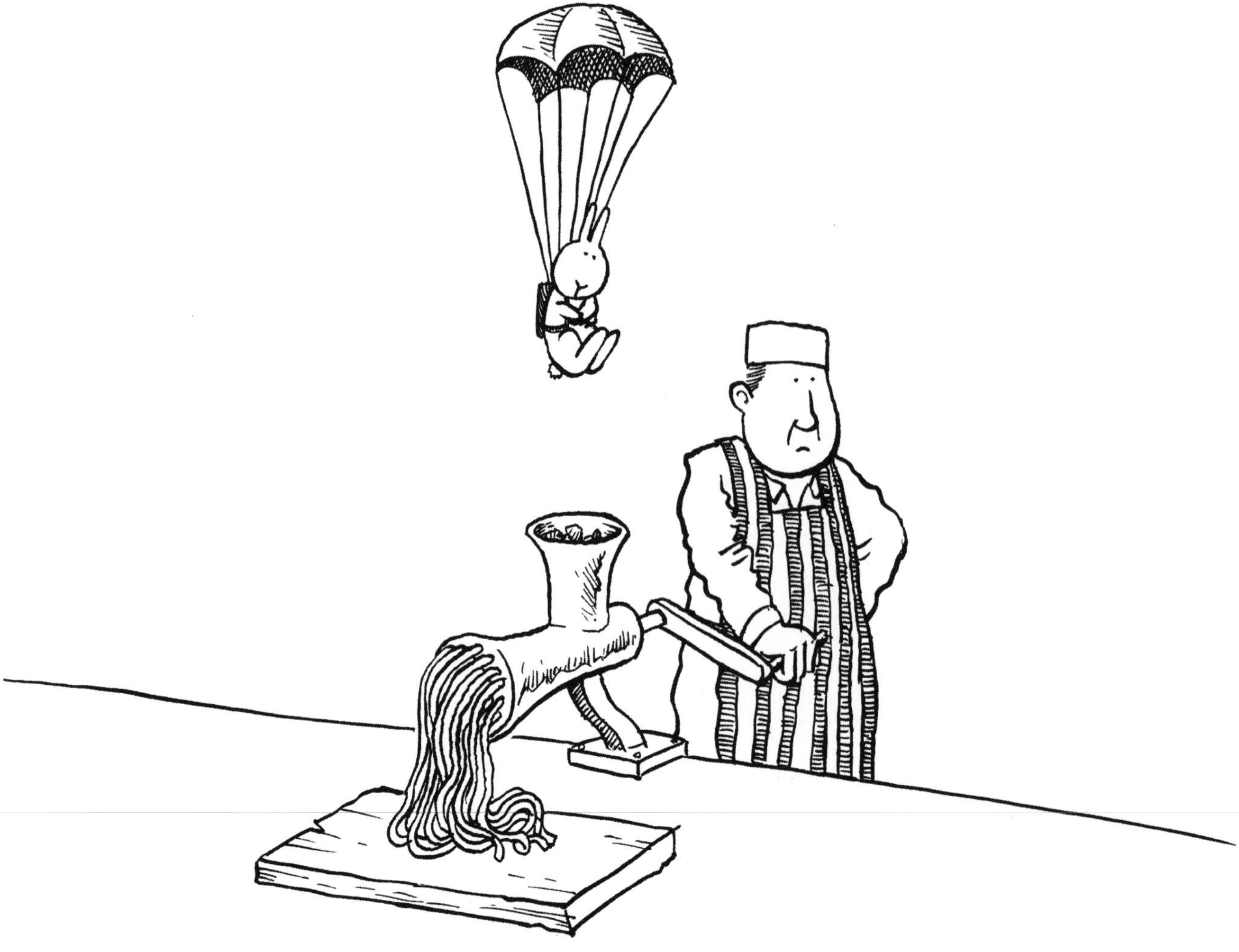

DO NOT PULL THIS LEVER
OFF
ON

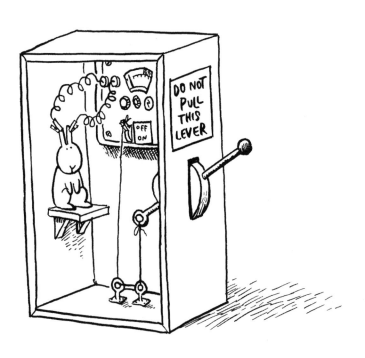

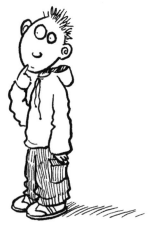

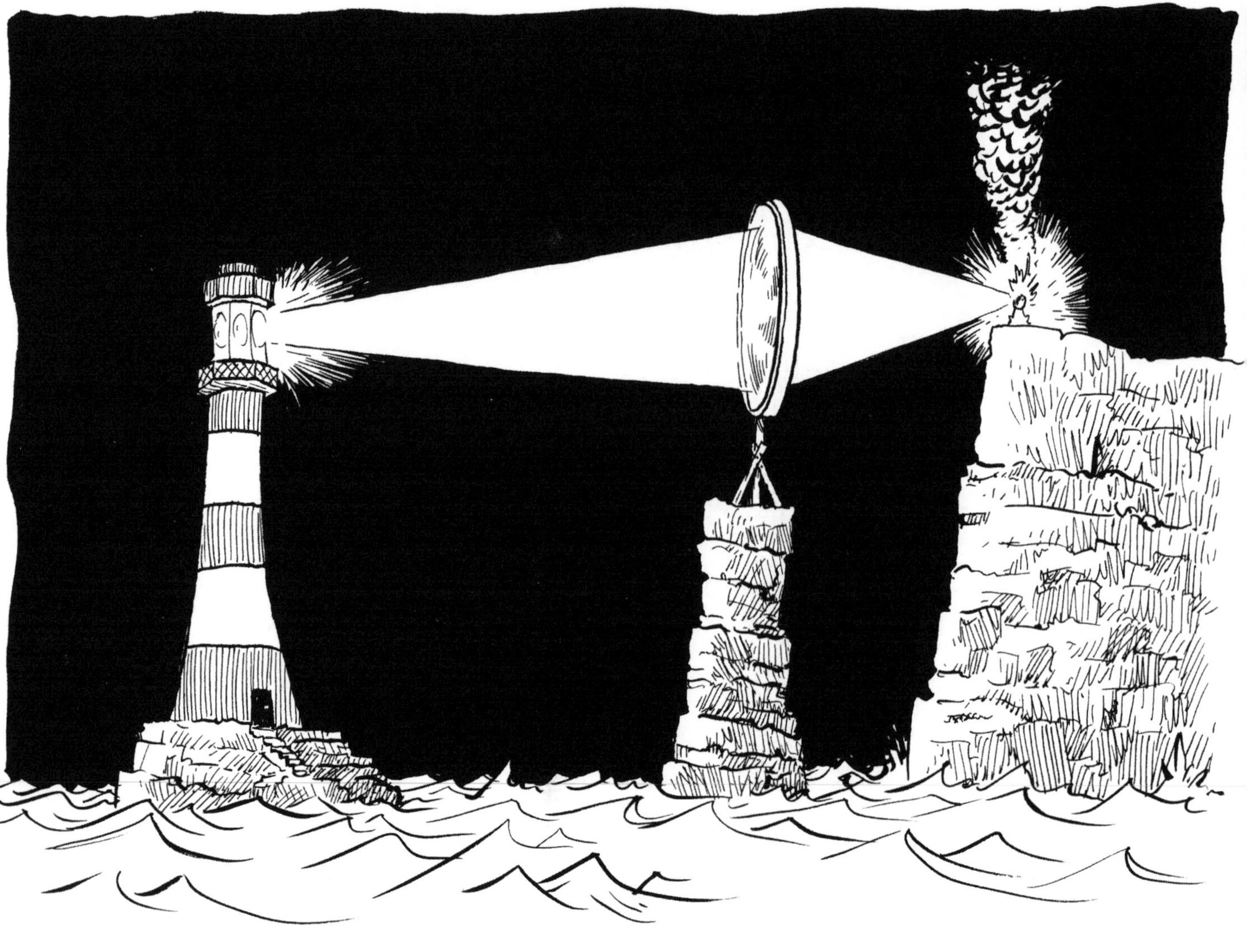

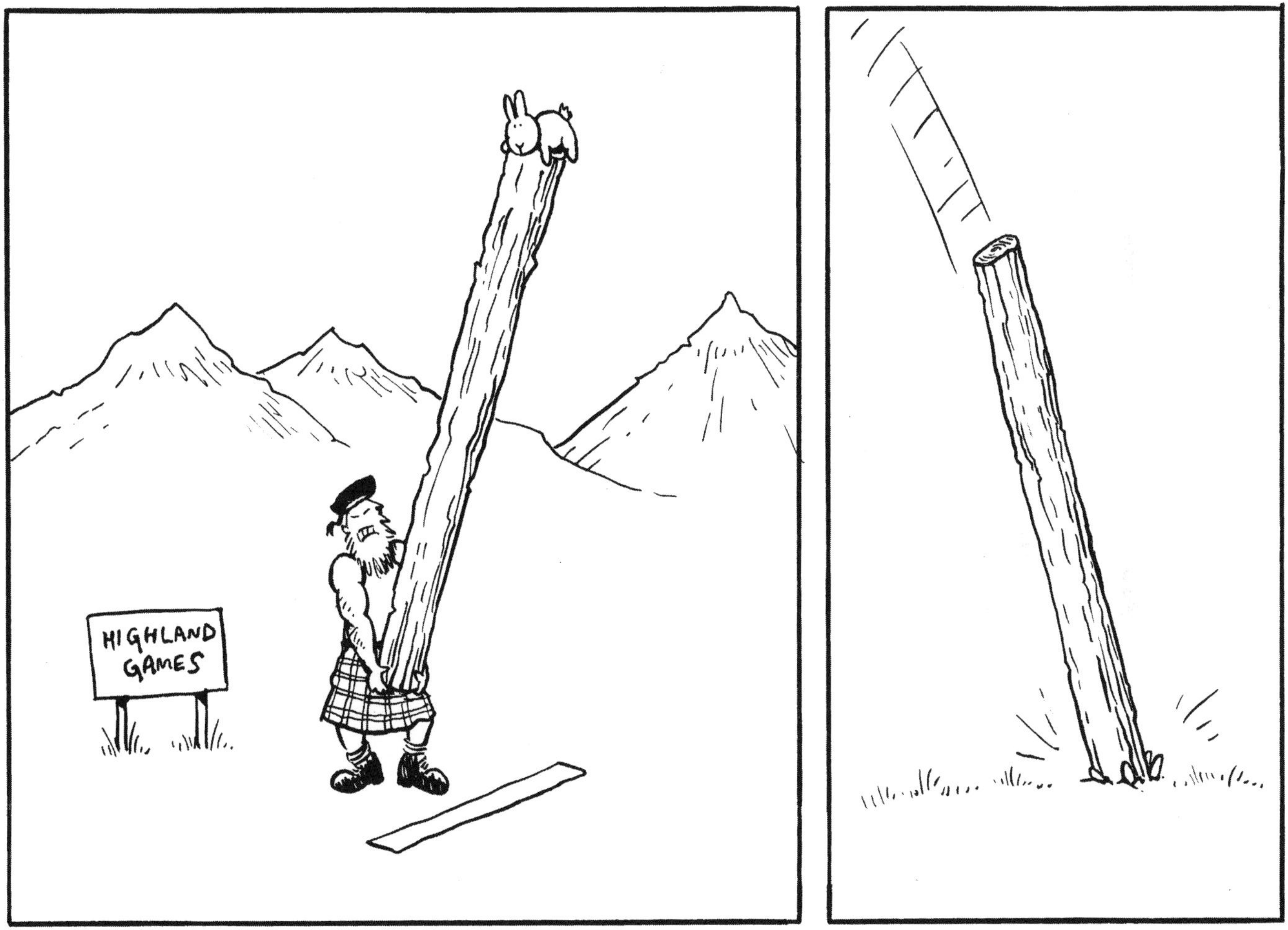
HIGHLAND
GAMES

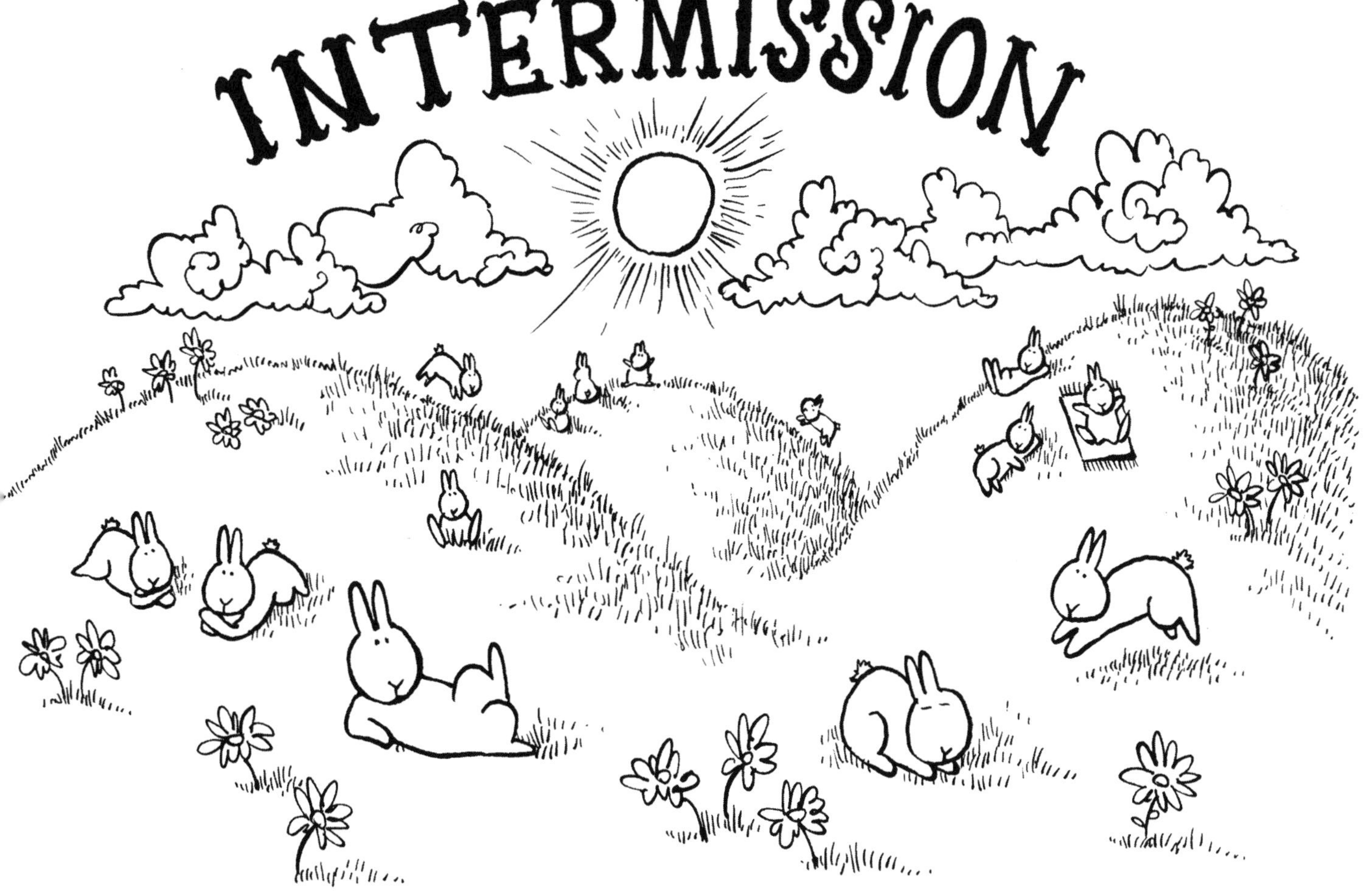
INTERMISSION

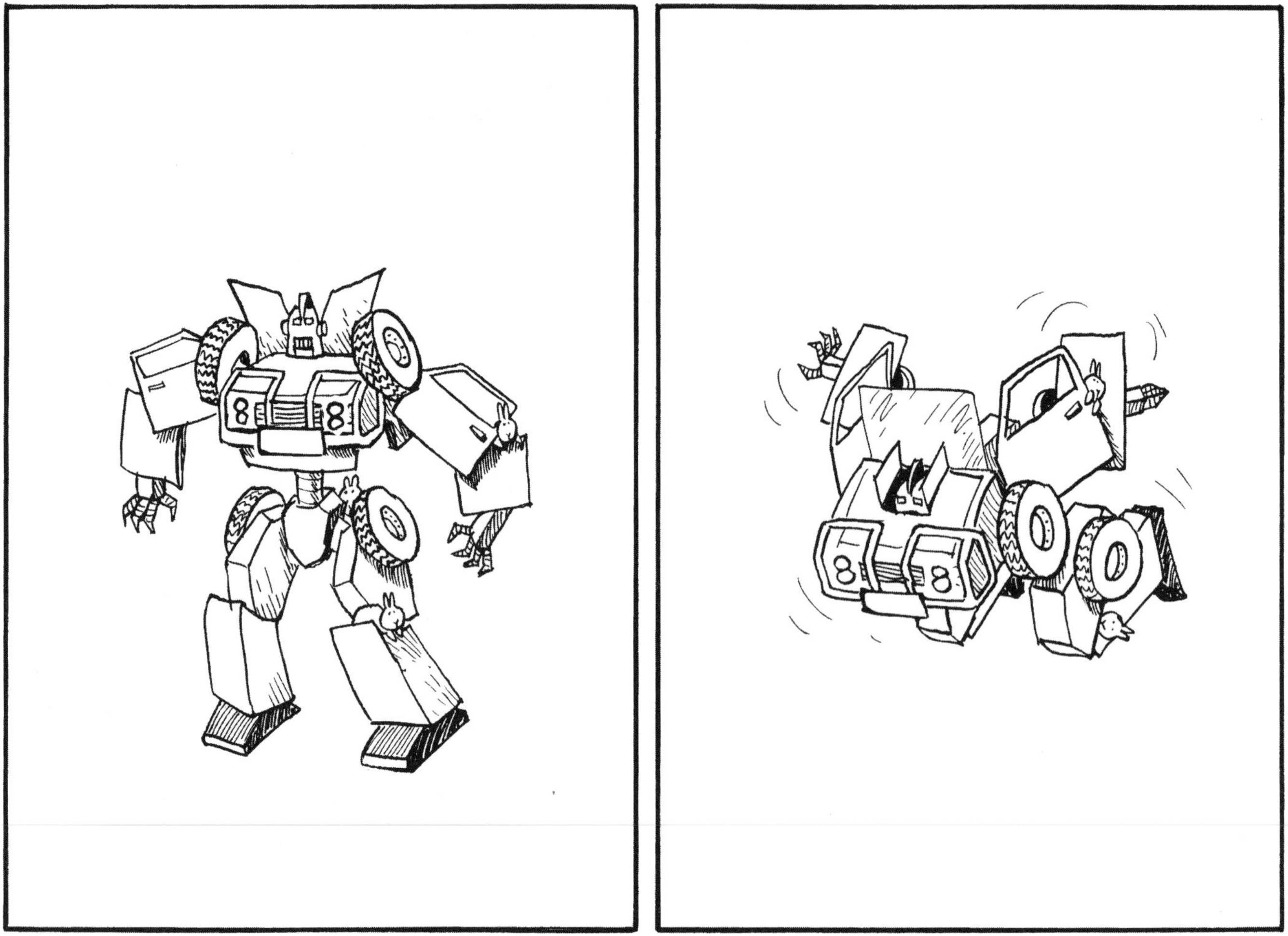

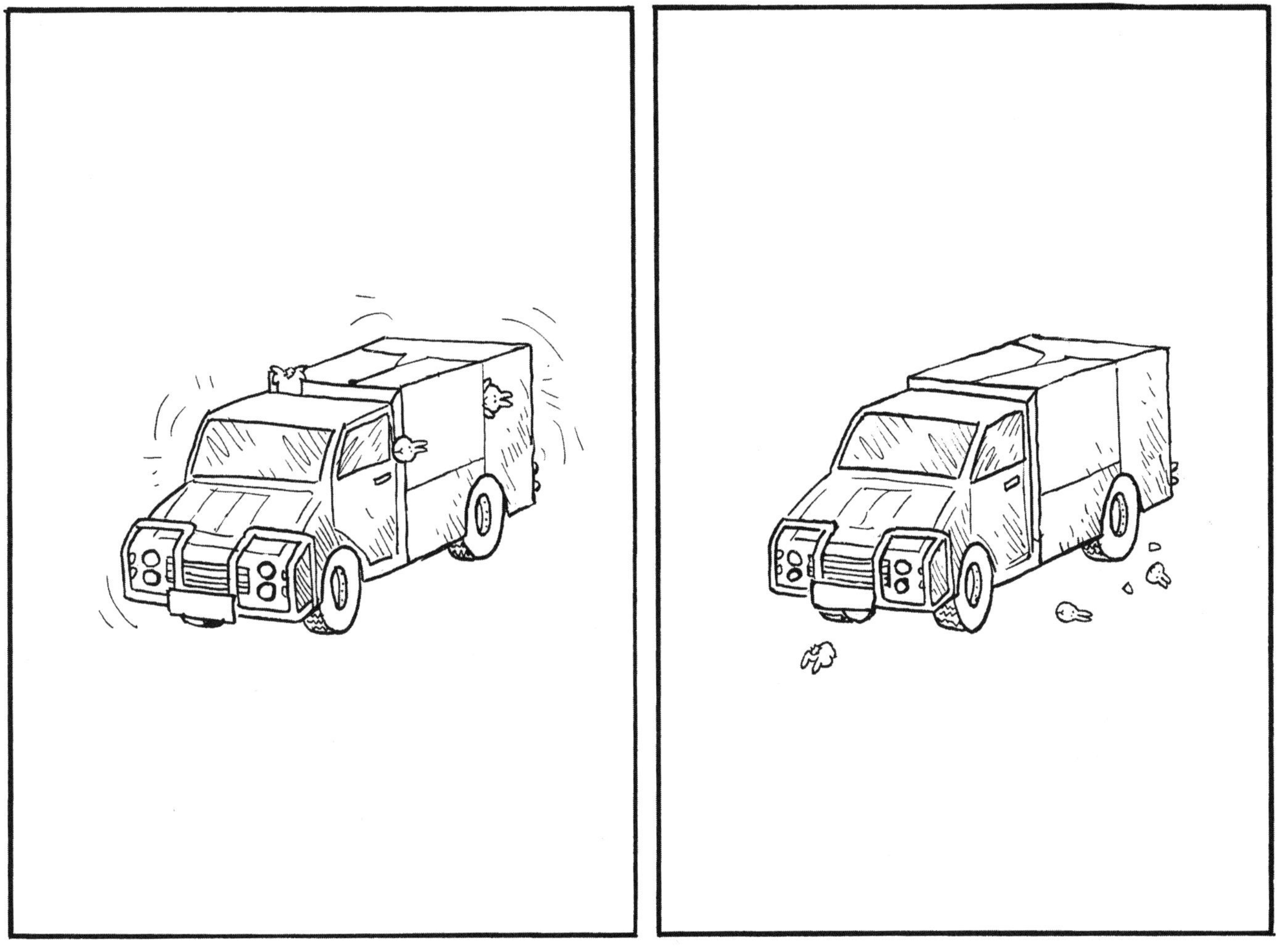

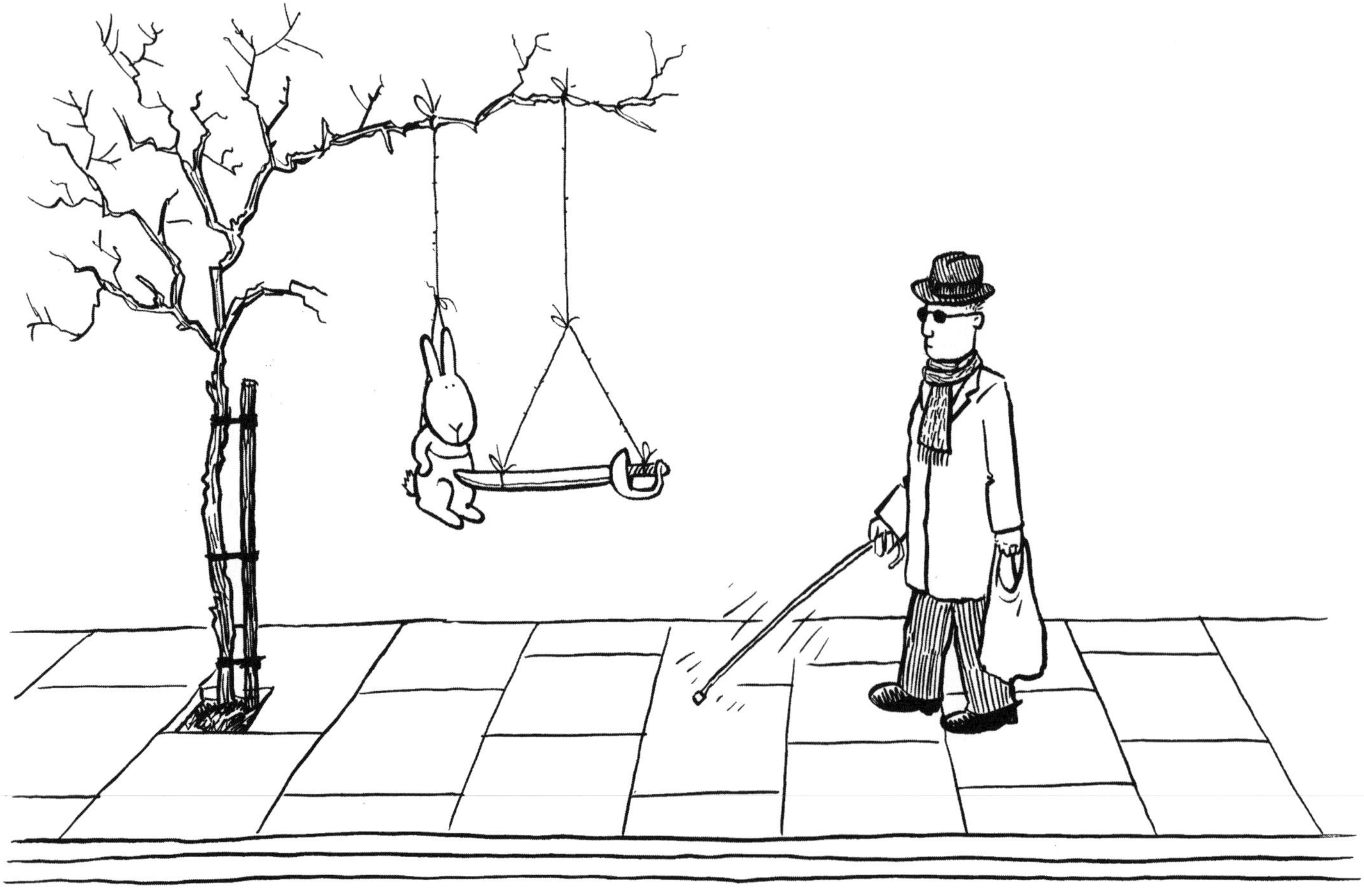

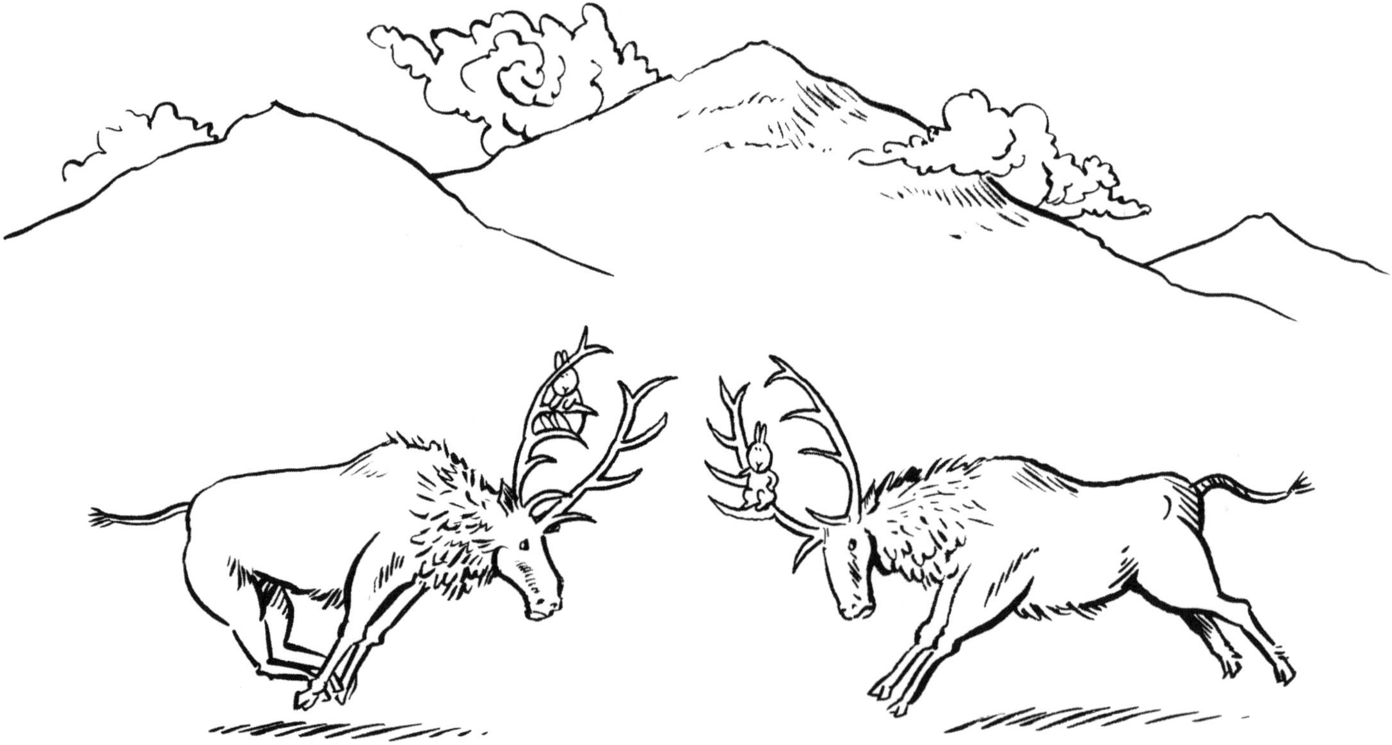

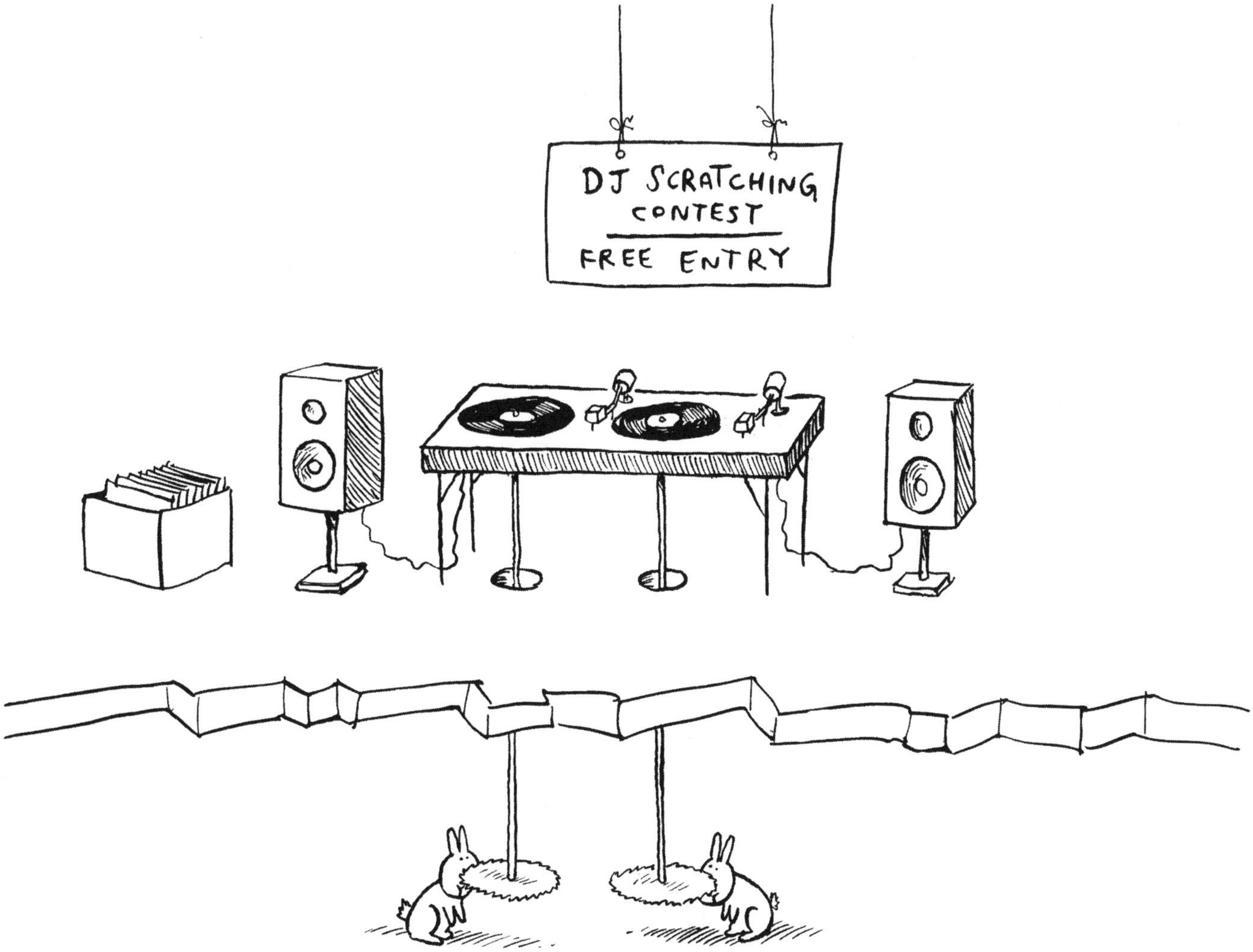
DJ SCRATCHING CONTEST
FREE ENTRY

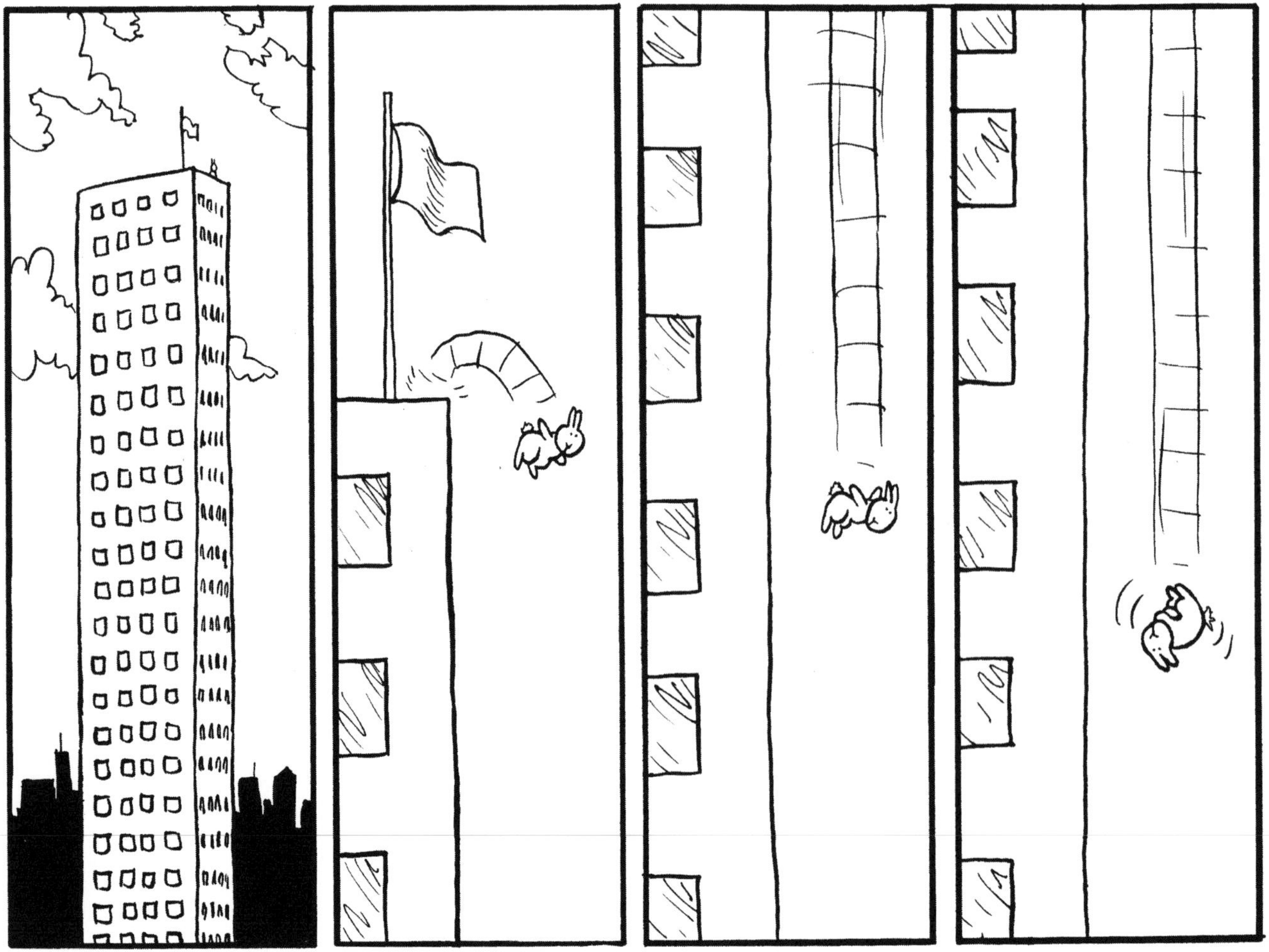

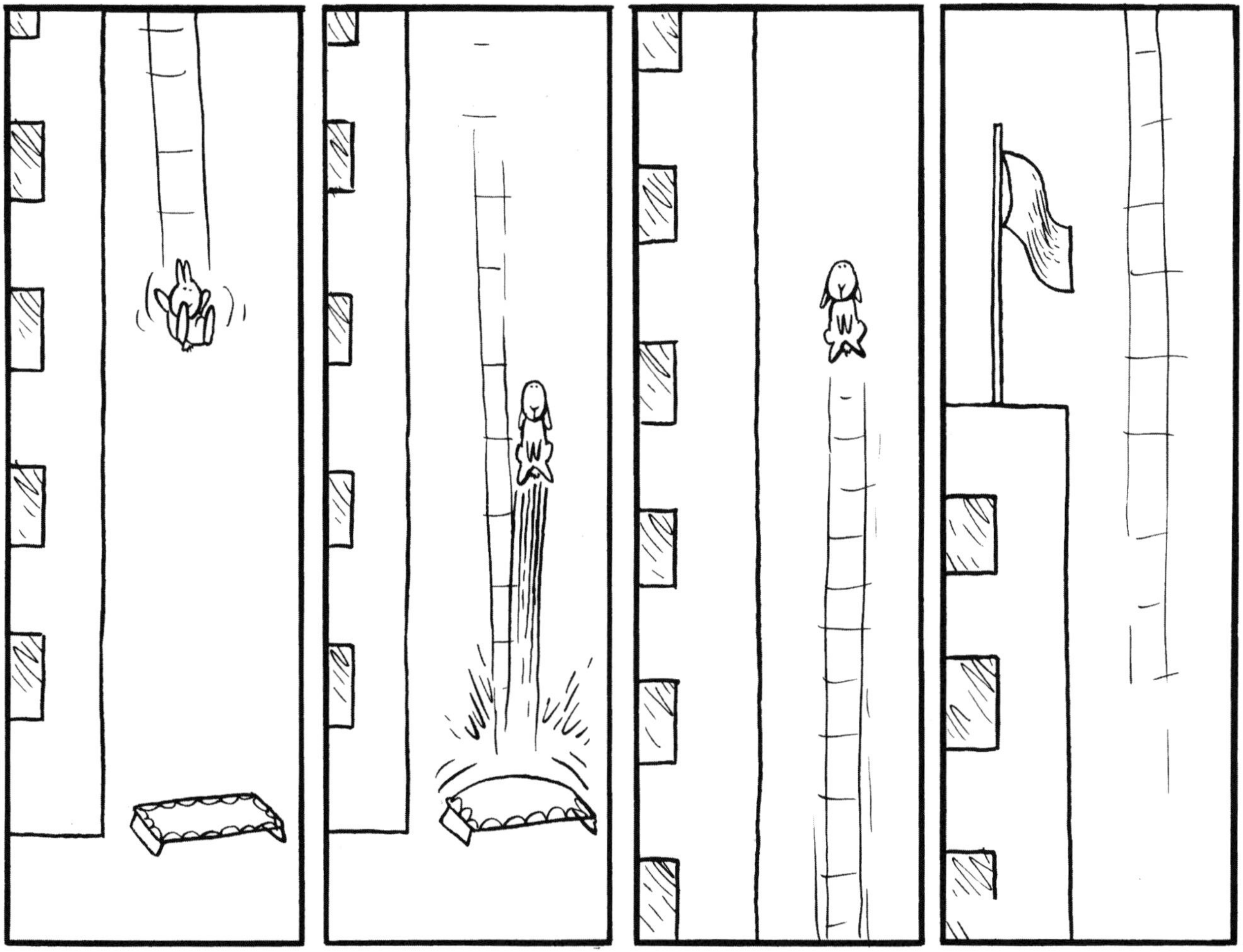

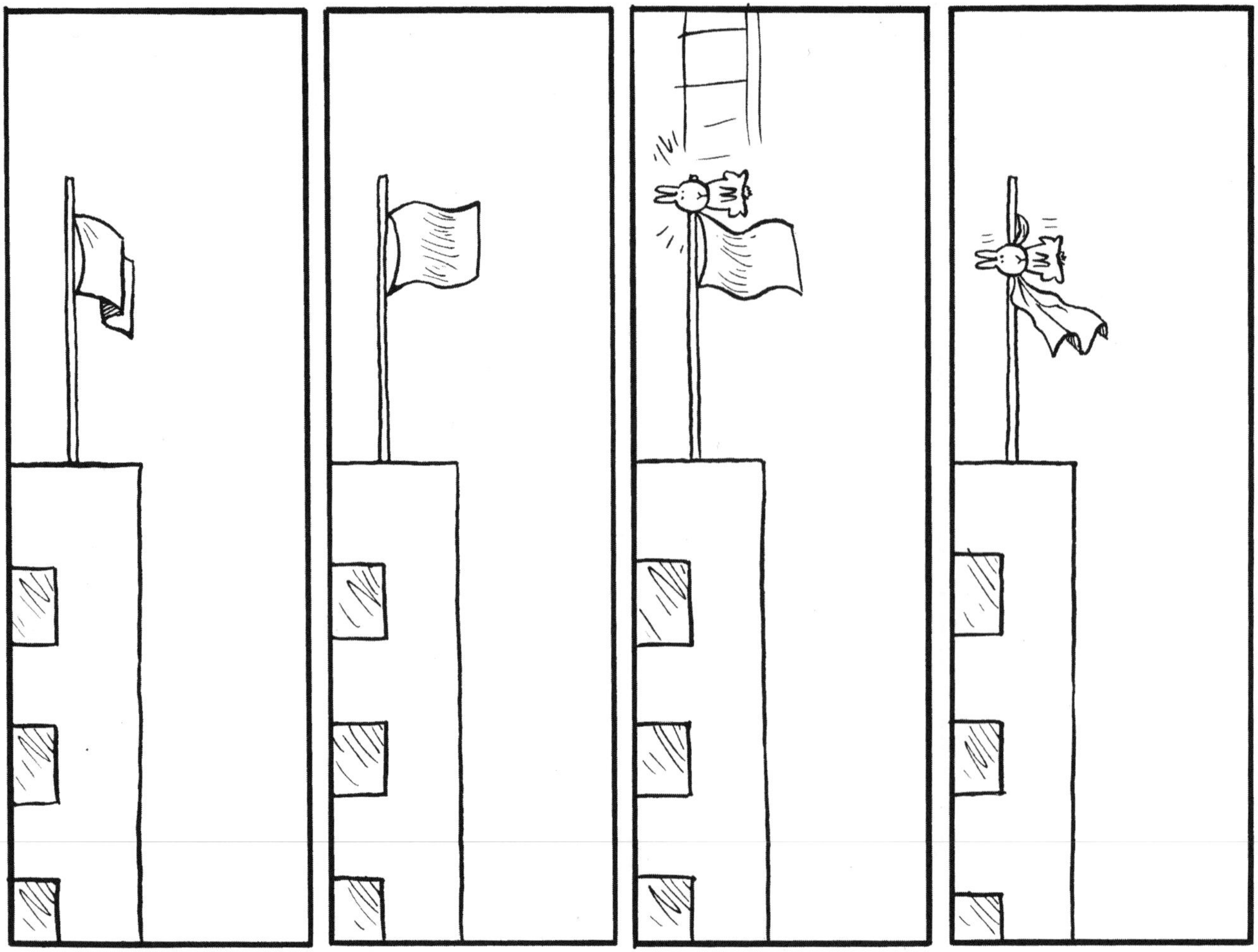

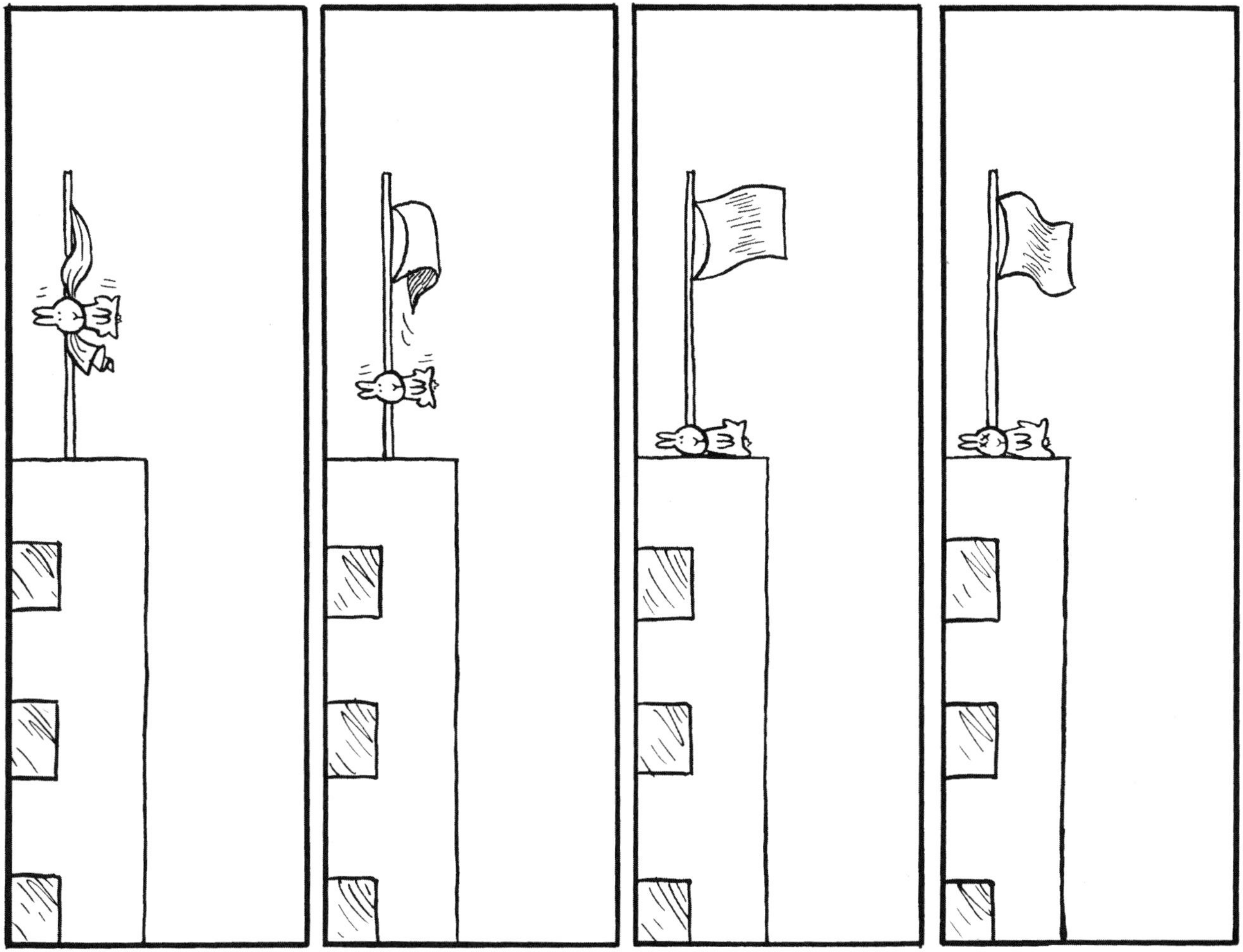

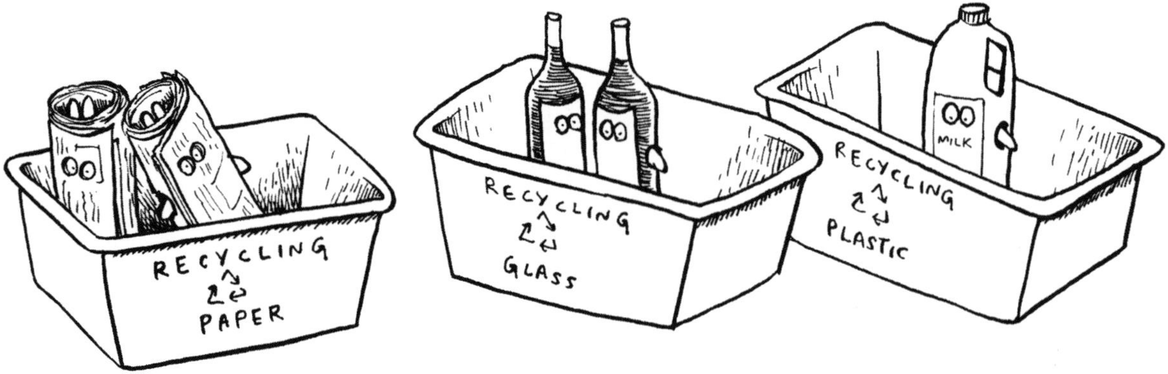
RECYCLING
PAPER
RECYCLING
GLASS
RECYCLING
PLASTIC
MILK

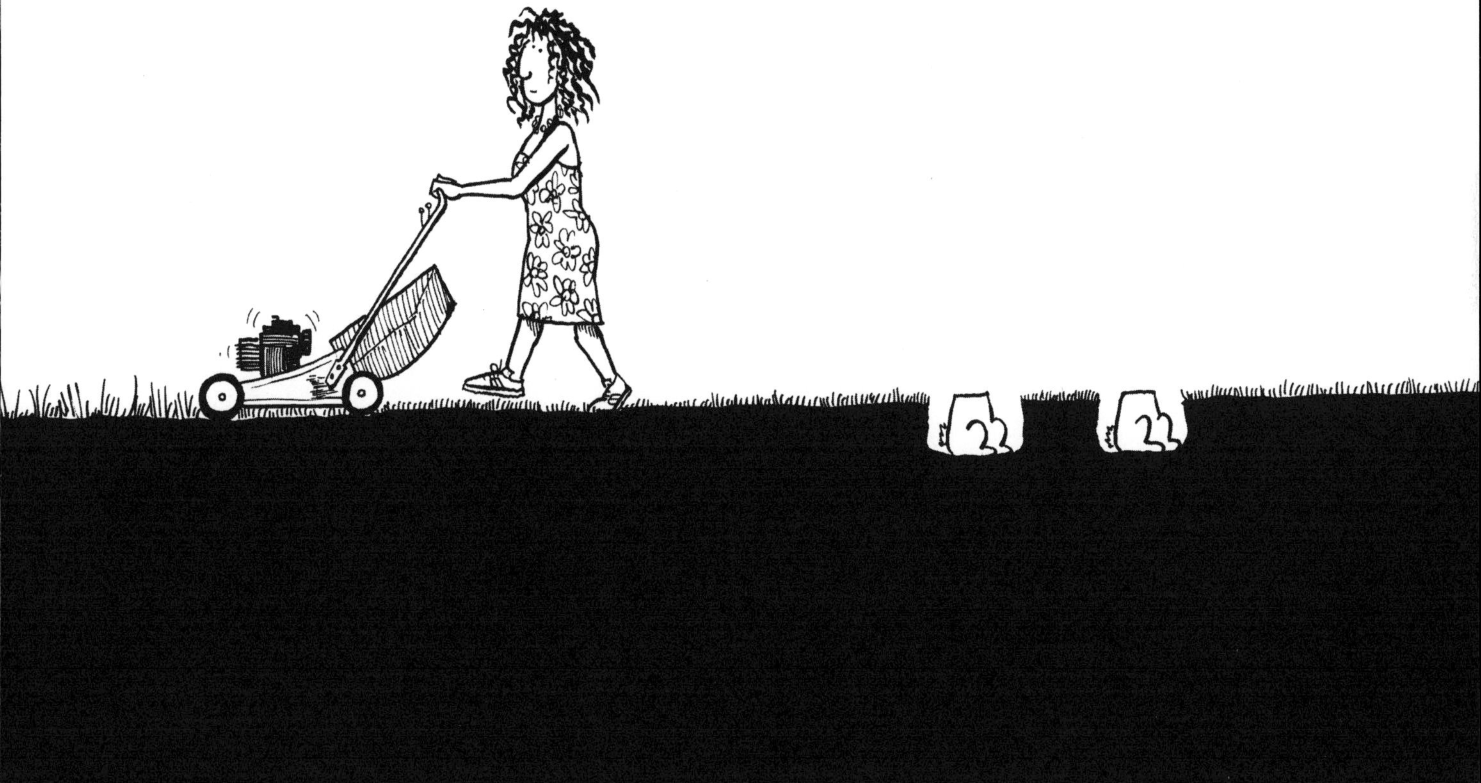

1000 W
600 W
400 W

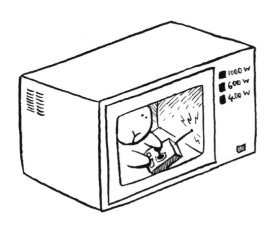

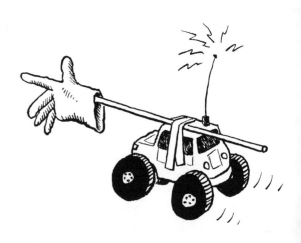

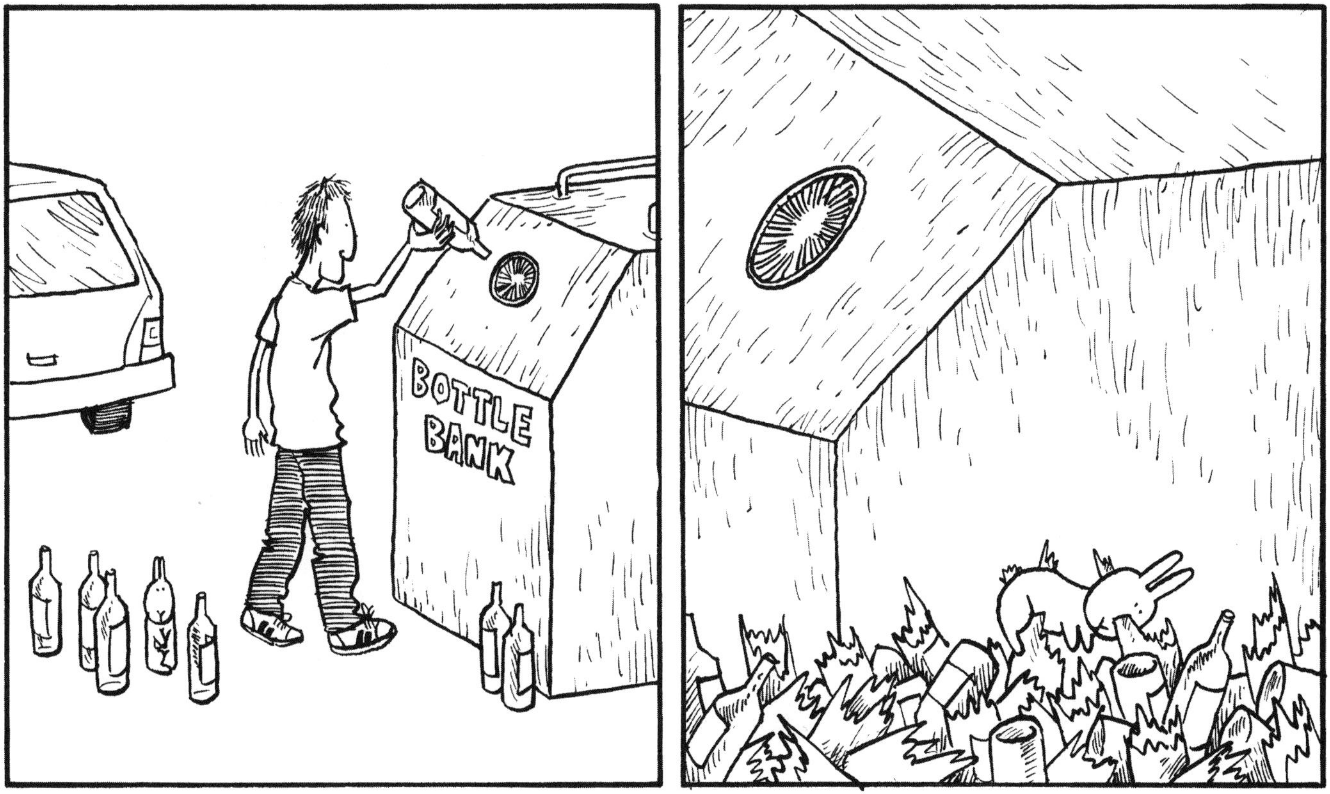
BOTTLE
BANK

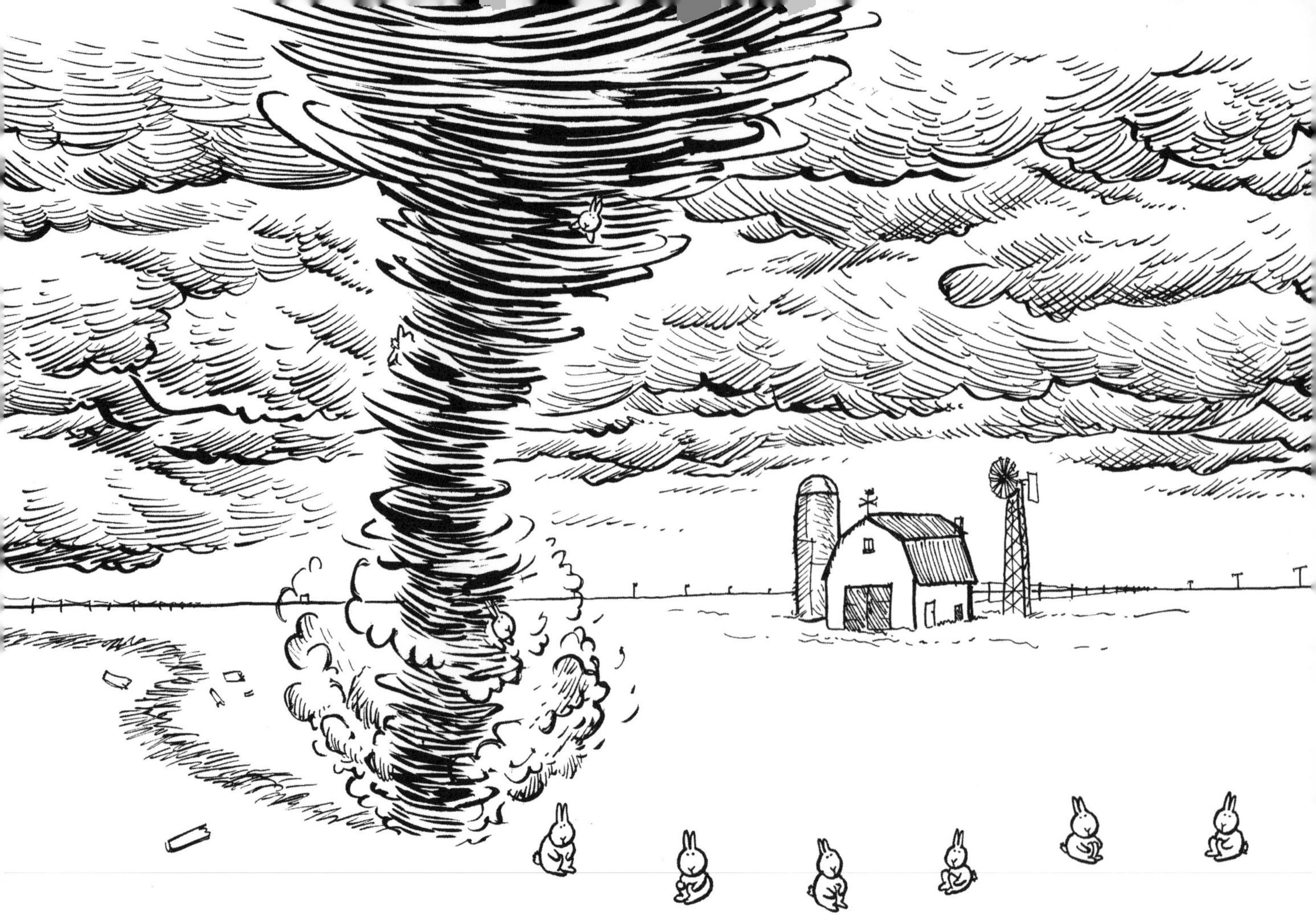

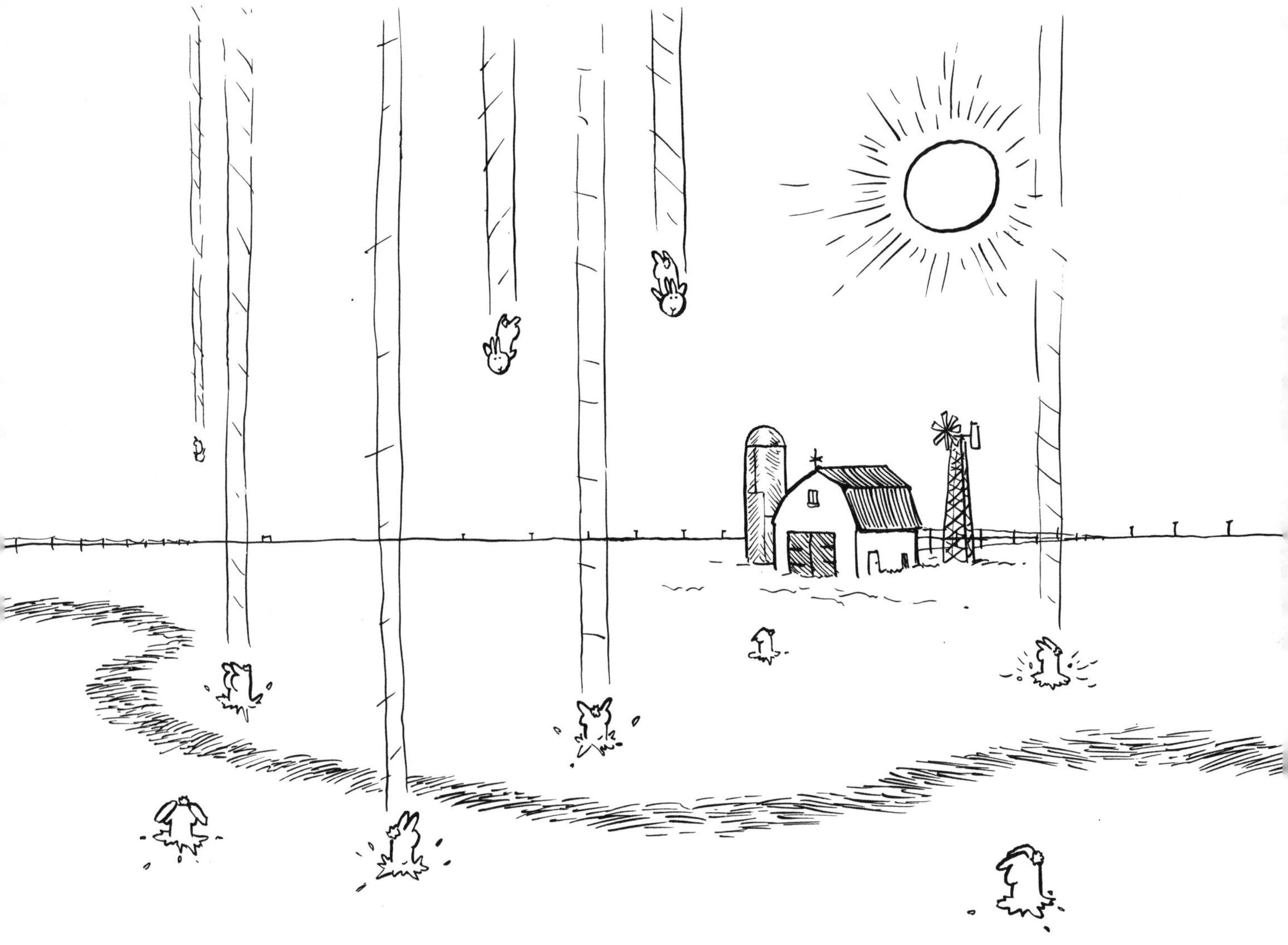

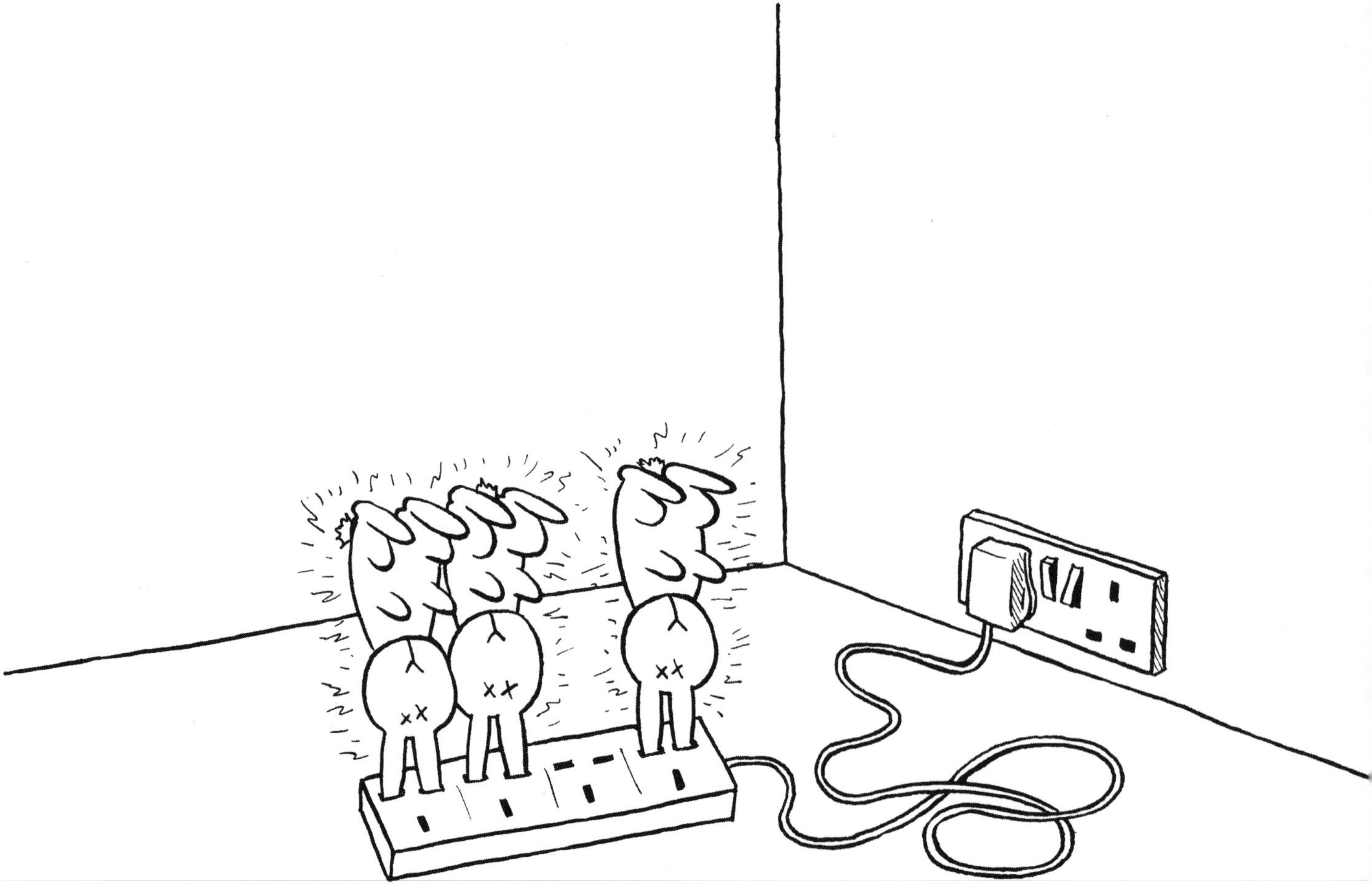

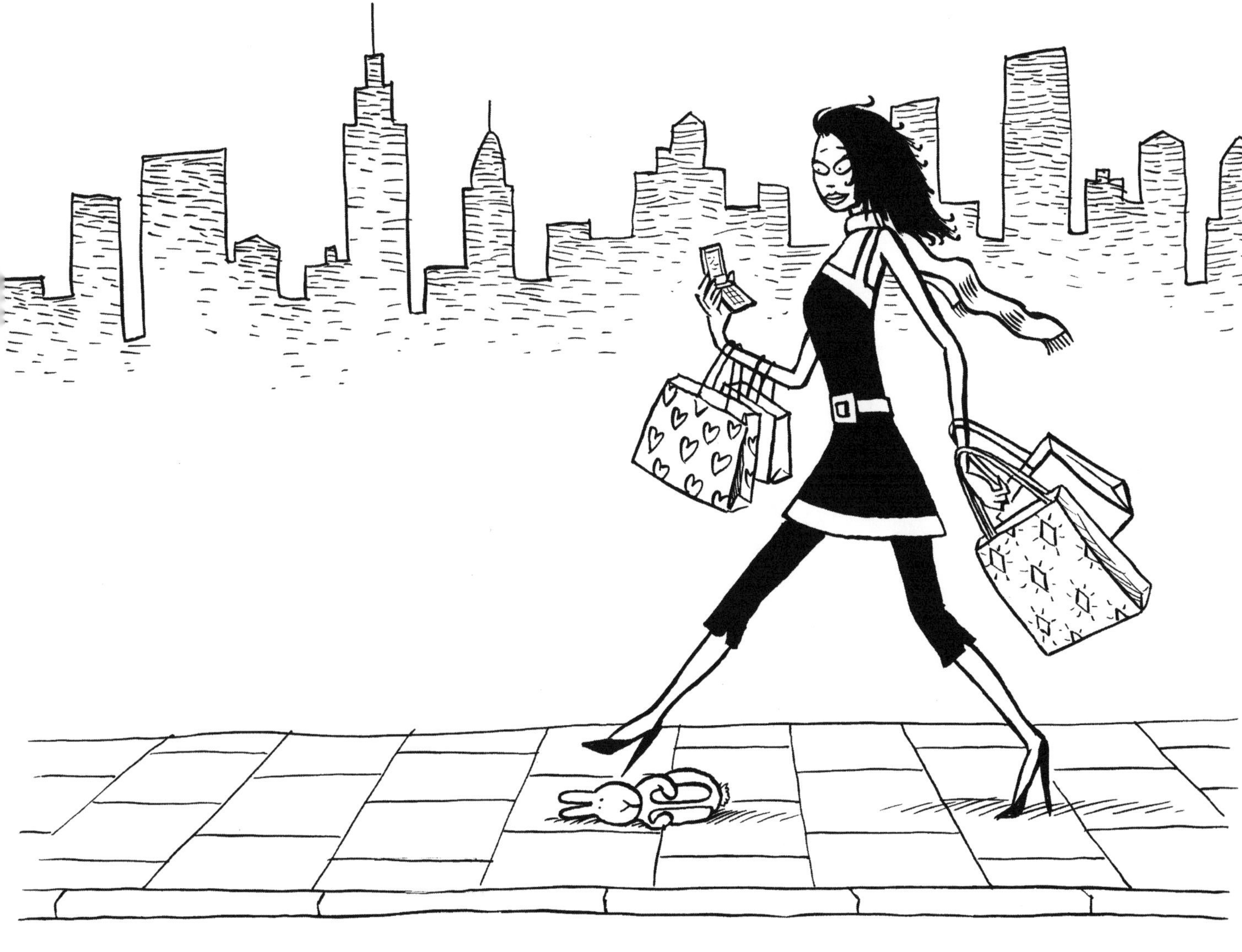

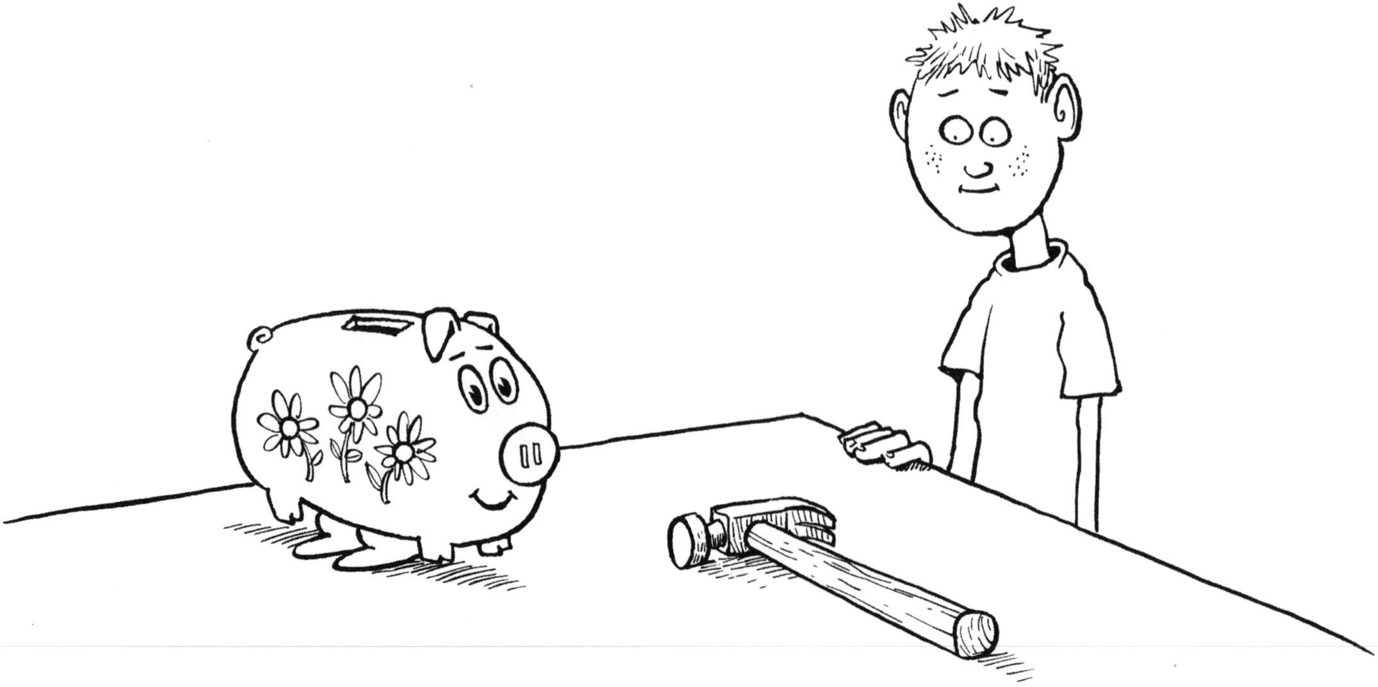

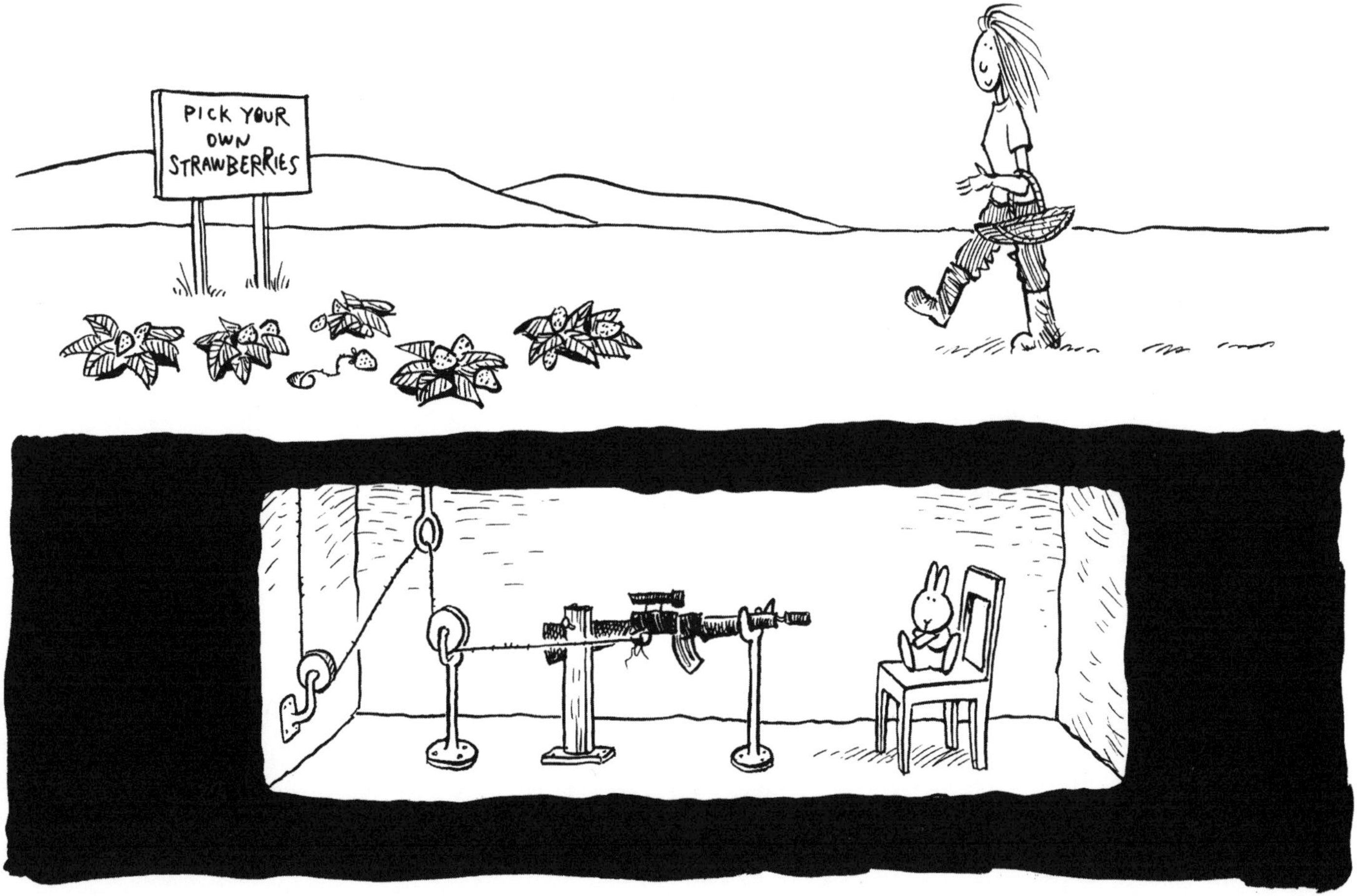
PICK YOUR
OWN
STRAWBERRIES

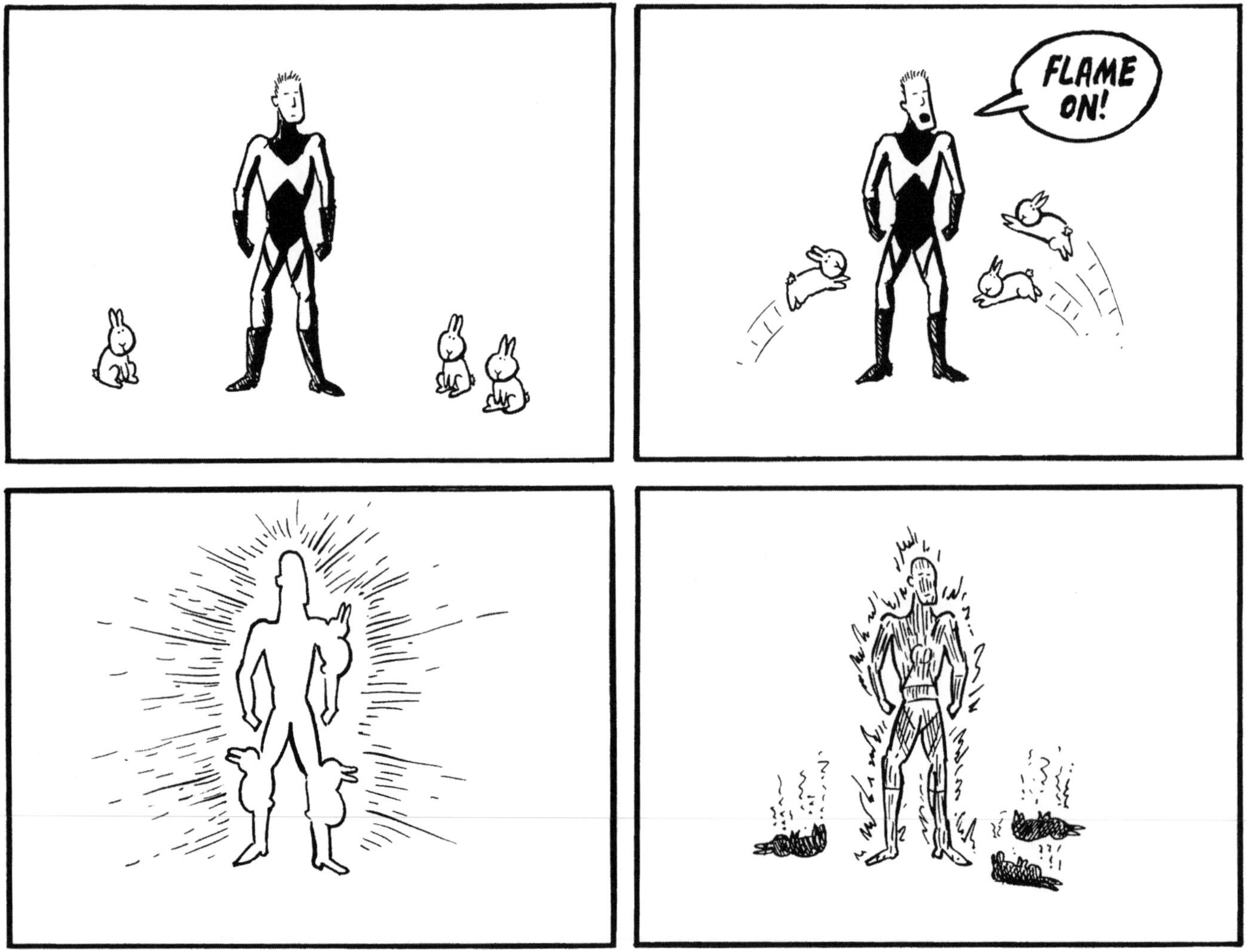
FLAME ON!

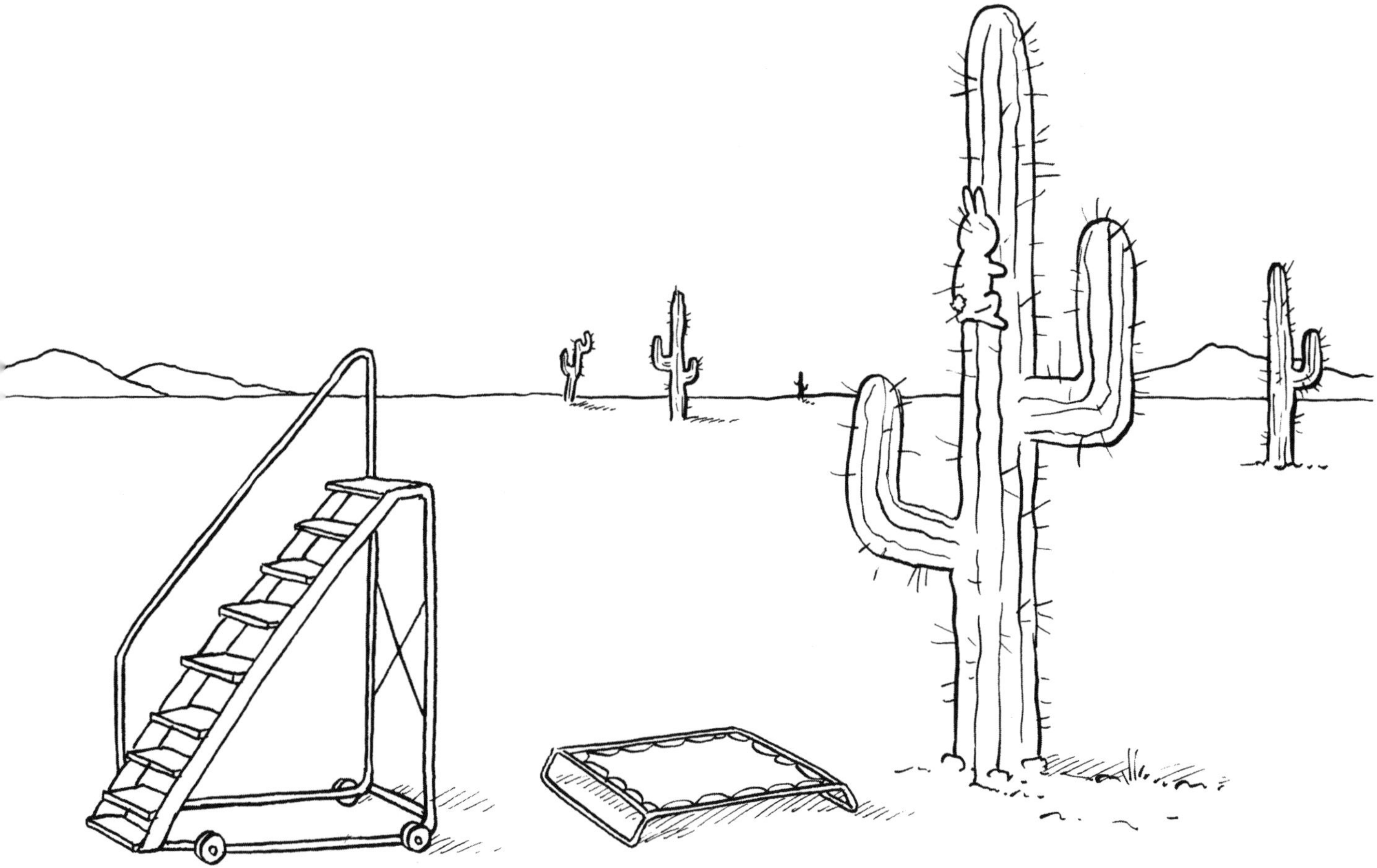

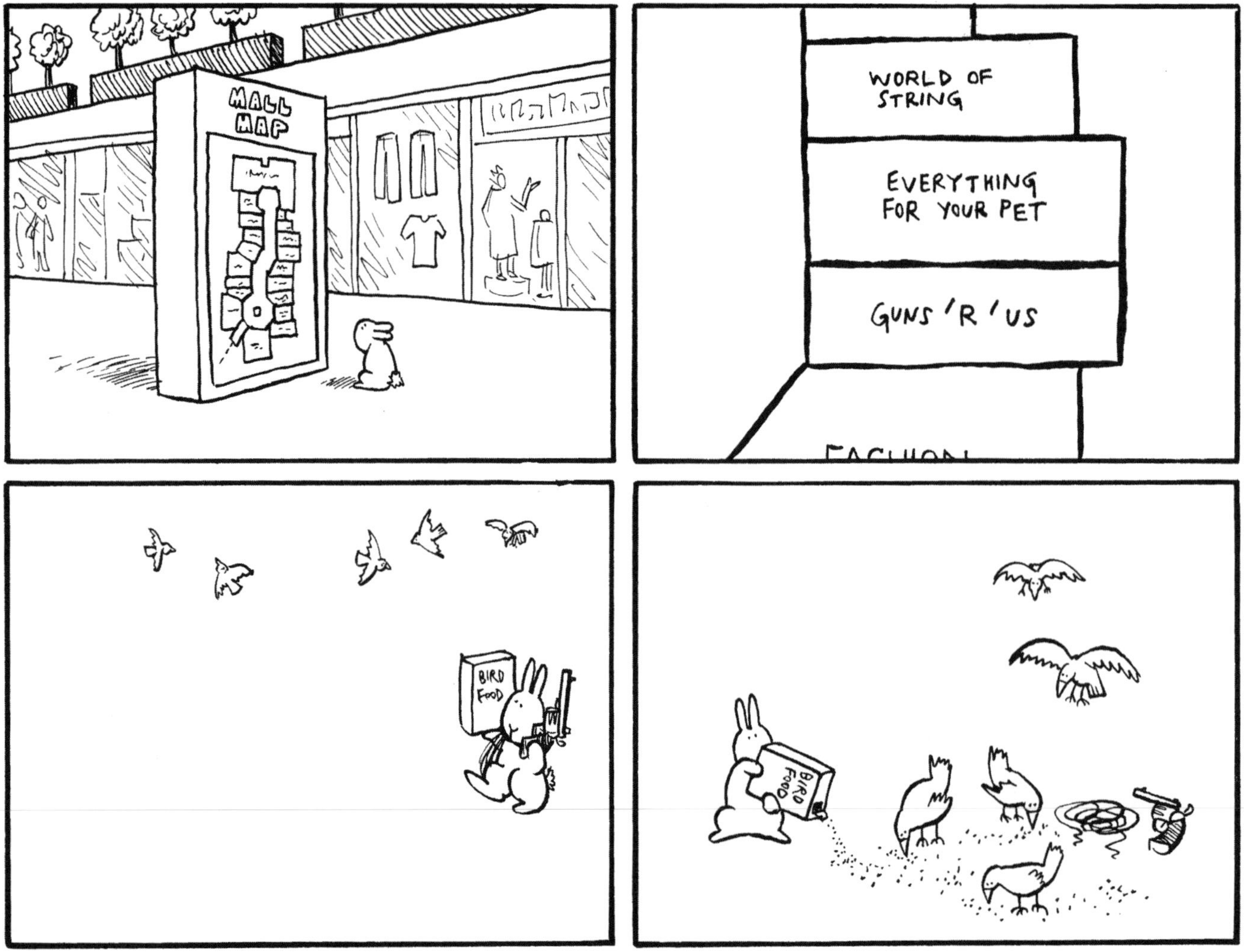
MALL MAP
WORLD OF STRING
EVERYTHING FOR YOUR PET
GUNS 'R' US
BIRD FOOD
BIRD FOOD

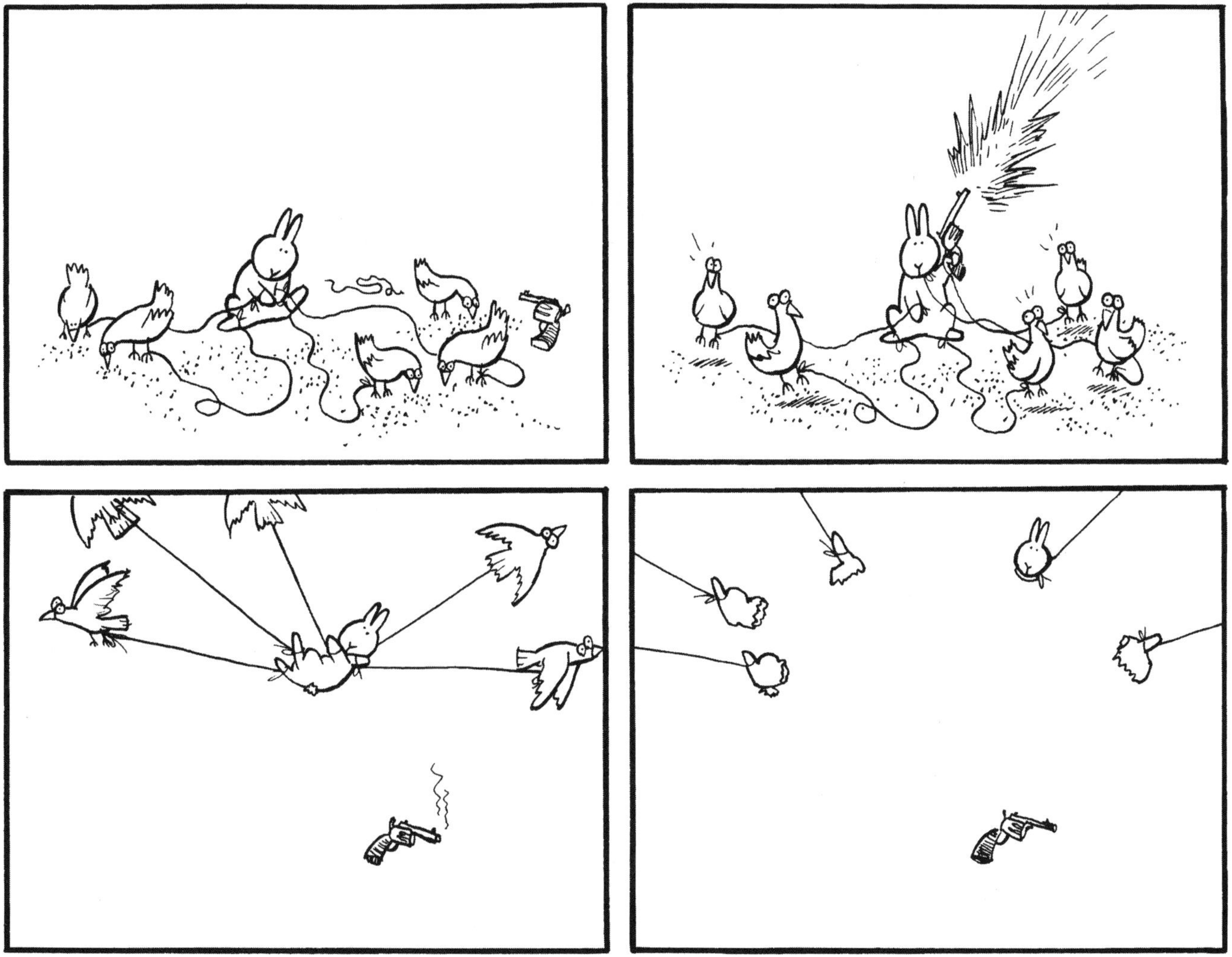

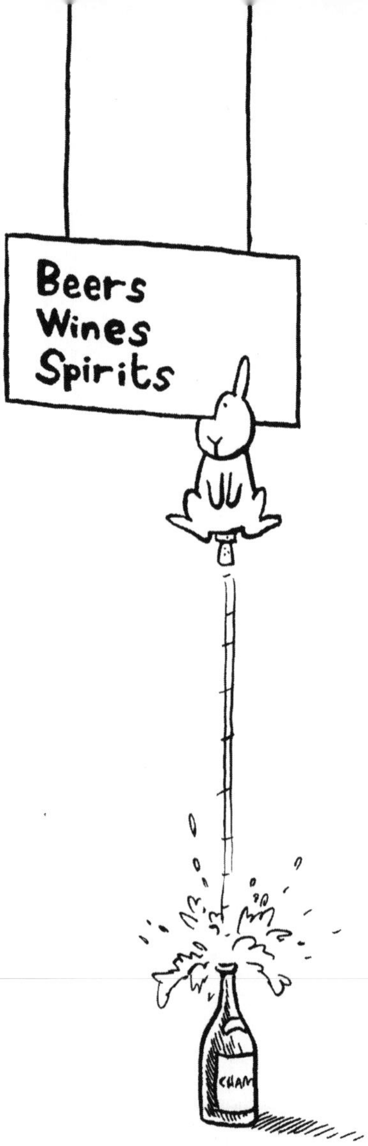
Beers
Wines
Spirits
CHAM

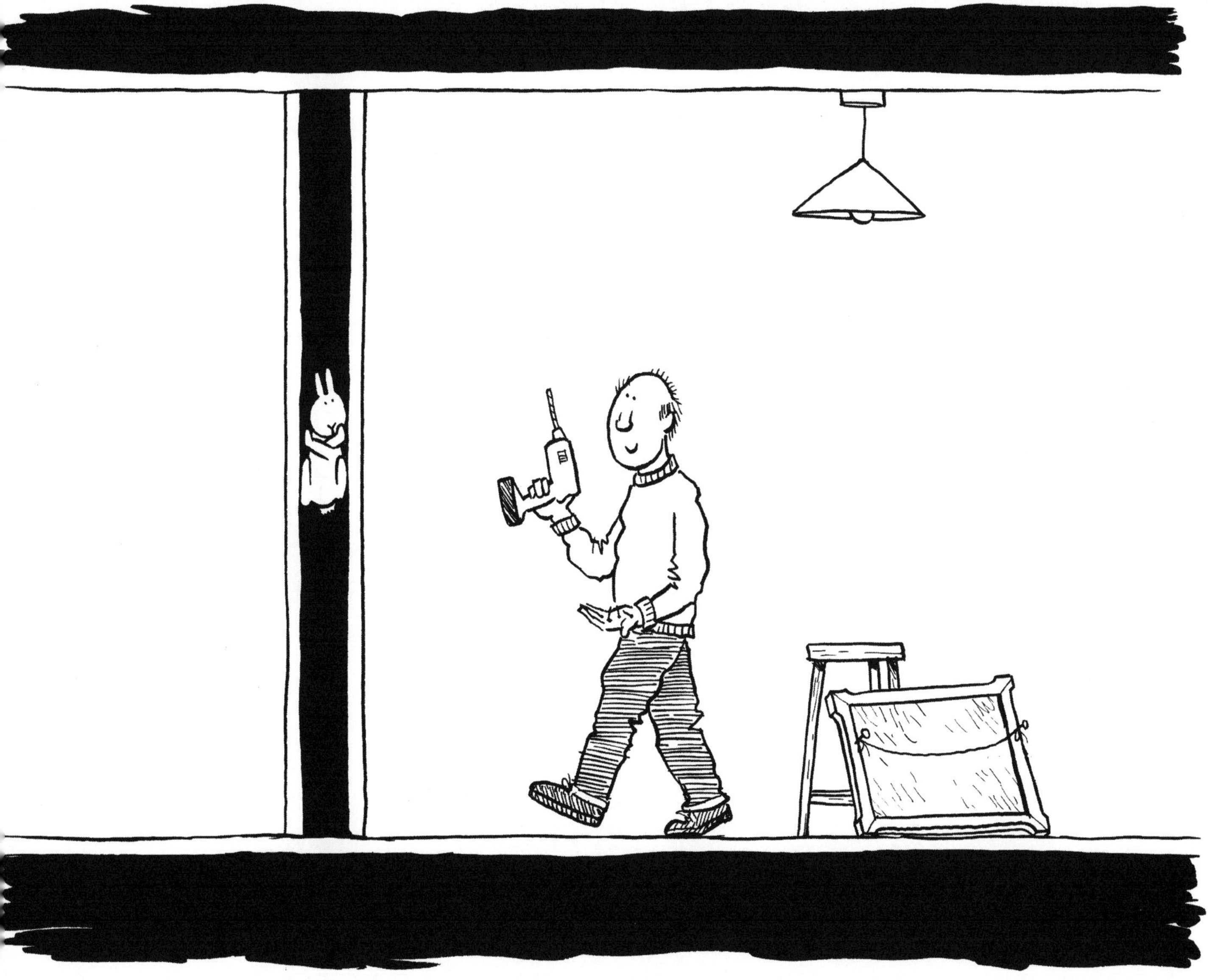

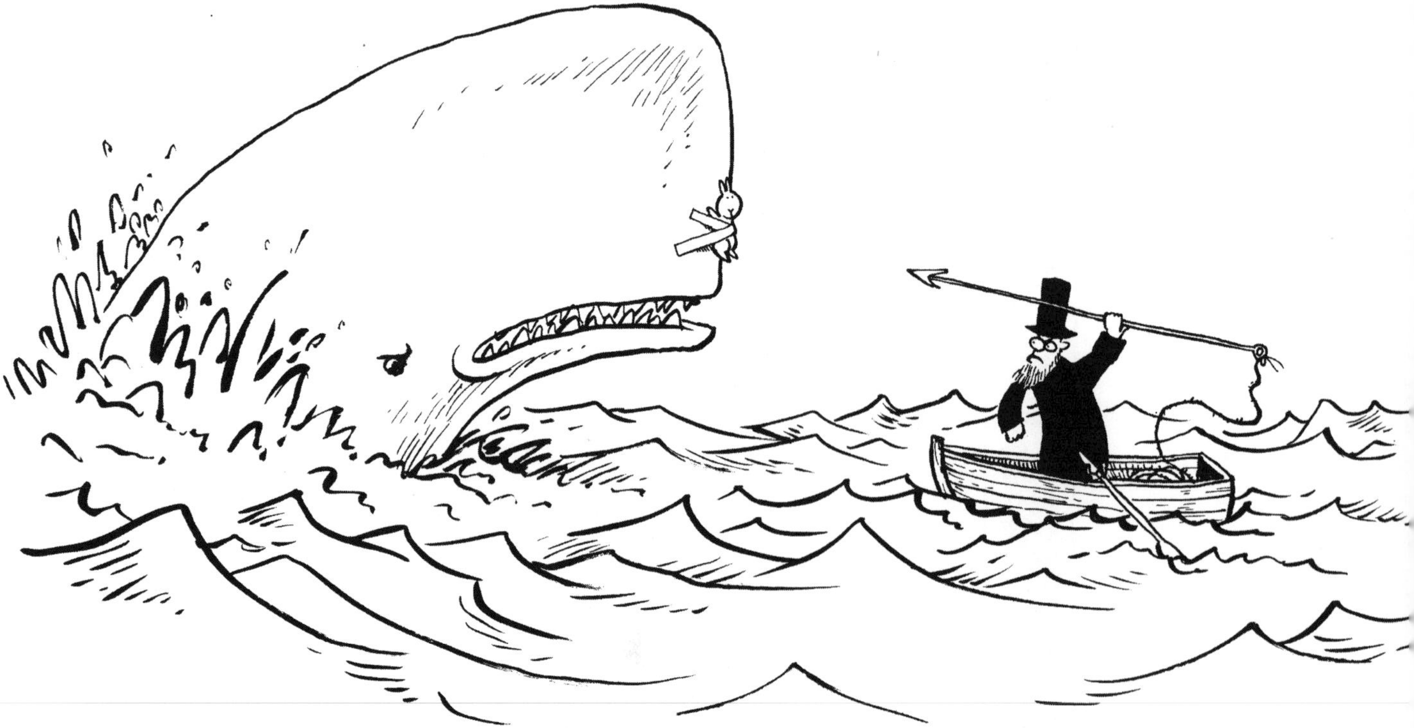

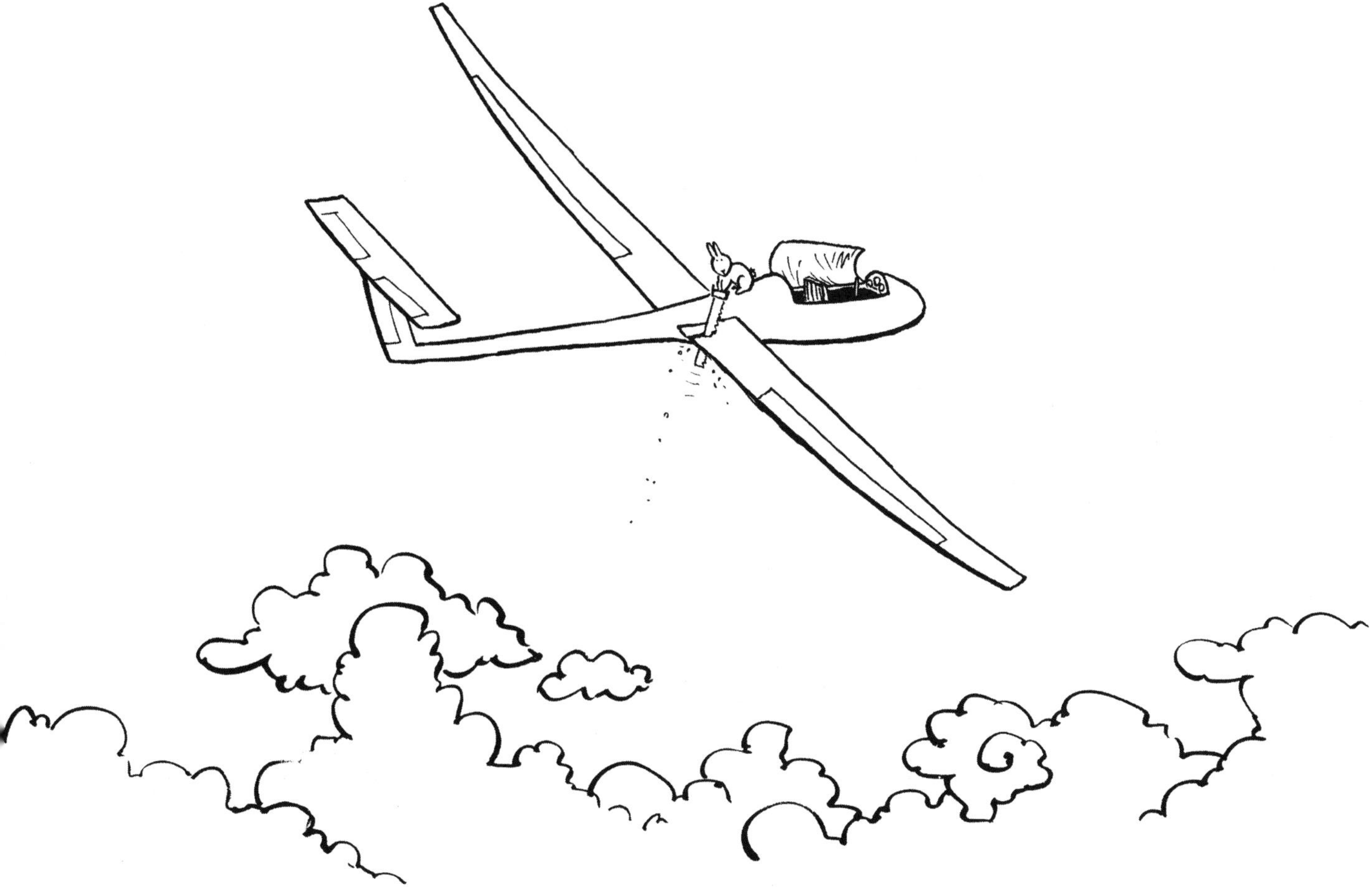

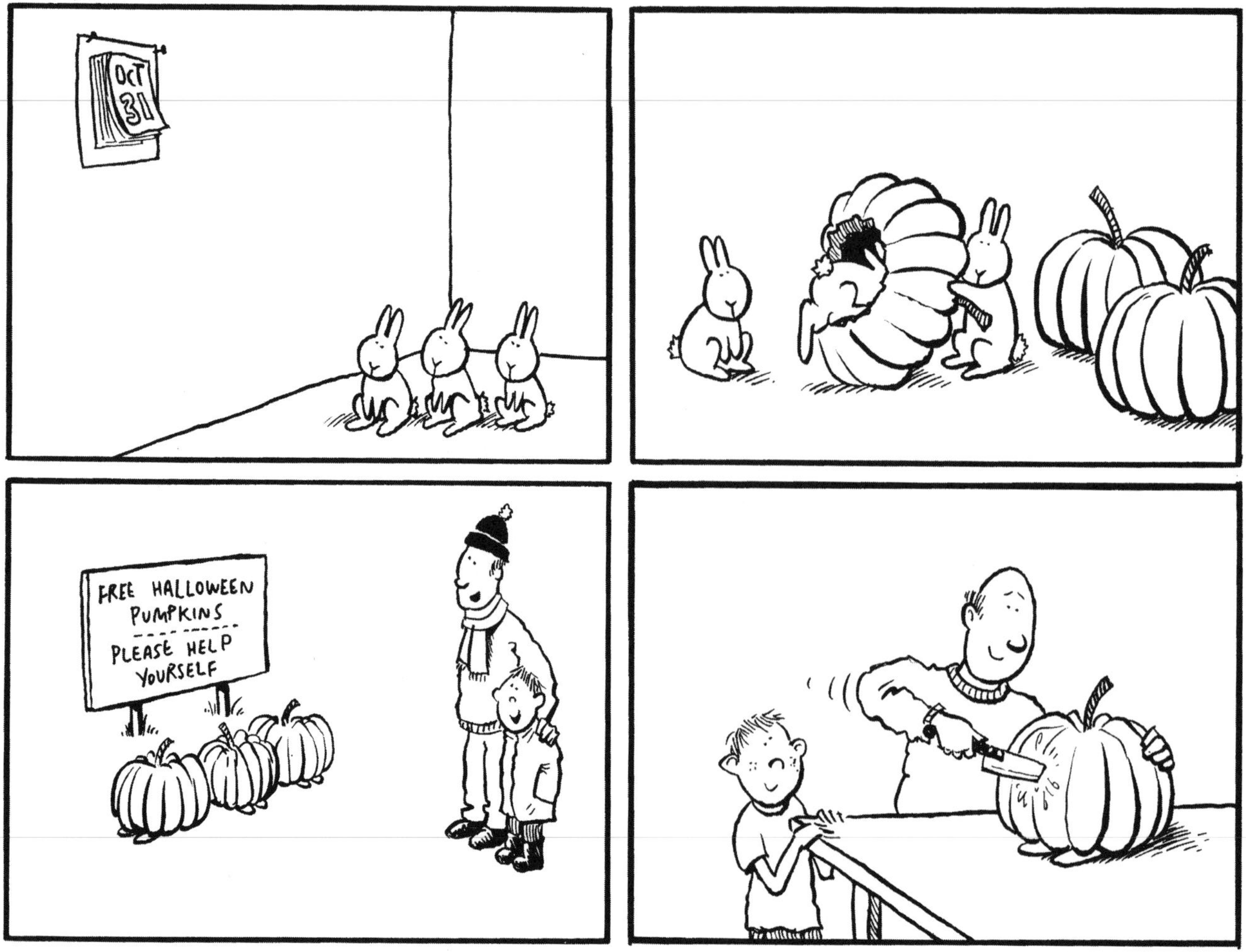
OCT
31
FREE HALLOWEEN PUMPKINS
PLEASE HELP YOURSELF

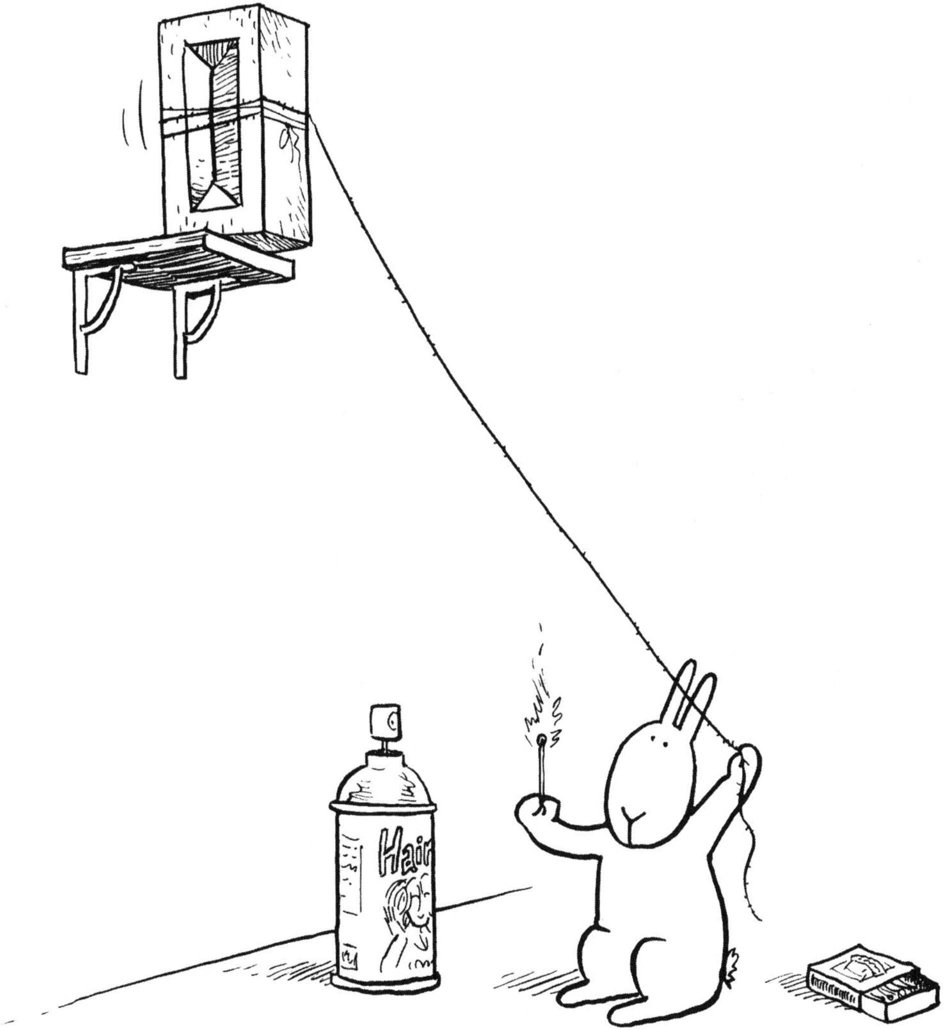
Hair

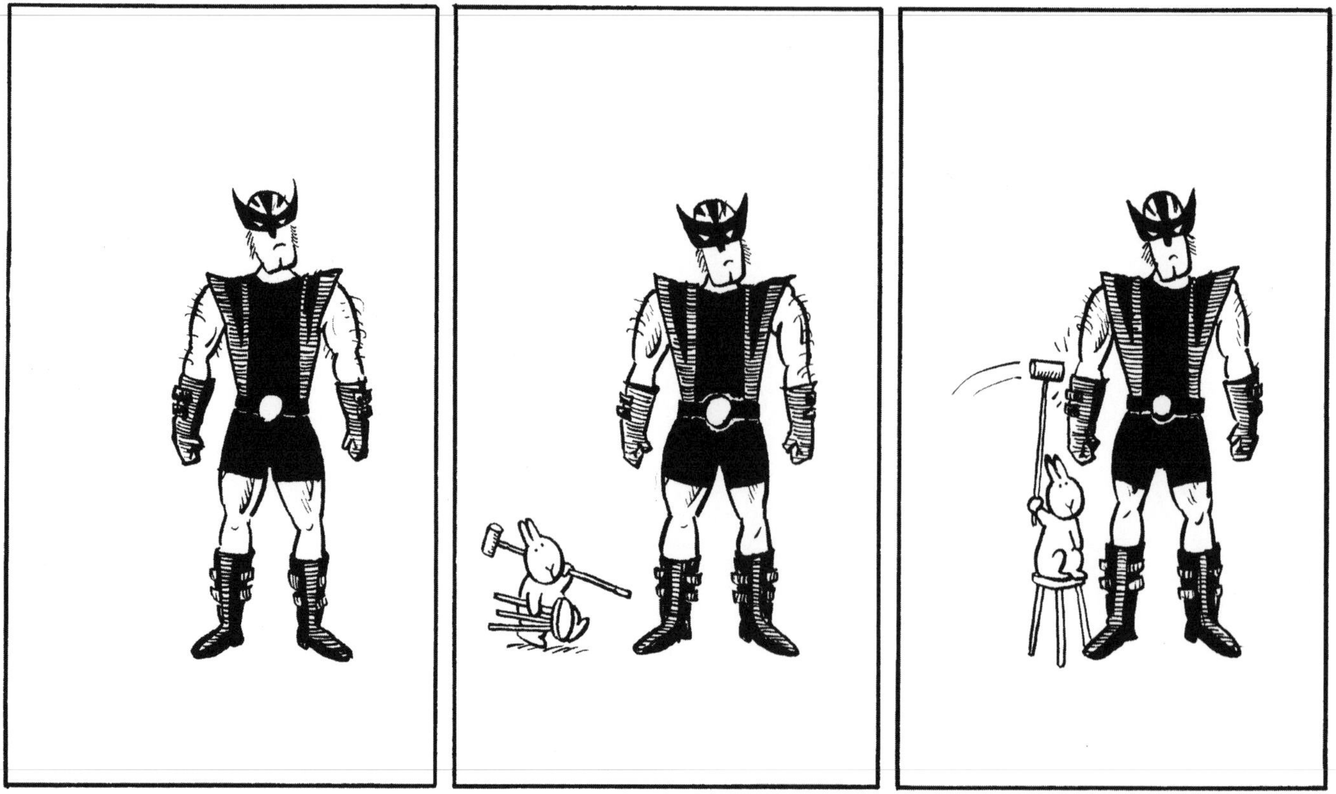

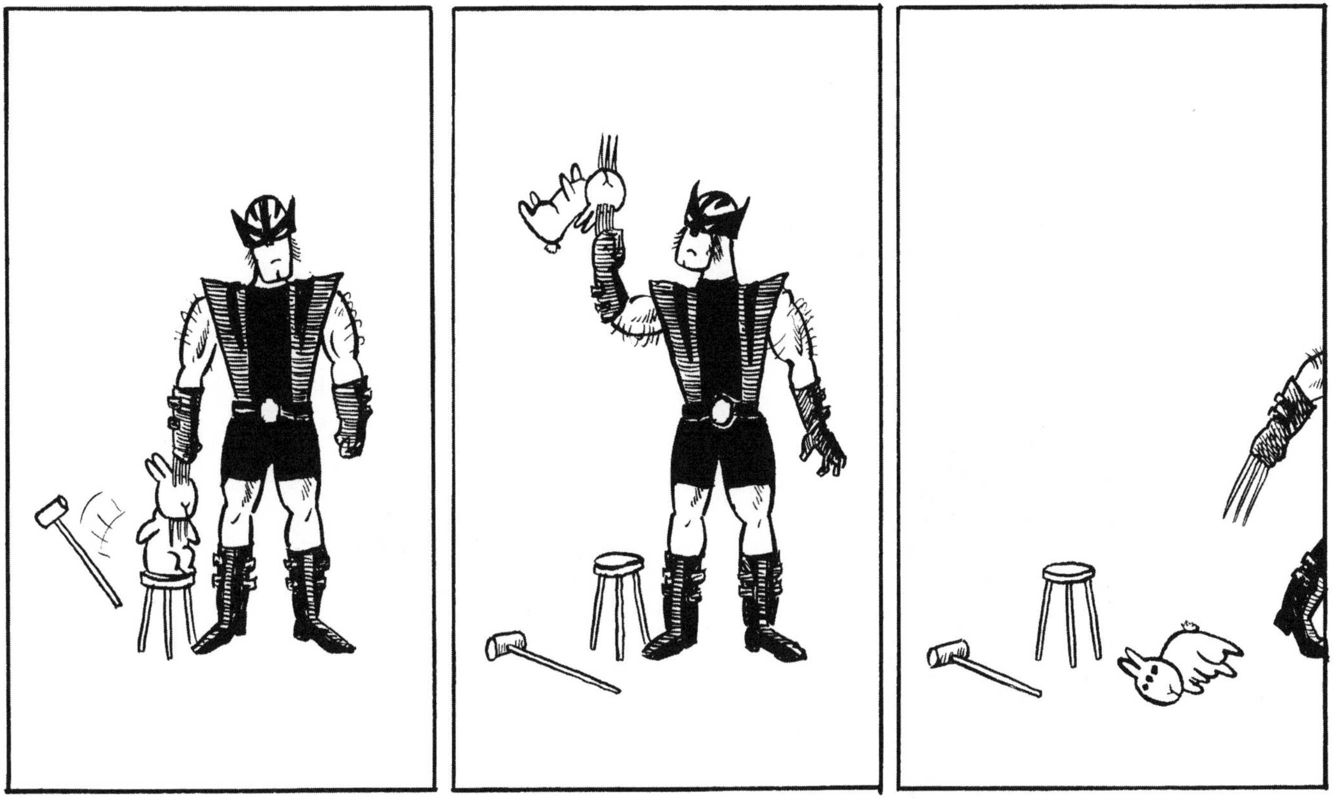

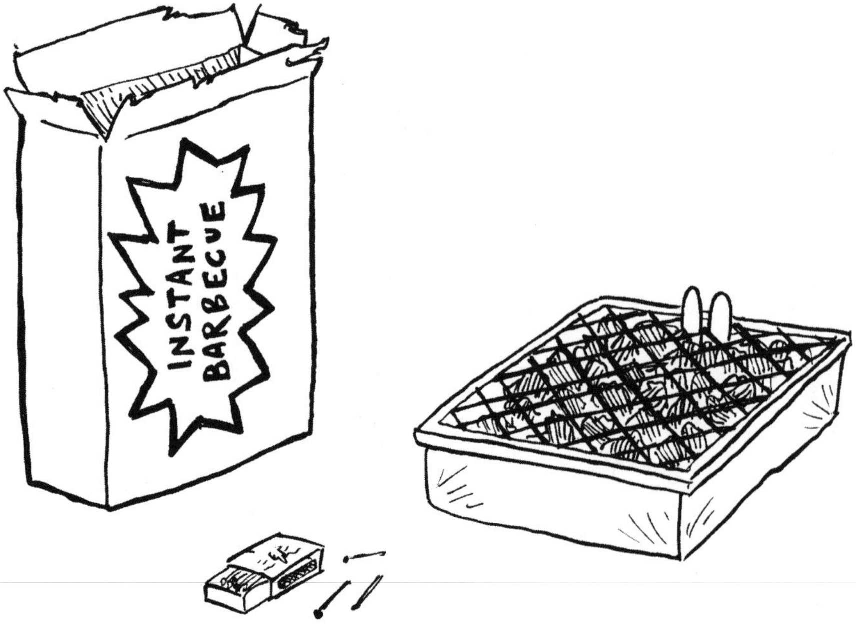
INSTANT
BARBECUE

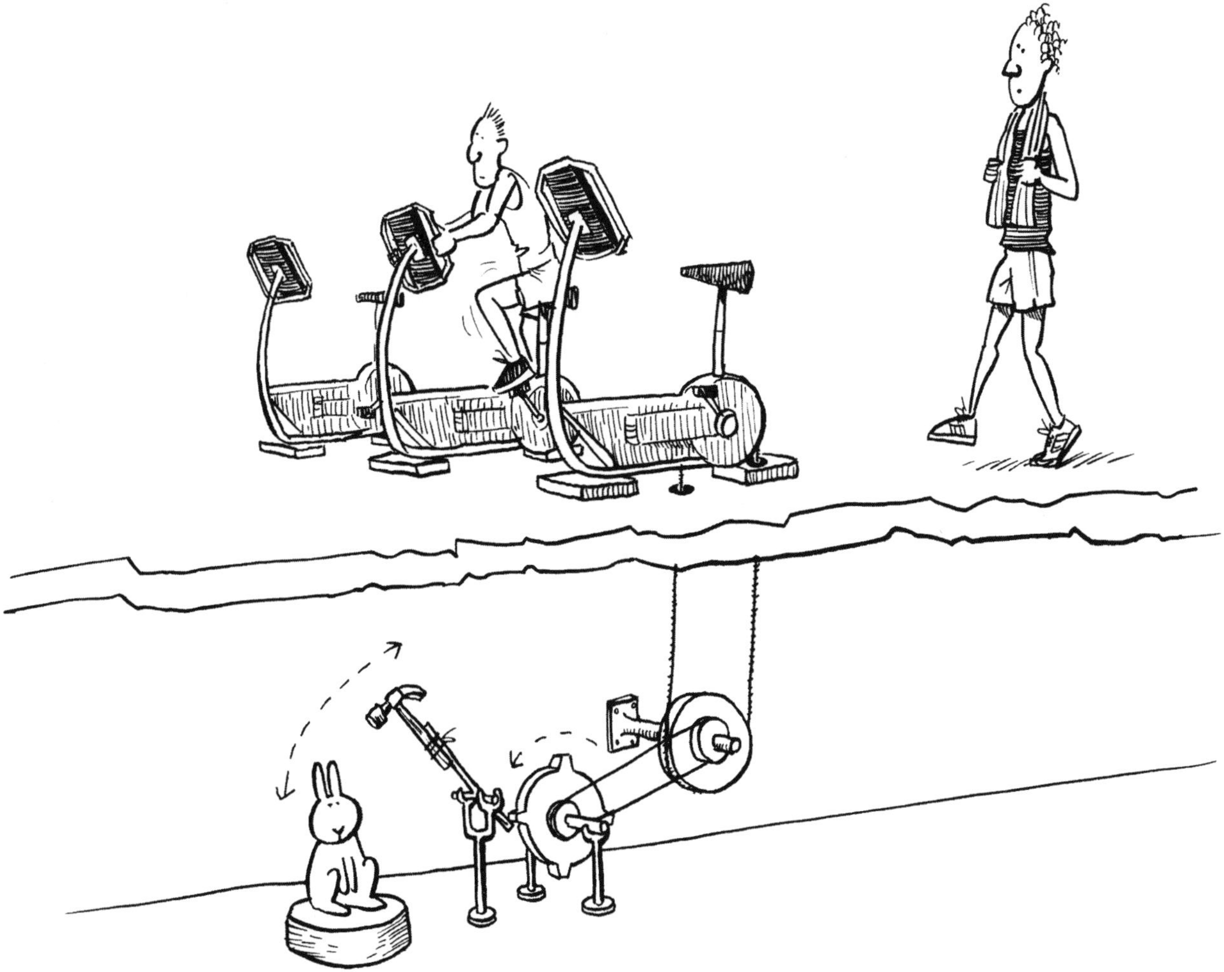

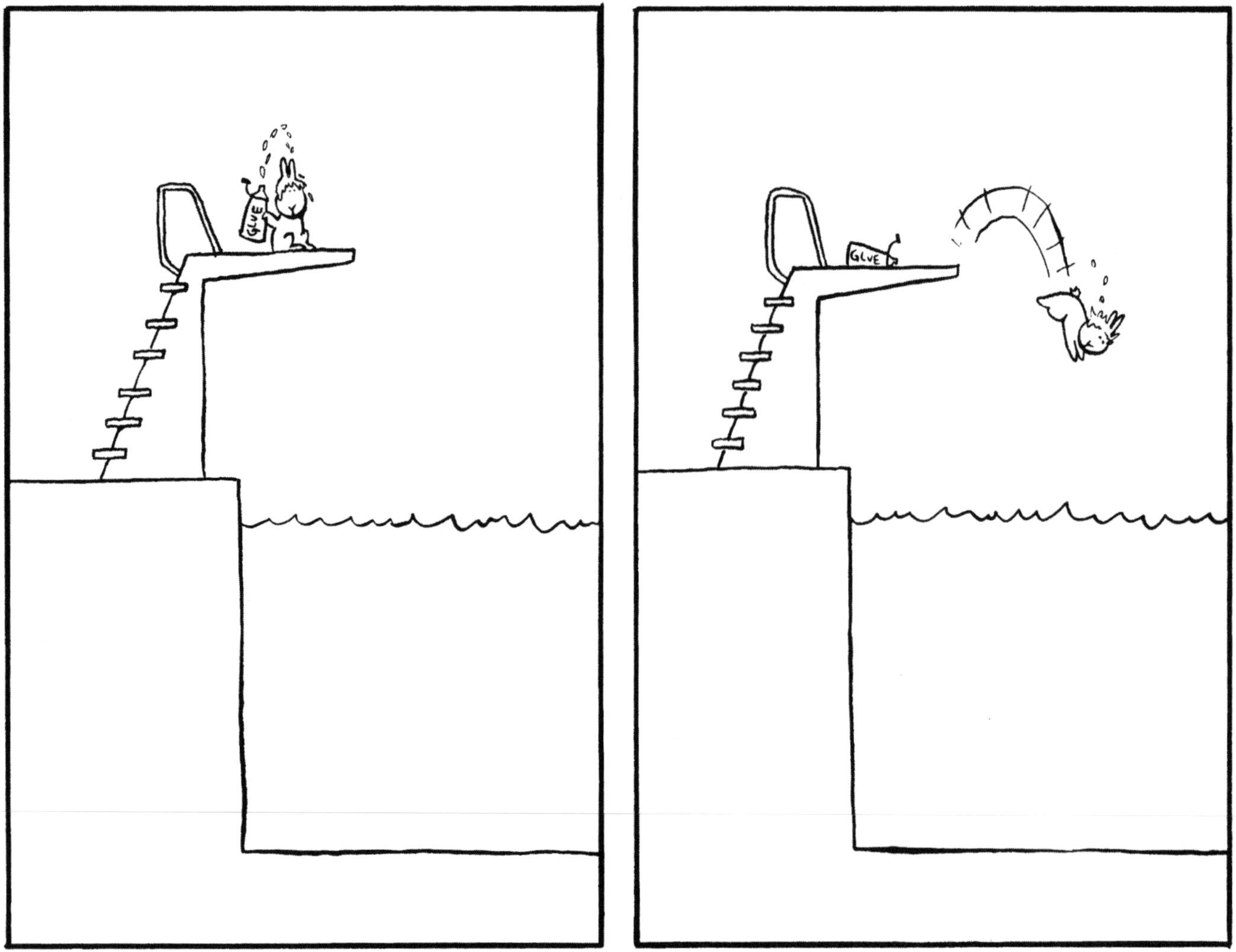
GLUE
GLUE

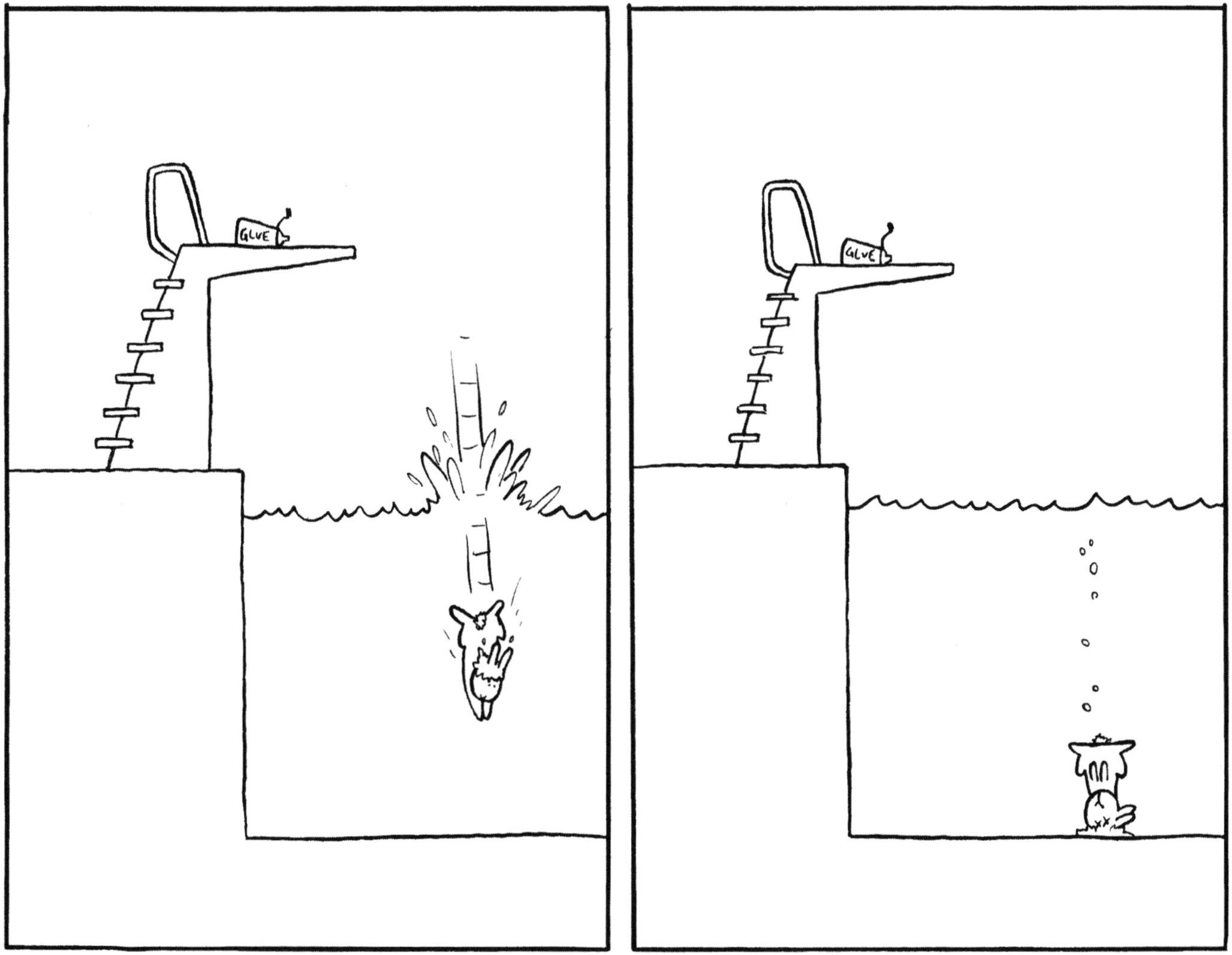
GLUE
GLUE

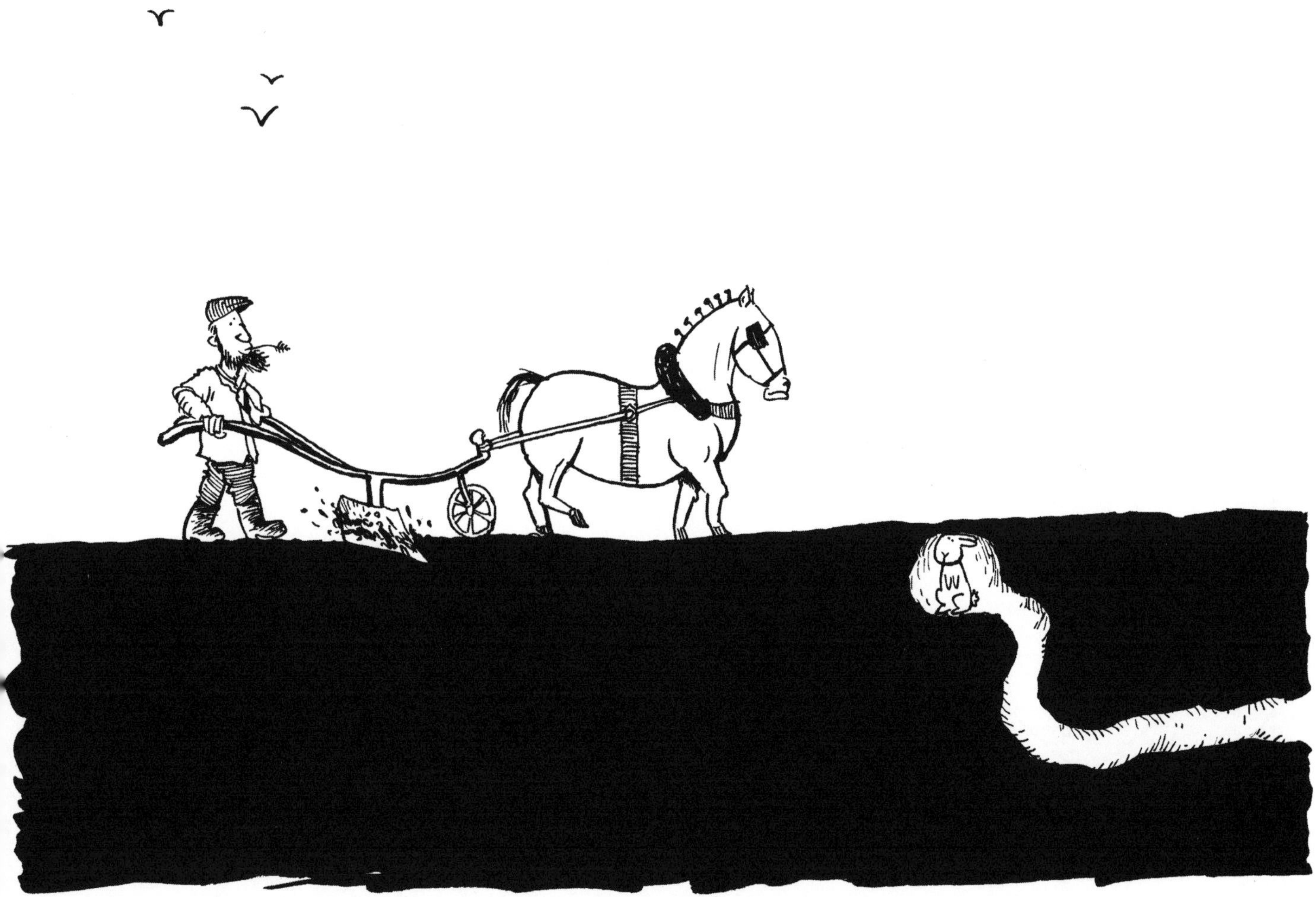

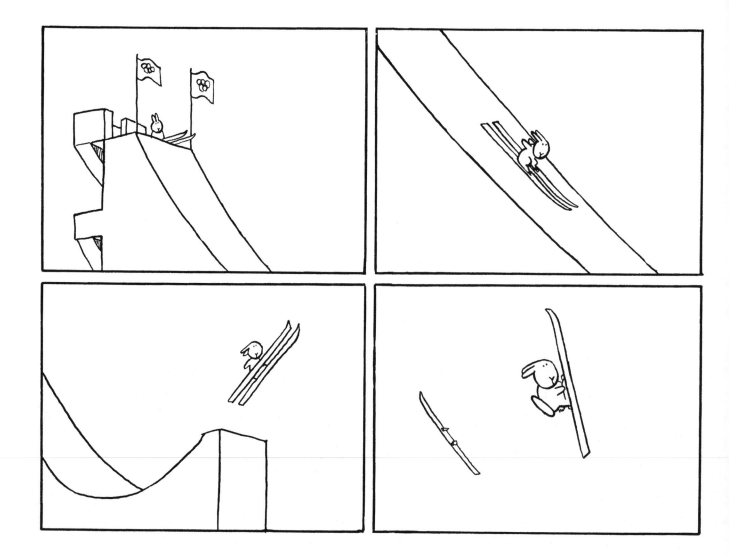

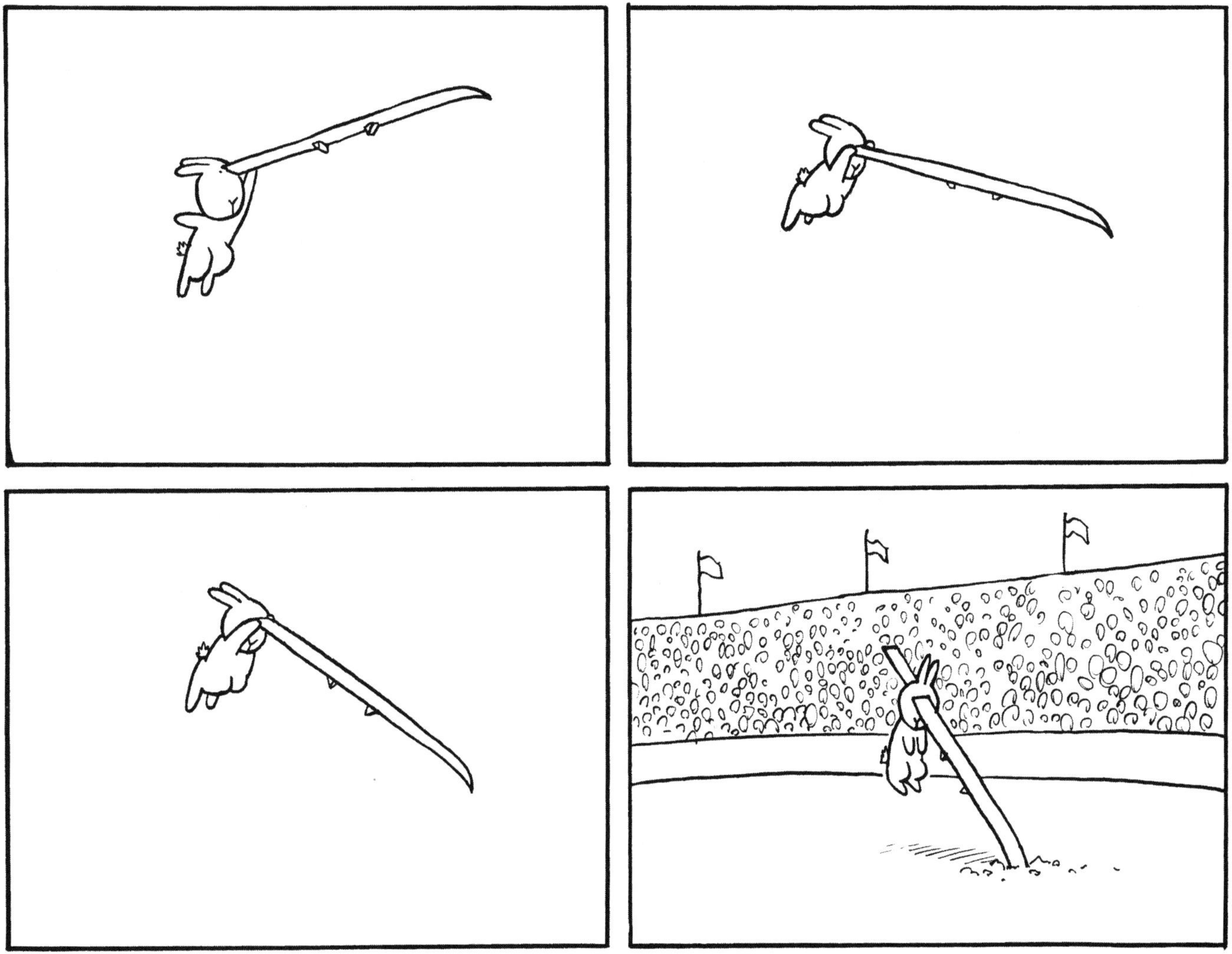

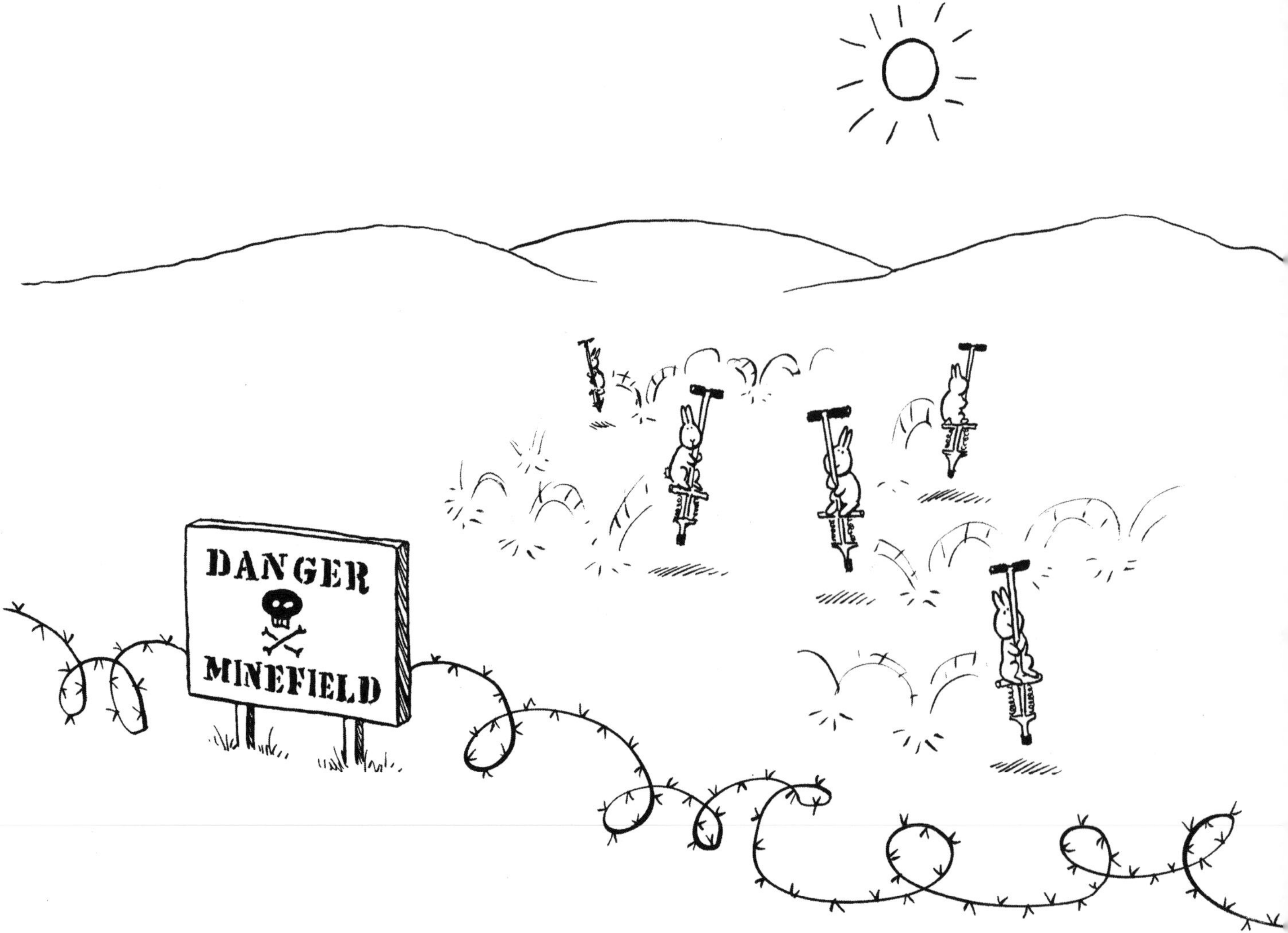
DANGER
MINEFIELD

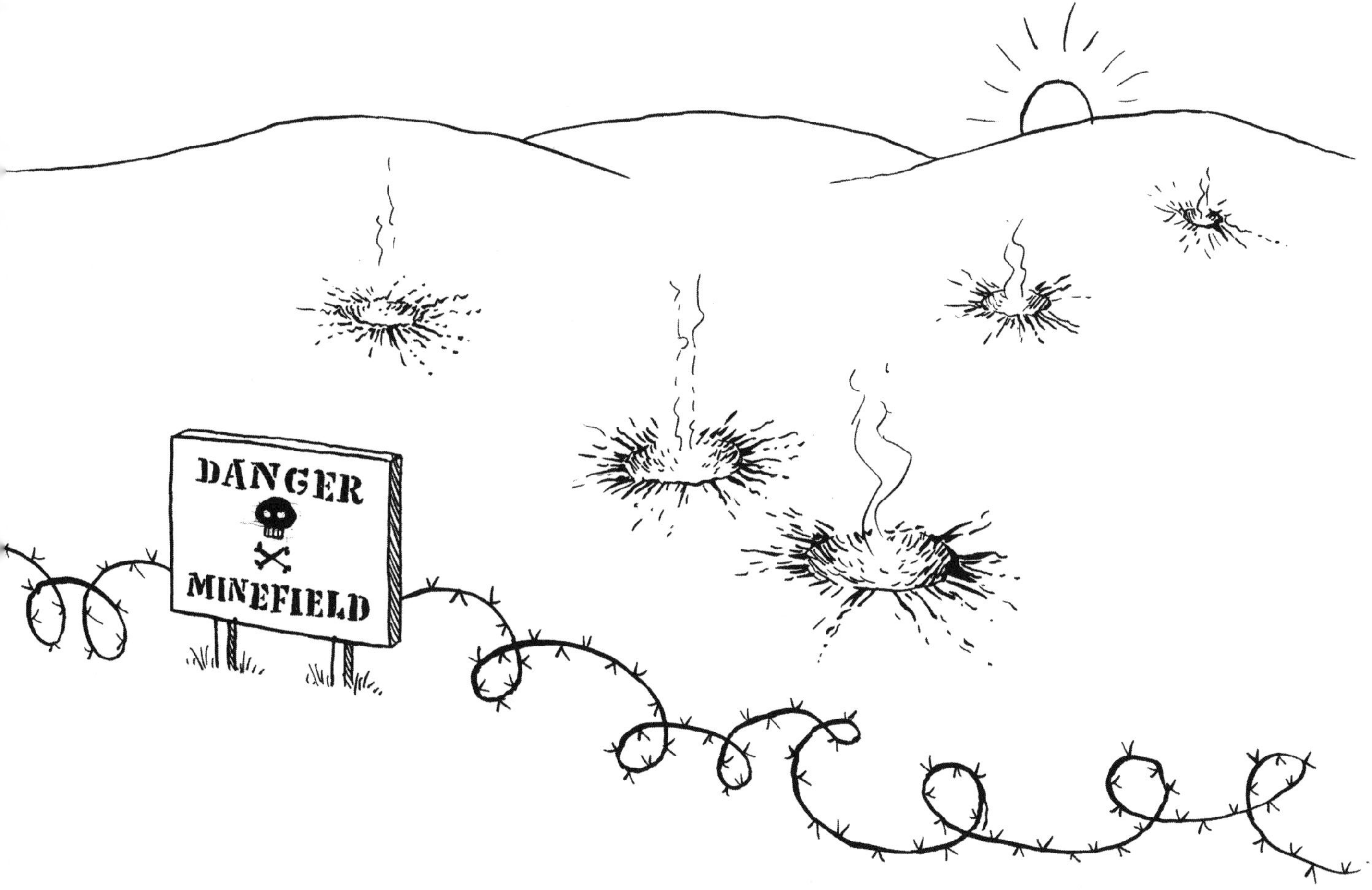
DANGER
MINEFIELD

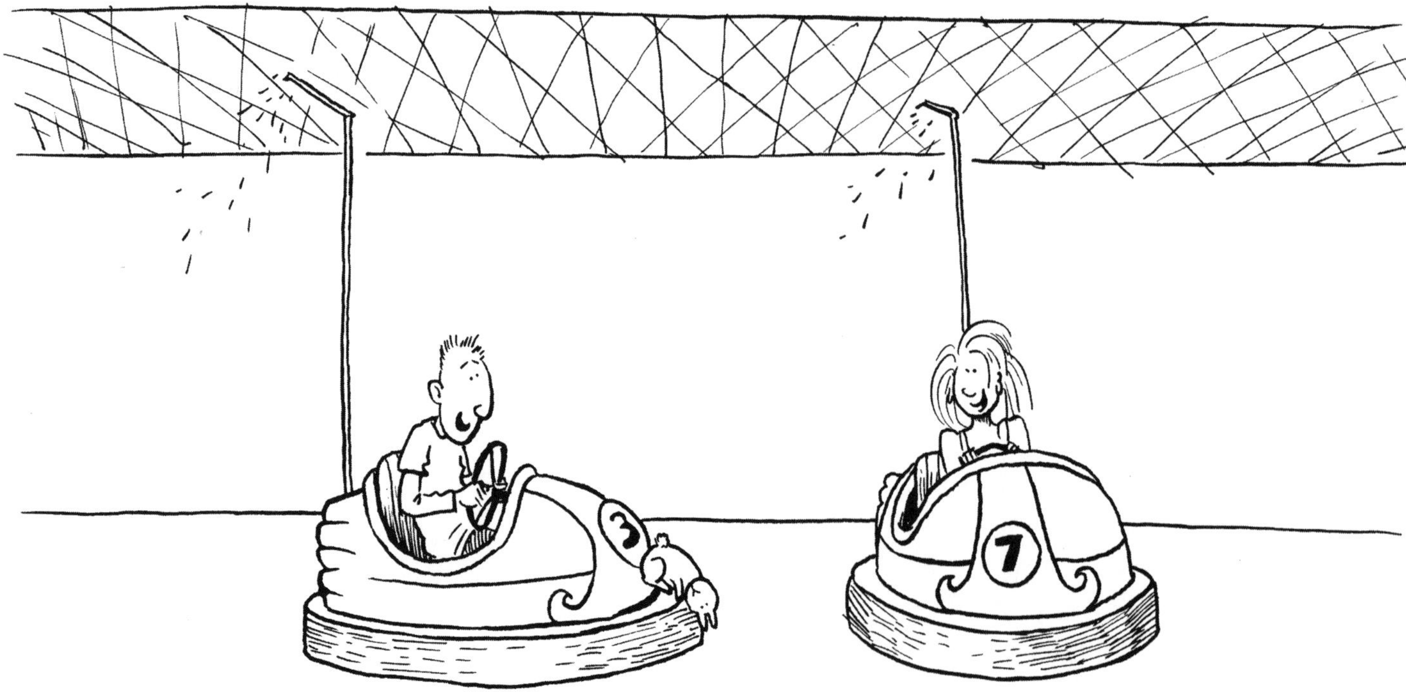
3
7

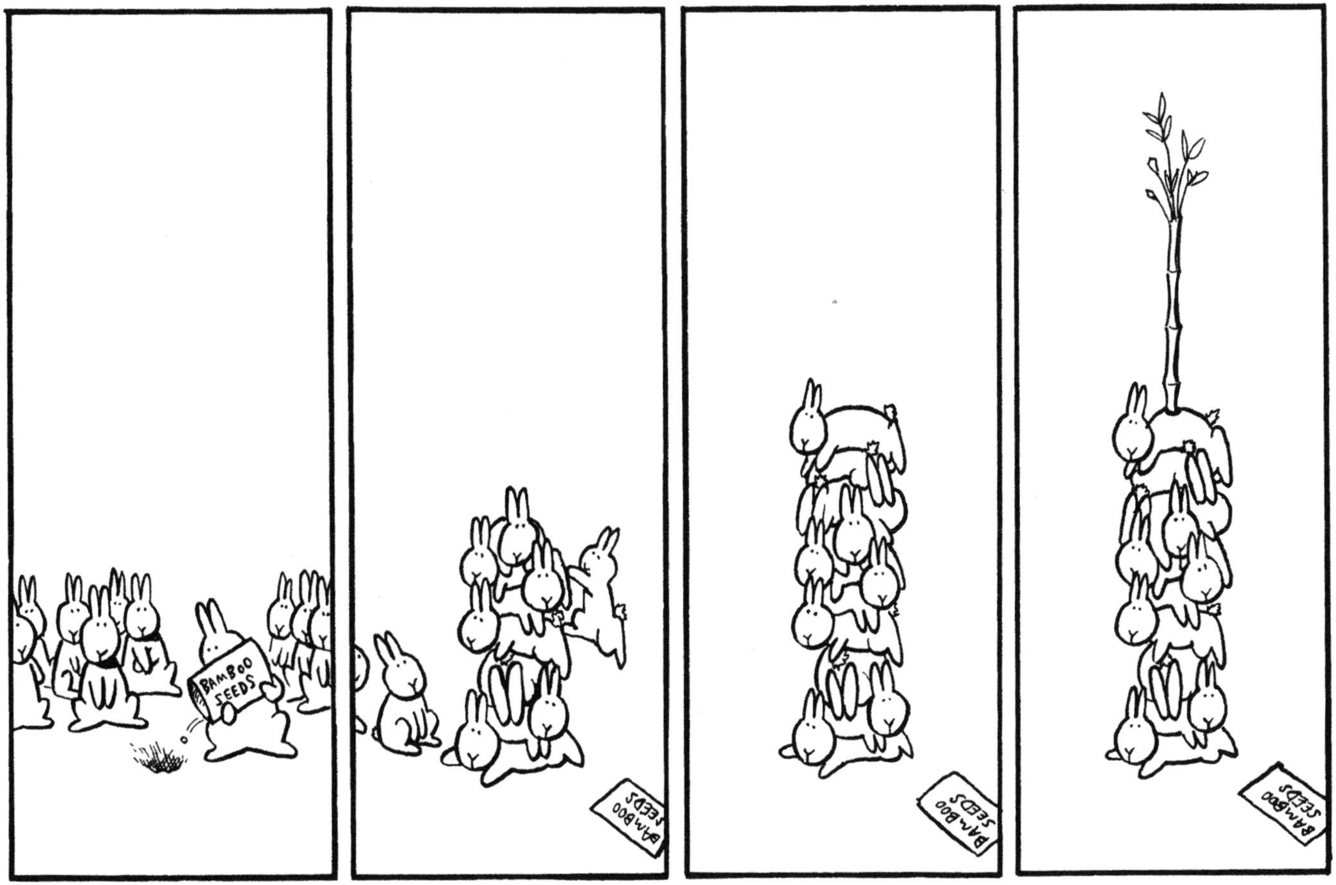
BAMBOO SEEDS
BAMBOO SEEDS
BAMBOO SEEDS
BAMBOO SEEDS

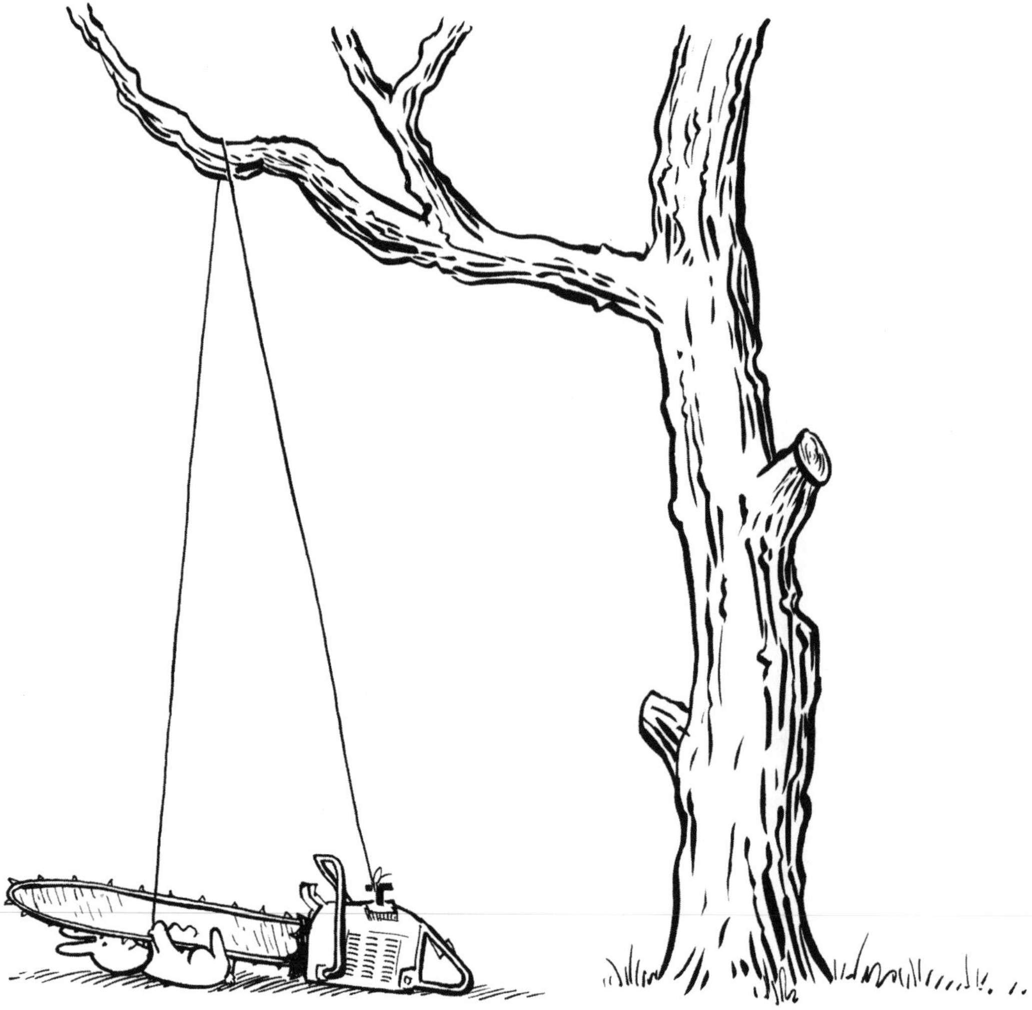

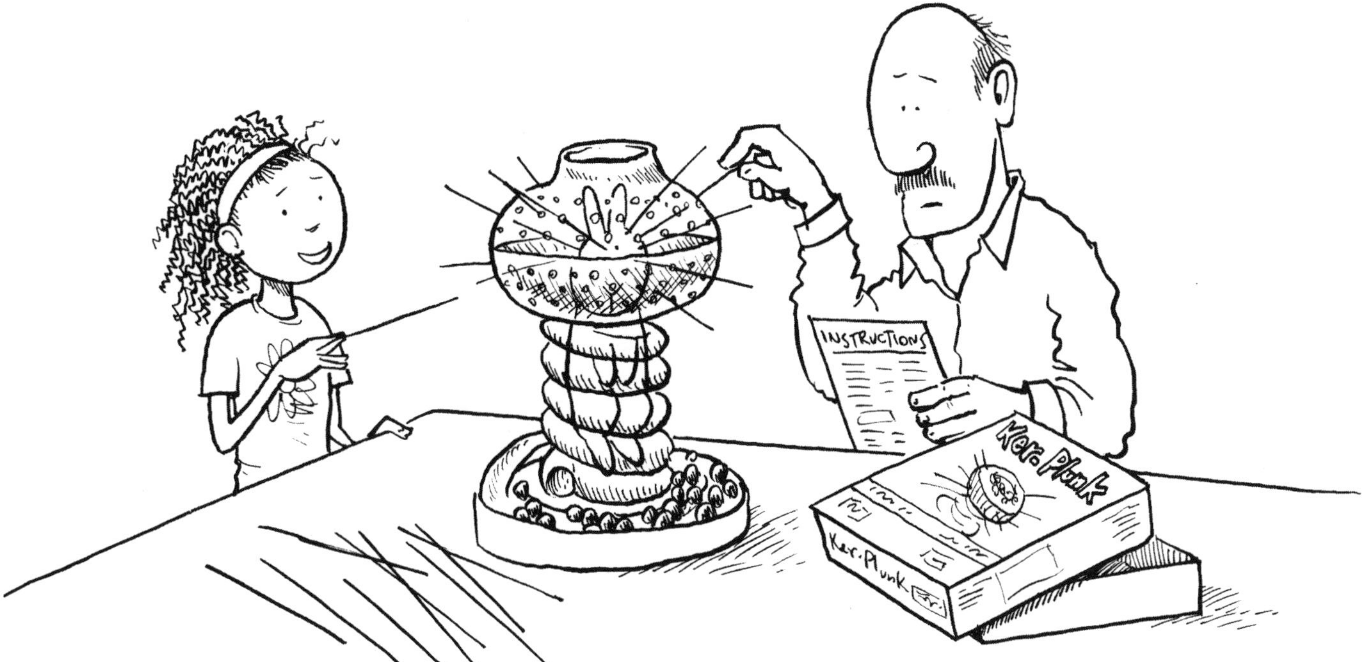
INSTRUCTIONS
Ker-Plunk
Ker-Plunk

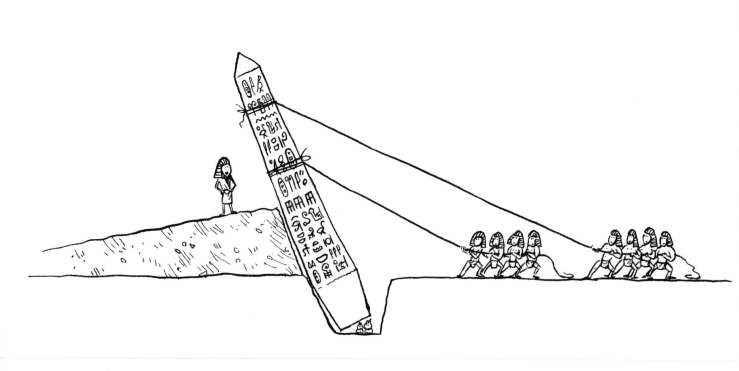

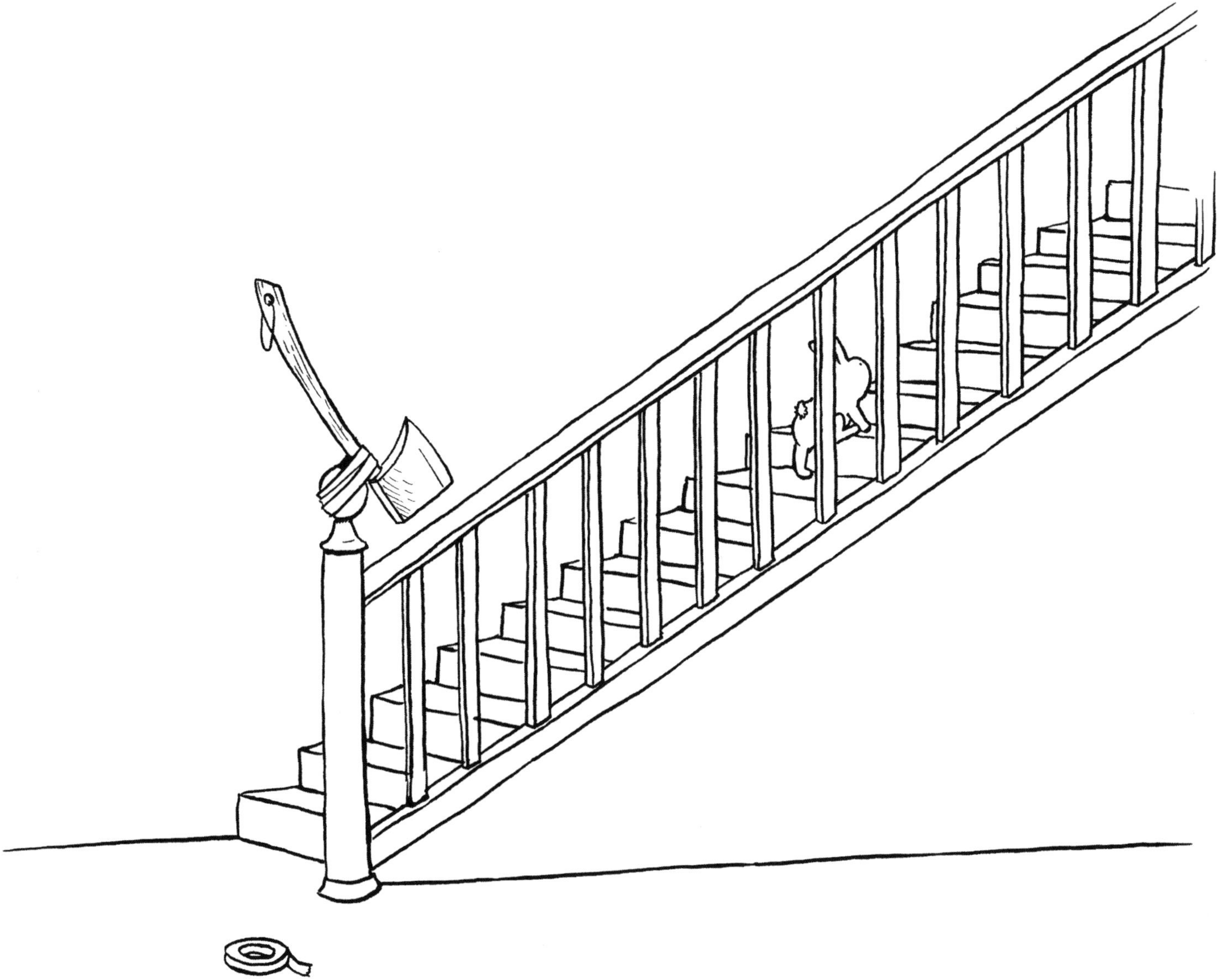

FRESHLY
SQUEEZED
ORANGE
JUICE

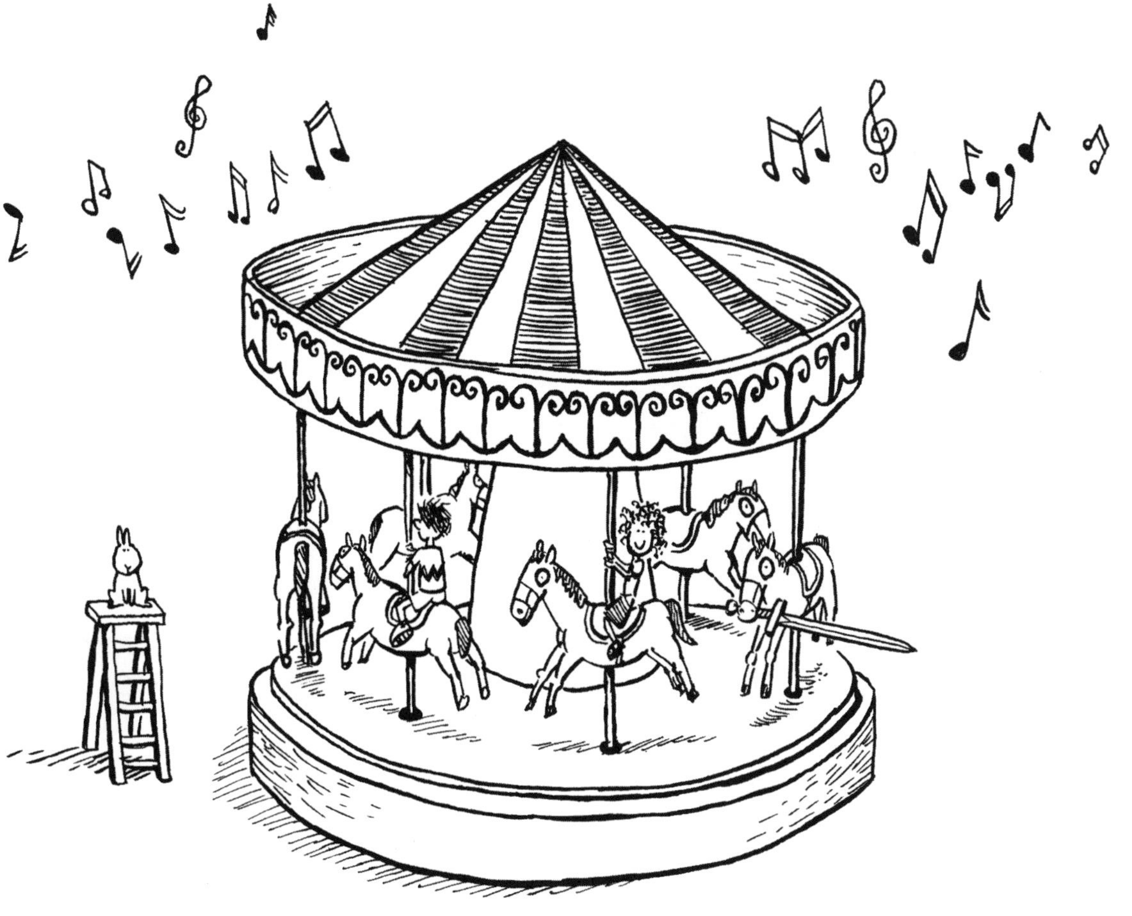

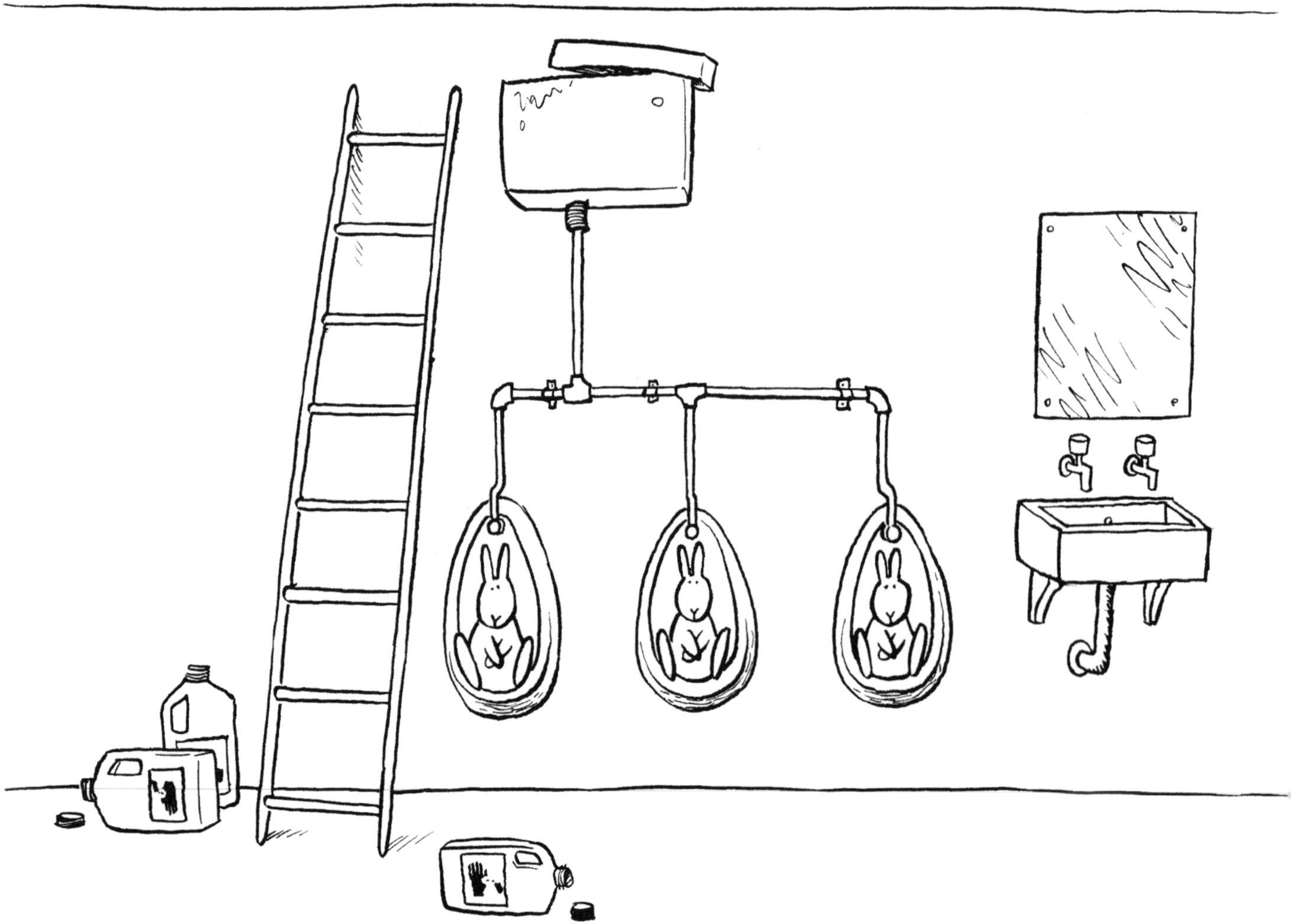

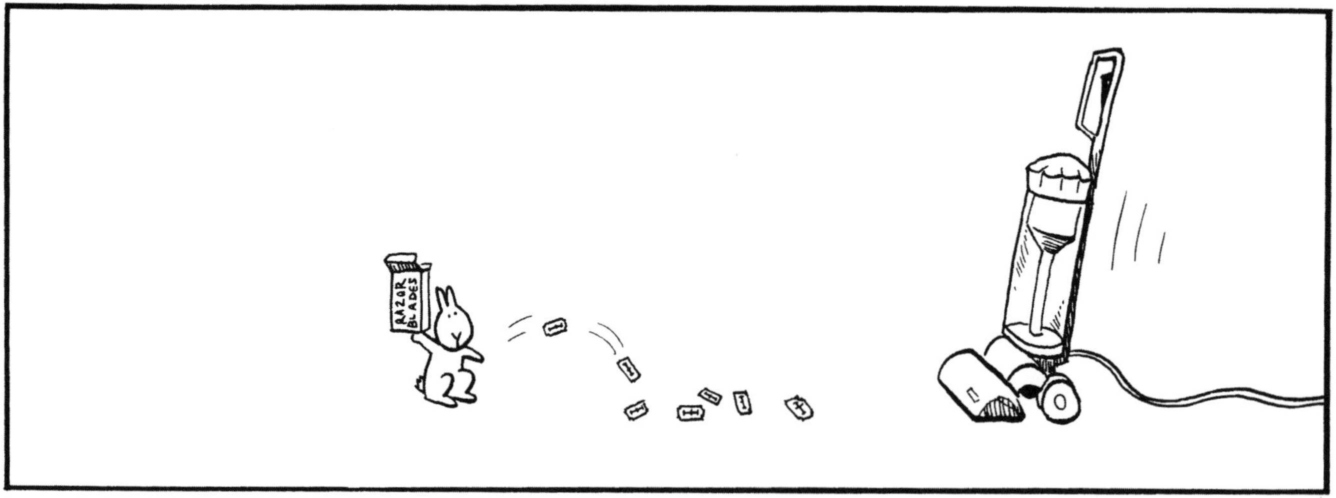
RAZOR BLADES

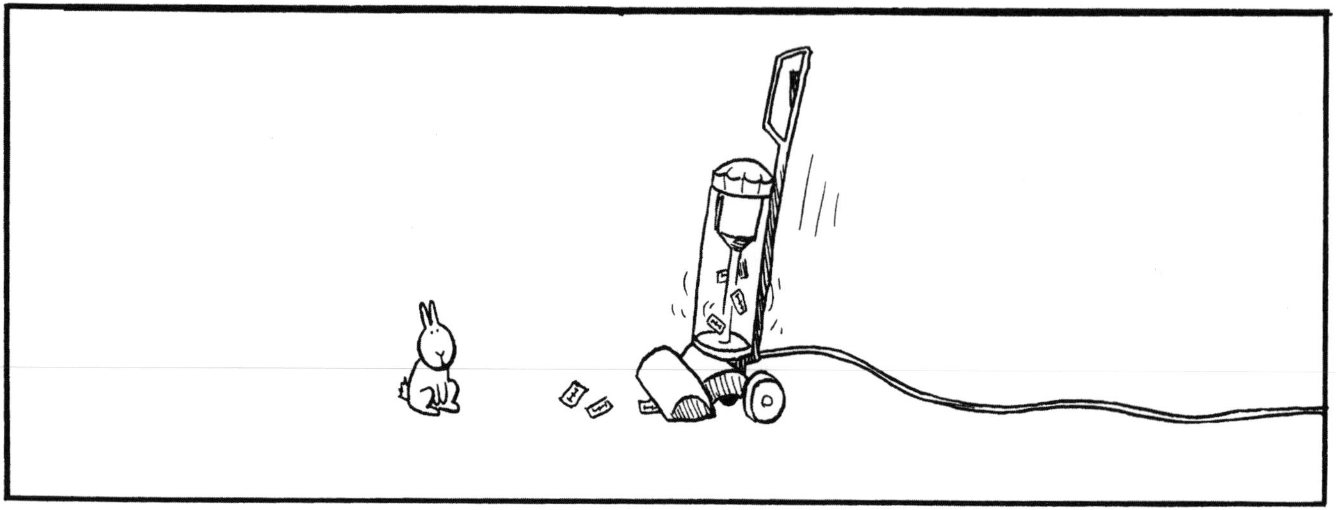

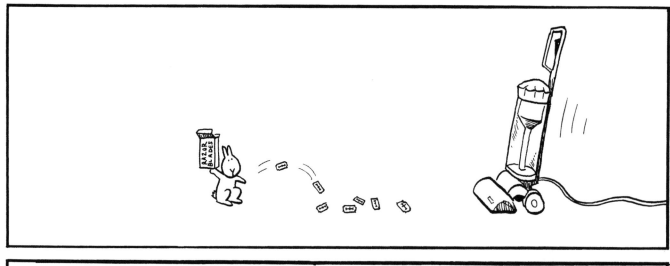

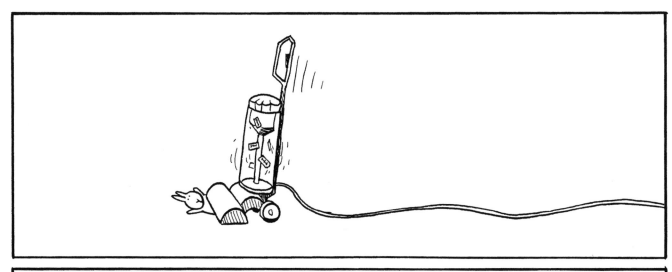

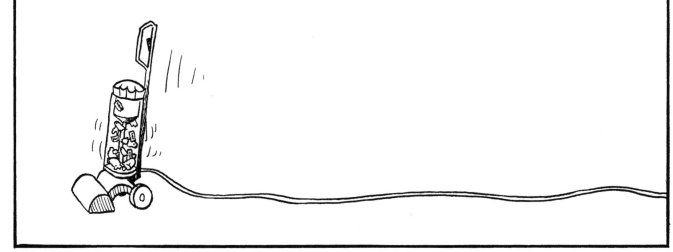

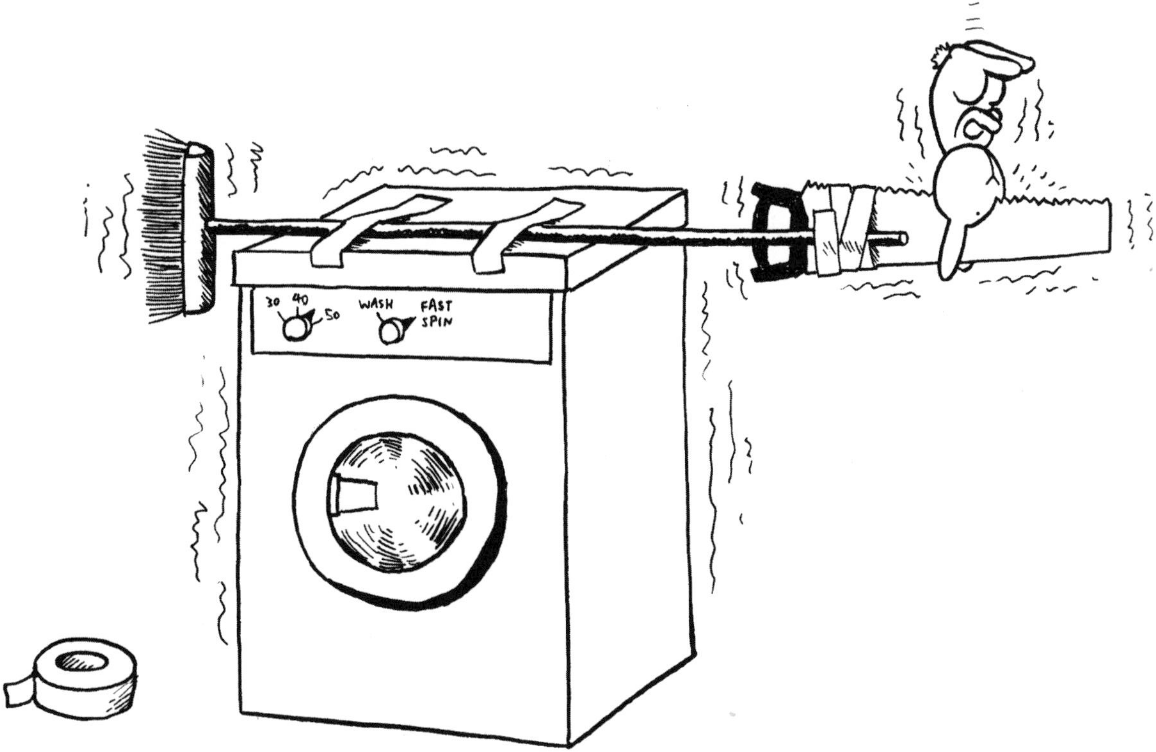

30
40
50
WASH
FAST SPIN

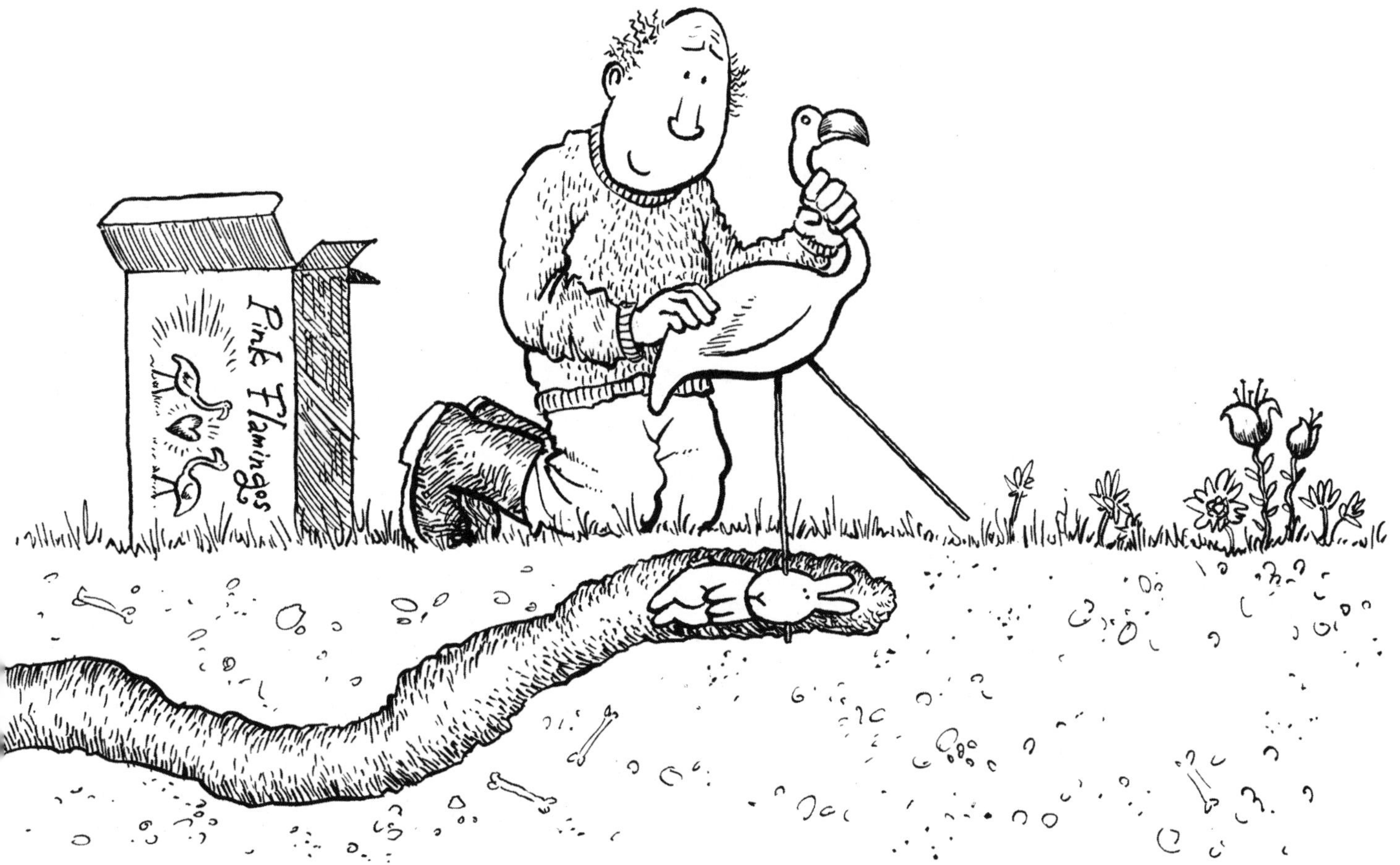
Pink Flamingos

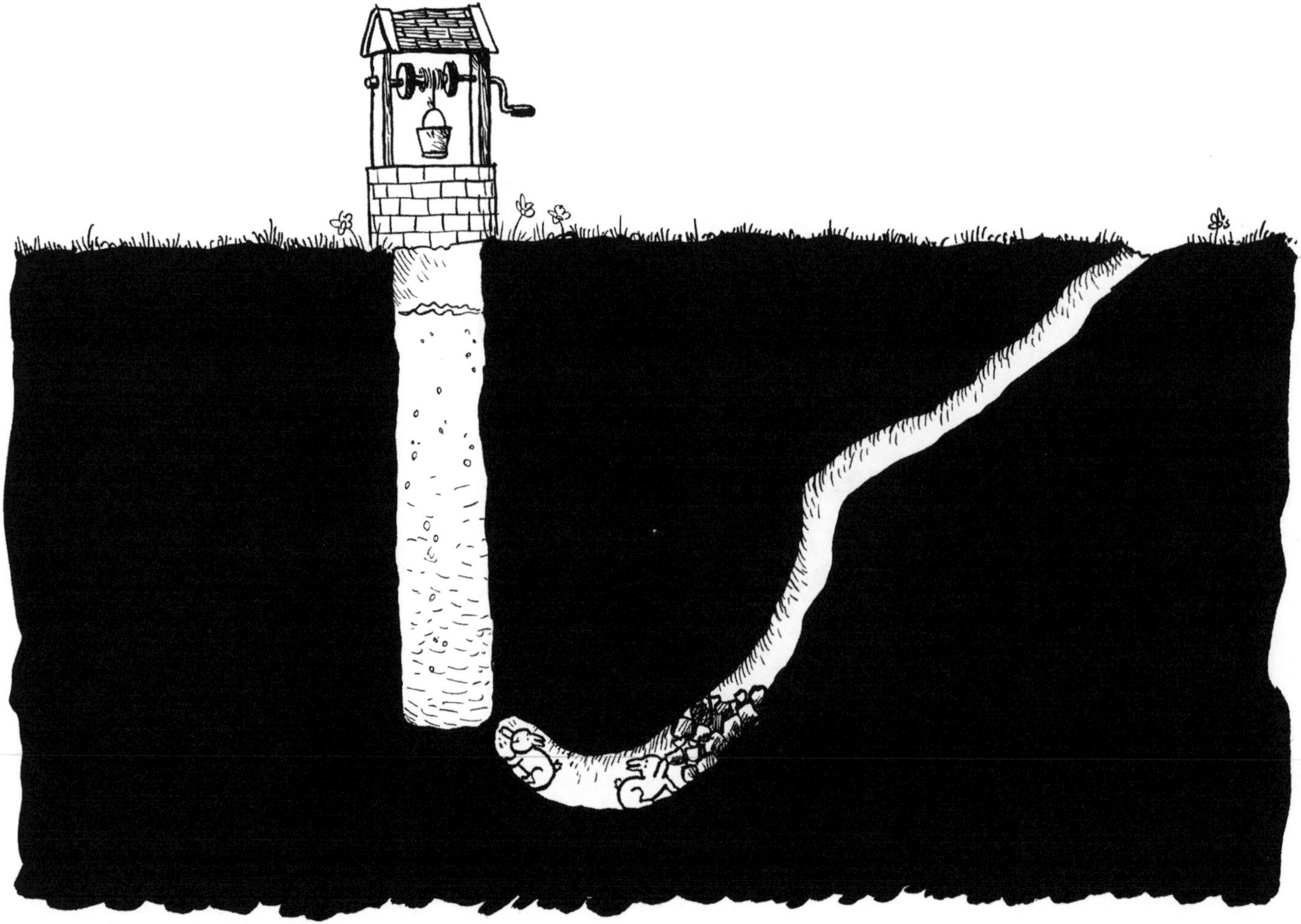

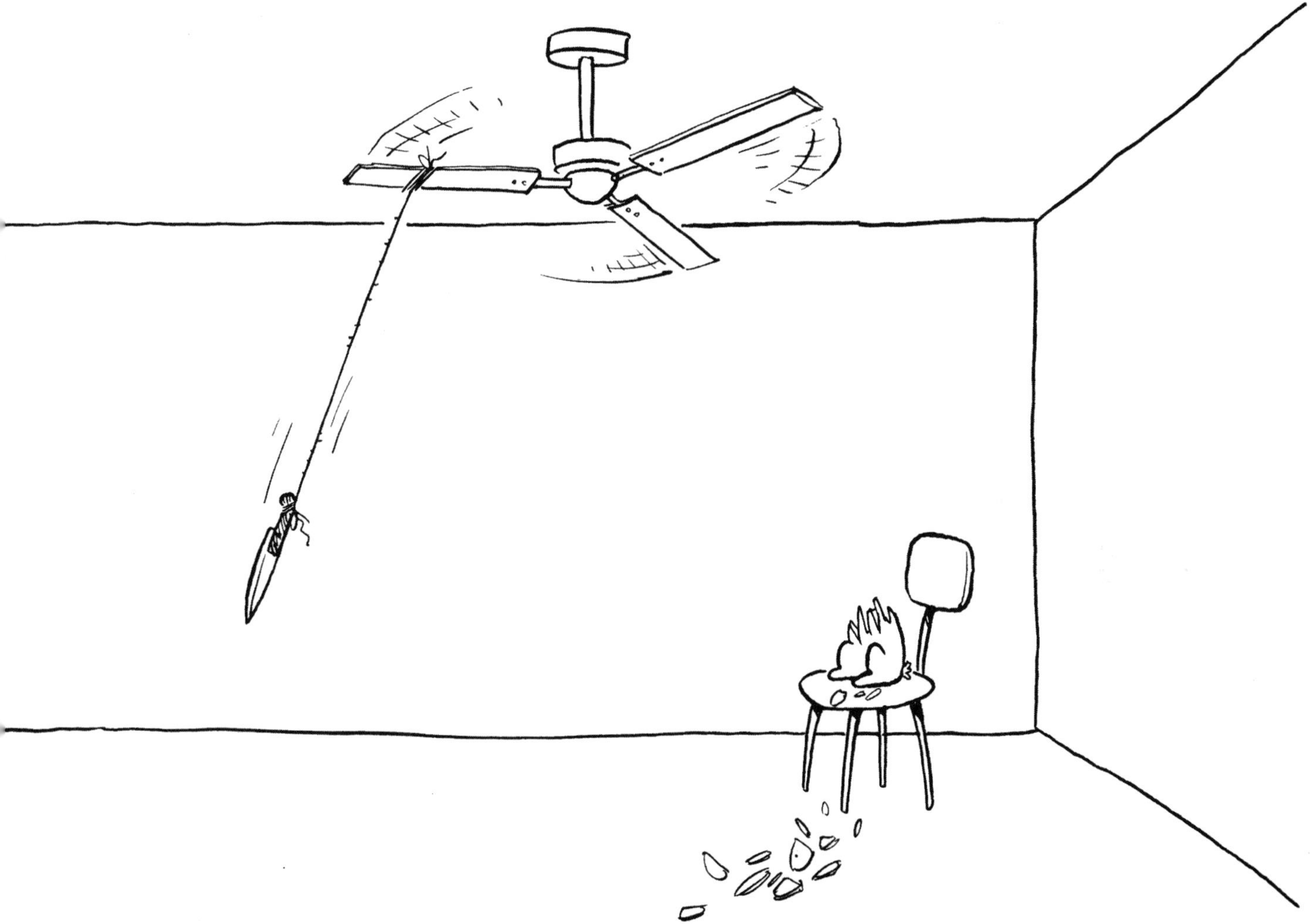

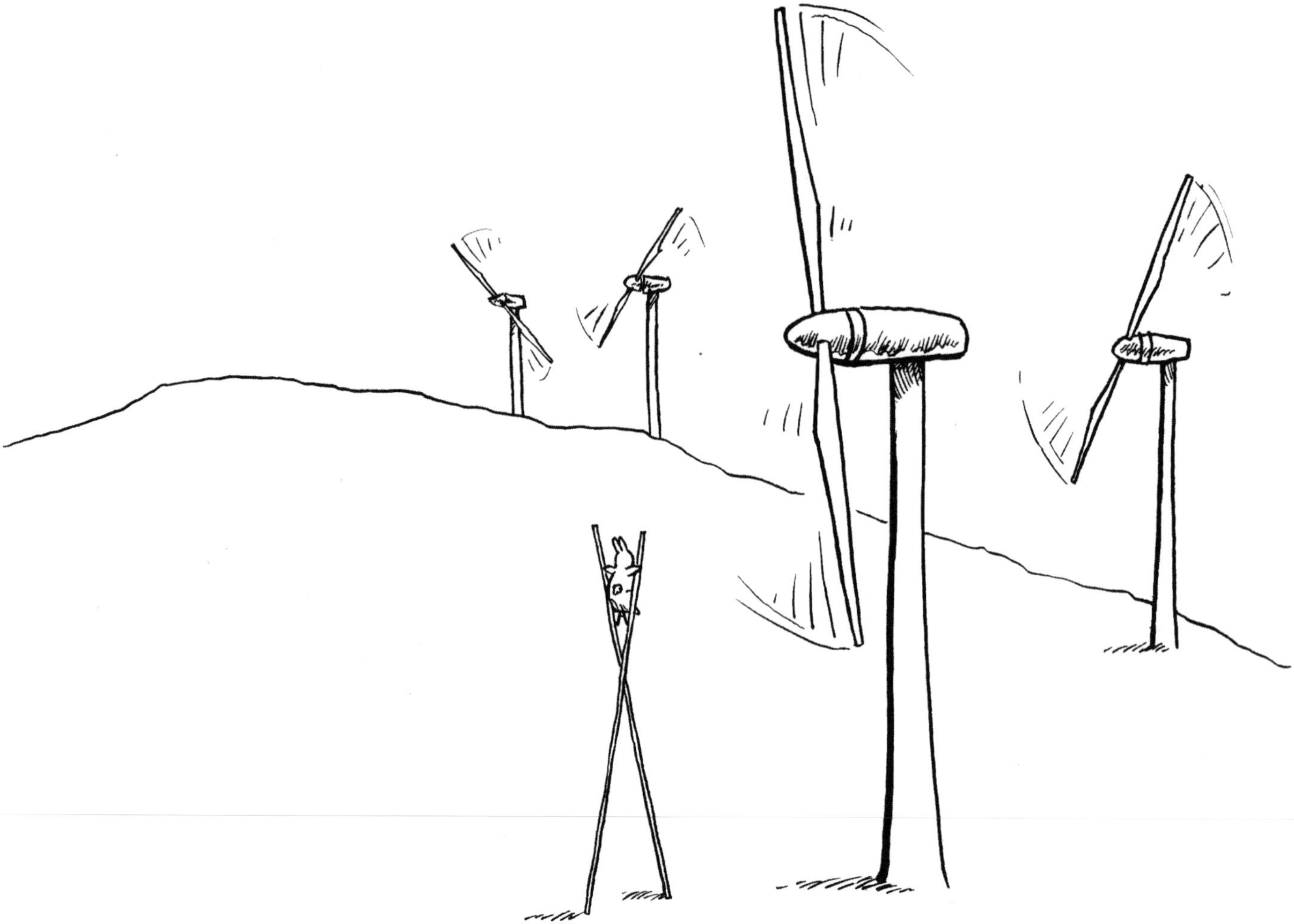

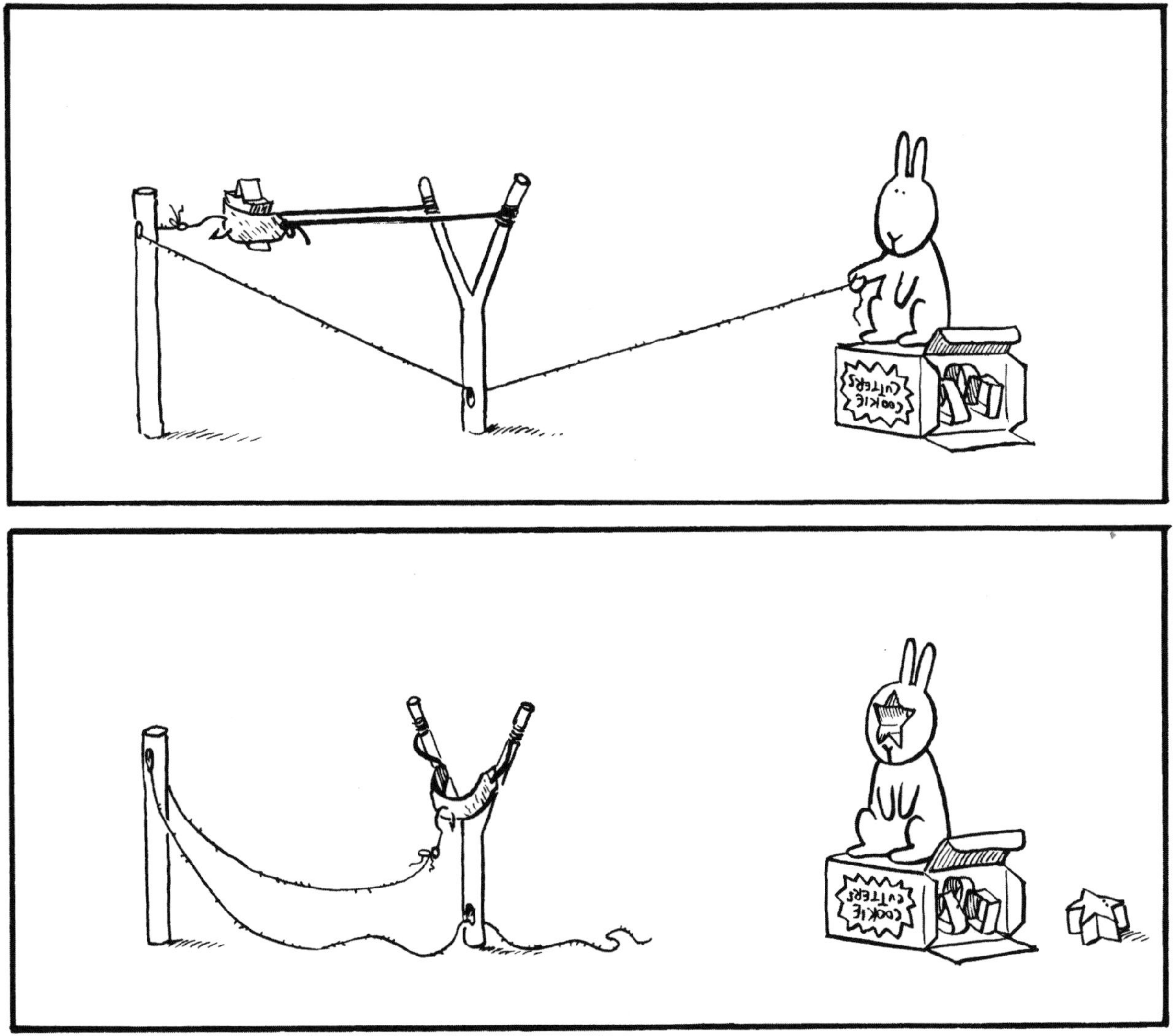
COOKIE CUTTERS
COOKIE CUTTERS

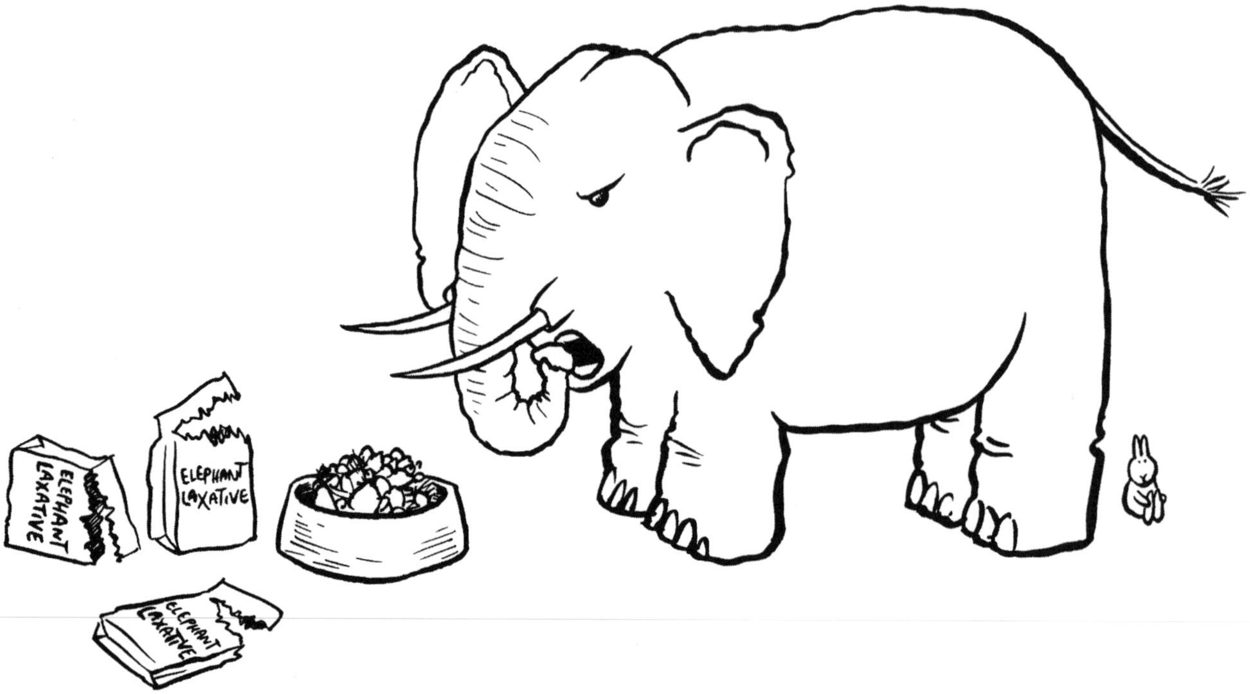
ELEPHANT LAXATIVE
ELEPHANT LAXATIVE
ELEPHANT LAXATIVE

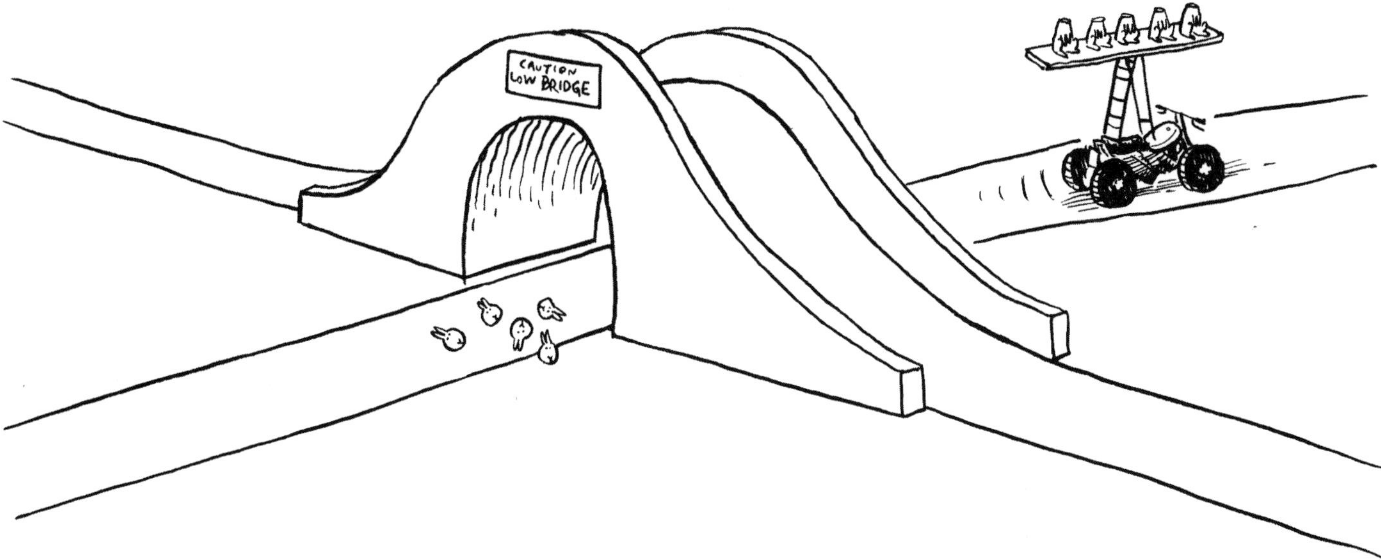
CAUTION
LOW BRIDGE

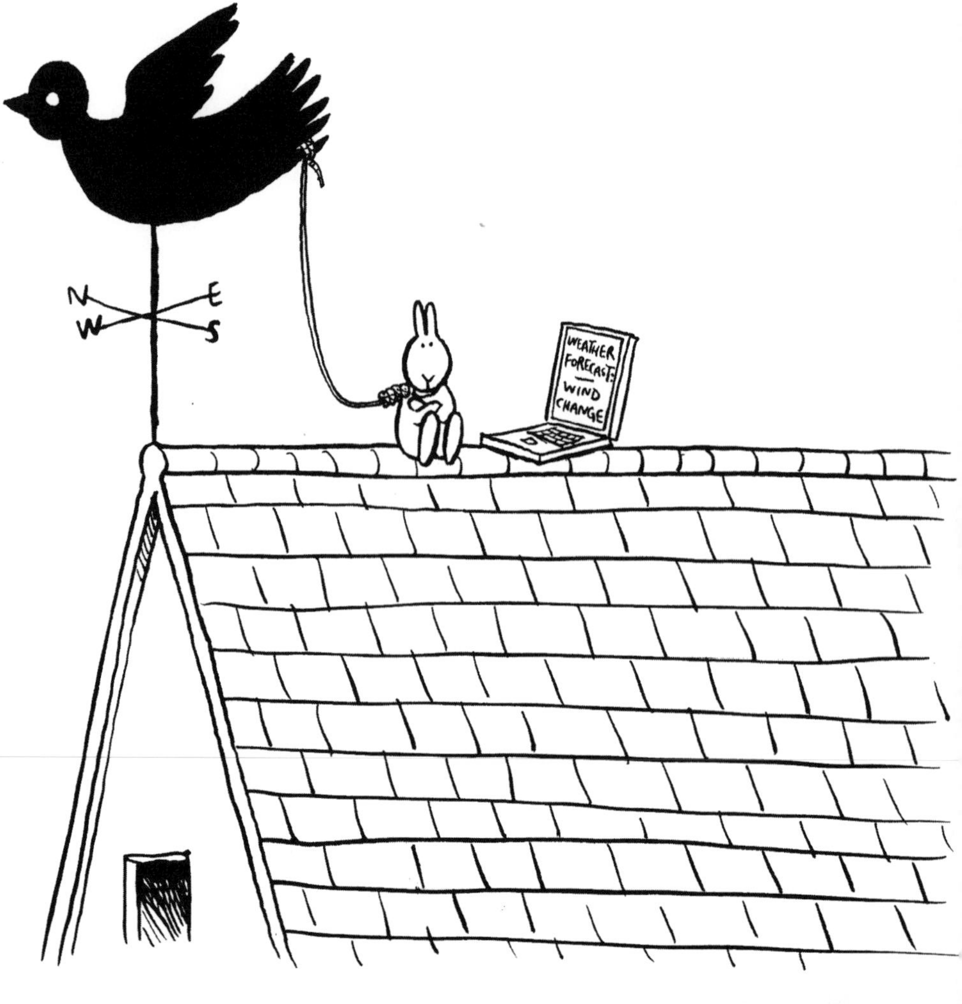
N
E
W
S
WEATHER FORECAST:
WIND CHANGE

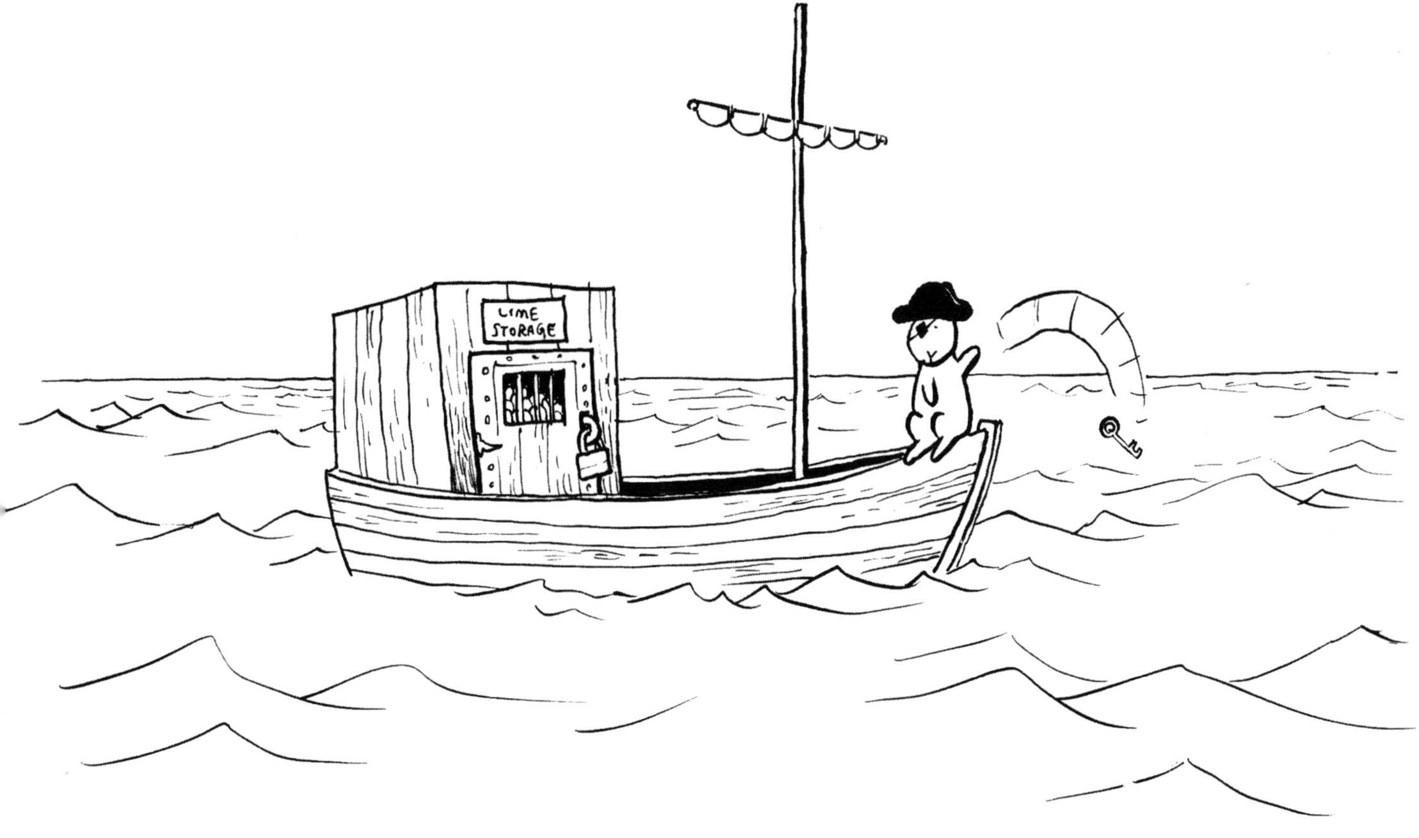
LIME
STORAGE

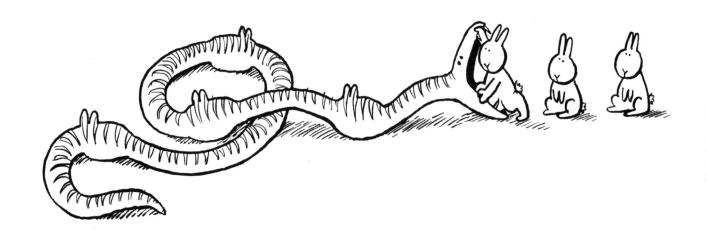

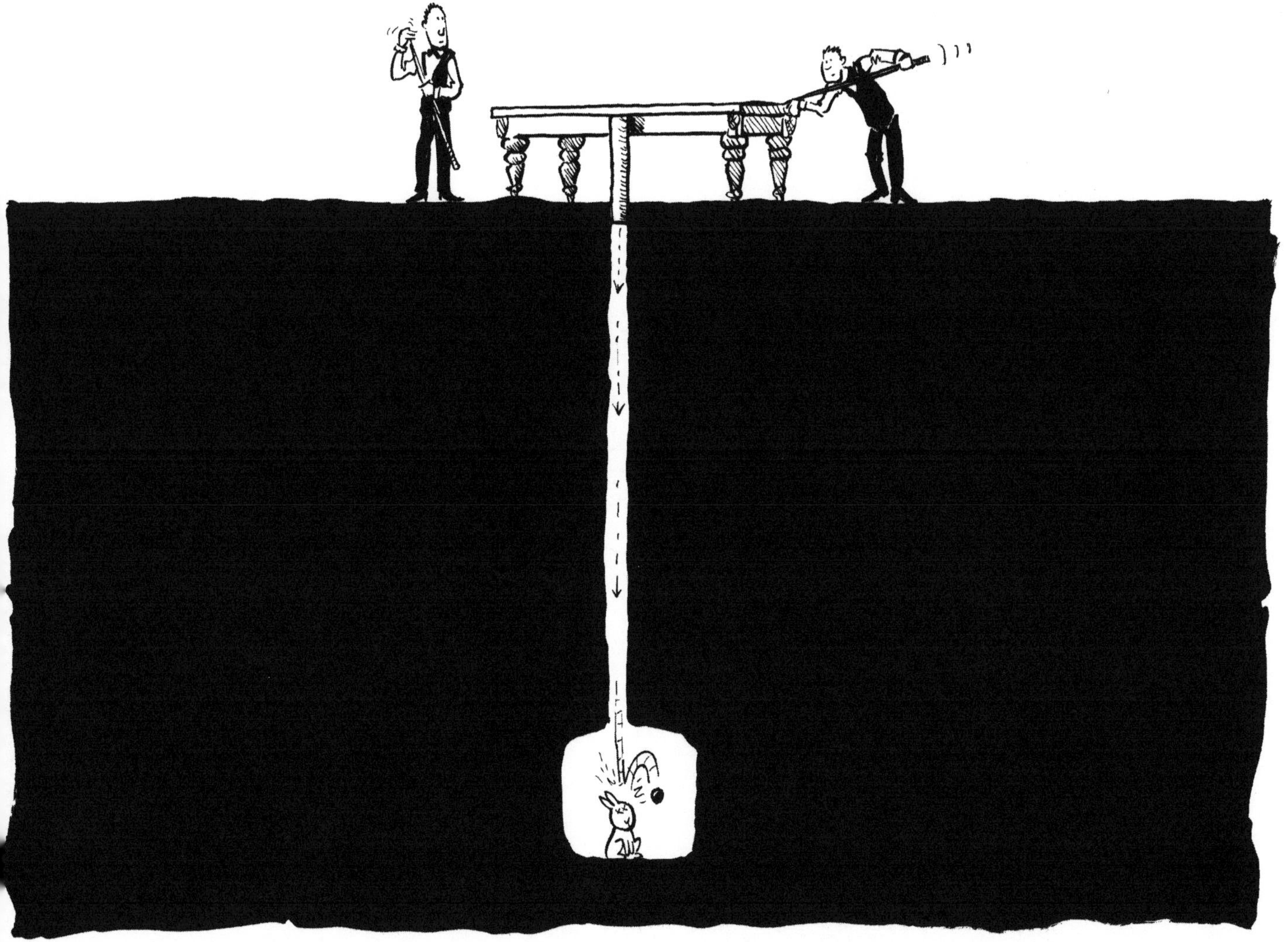

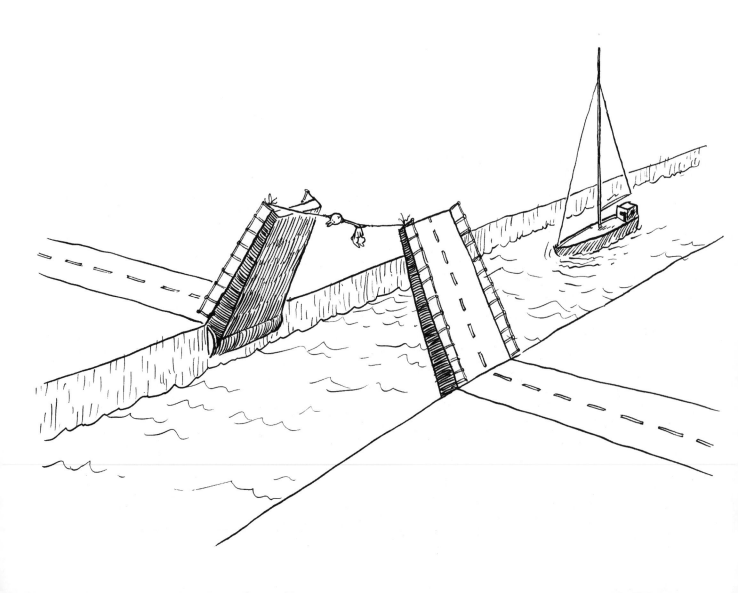

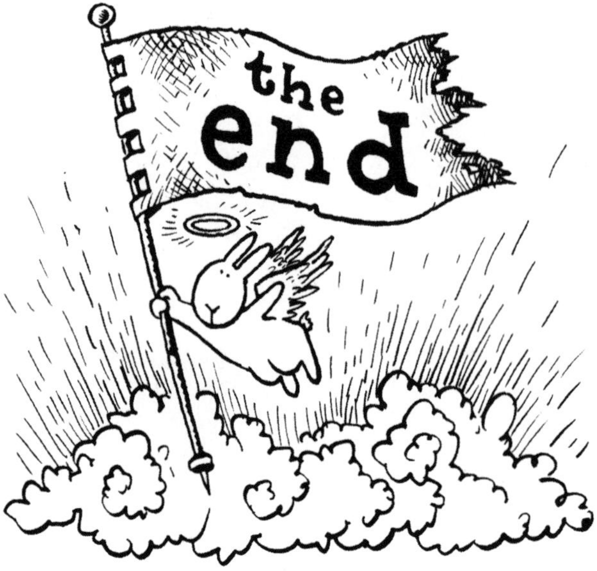
the
end

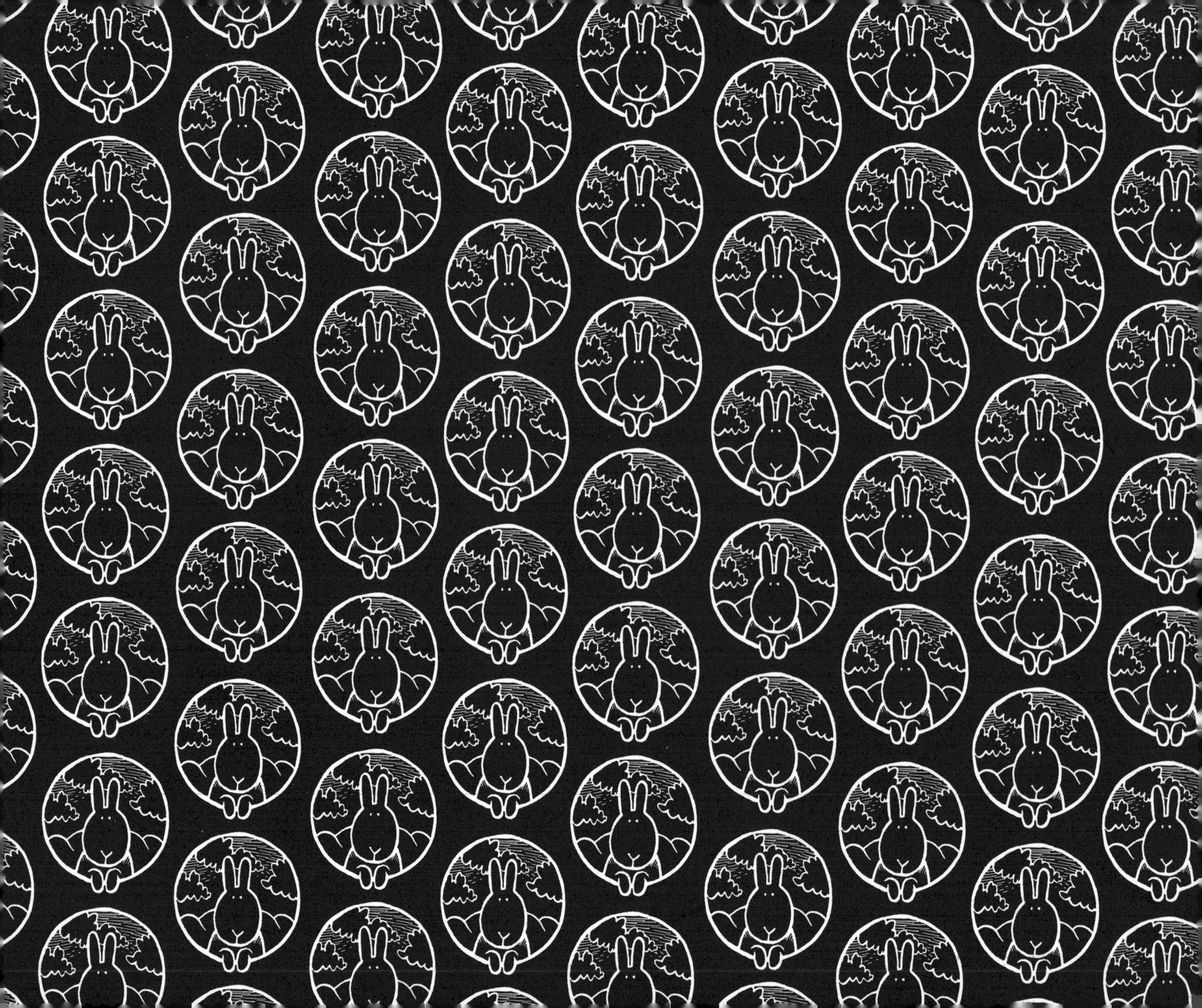